How to Read a Novelist

John Freeman

corsair

Constable & Robinson Ltd
55-56 Russell Square
London WC1B 4HP
www.constablerobinson.com

First published in Australia, in different form, by Text Publishing, 2012

First published in the US by Farrar, Straus and Giroux,
an imprint of Macmillan Publishers, 2013

First published in the UK by Corsair,
an imprint of Constable & Robinson Ltd, 2013

A copy of the British Library Cataloguing in Publication
Data is available from the British Library

ISBN 978-1-47210-937-8 (trade paperback)
ISBN 978-1-47210-938-5 (ebook)

Printed and bound in the UK by CPI Group (UK) Ltd, Croydon, CR0 4YY

1 3 5 7 9 10 8 6 4 2

For my father, who asked the right questions

Contents

How to Read a Novelist

U and Me: The Hard Lessons of Idolizing John Updike

My first apartment in New York was in a Brooklyn brownstone owned by a magazine editor and her silent, bookish husband. I spent a lot of time before a long, dusty bookshelf that ran parallel to the staircase in their home. To get a volume from the *F* section, you had to climb halfway up the stairs and lean out over the banister. One day, the silent, bookish husband caught me craning over the ten-foot drop, Flaubert's *Sentimental Education* in my hands. He became talkative. He told of disappearing into Proust over a teenage summer on Fire Island. How Tolstoy was a passionate college-age fling. I came late to reading, and so I envied his library and these summers spent in a book. Mine were spent performing rebound drills at basketball camps. I asked him what I should read. First he pulled down a volume of short stories by John Cheever, then he gave me *Rabbit, Run* by John Updike.

The Cheever I put down without finishing: The stories felt whiny and overdetermined, their trick endings too neatly engineered. But Updike was another thing. I blasted through *Rabbit, Run* in a few days, ferrying it into the city on the A train in a muggy trance. In college, I had fallen for Jack Kerouac's novels, particularly *On the Road*. Here was that book's exquisite opposite—the story of a man who made himself a prison of small-town domestic life, a man whose big countercultural act was not to light out for the open highway but to get in a car and drive across town to sleep with his mistress.

I felt an instant connection with Updike's fiction. I had lived in eastern Pennsylvania for six years as a child, and the region's gentle embrace felt like a third parent to me growing up. Now that I was an adult, I could see how such a life might have become stifling. In Updike's prose, it was gorgeously so.

One book led to another, and before long my Updike appreciation had turned to mania. I amassed an almost complete set of first editions of his books—more than fifty in all; I was missing just his tales for children—and my girlfriend, bemused and never smitten by Updike, often accompanied me to bookstores to get them signed. When I decided I, too, wanted to be a writer, I did what Updike had done forty years before me. I quit New York and moved with my girlfriend into a white clapboard house in New England. She took a job in technology re-search, and I began to write. Only I didn't. Instead, I spent my time reading Updike, aware that at my age he had published a volume of light verse and a short novel, but also increasingly conscious of his work's magnificent mel-ancholy—of the families broken up and destroyed, the repetitive failure of fleshly desire to relieve his characters' desire for transcendence. At night, I would occasionally look at the shelves in our bedroom and worry they might collapse from the black weight of their content, smother us in our sleep.

During the daytime, though, the air would clear and

my ever-expanding shelves of Updike titles became, again, a beacon. His industry and mindfulness of every detail of the visible world—so prevalent in even the soggiest of his novels—taught me a lot about the beauty of everyday things. If Updike himself functioned as my model for how to behave as a writer, his characters—whose lives mine was beginning to resemble—were the anti-models of how to behave as a person. Perhaps through the repetition of reading I might avoid the relationship immolation his characters provoked, again and again and again.

I took a job abridging *Tarzan of the Apes* for a children's publisher. It occurred to me that what I had been doing with Updike was similar to this tedious bit of hackery: tracing my life over that of another writer's. At the end of the workday, as the New England chill settled below the rafters, my girlfriend and I would snip at each other with the rancor of people looking for someone to blame. I was unhappy because I wasn't writing; she was unhappy for reasons I didn't quite understand. Even though we were only in our mid-twenties, a sense of opportunities lost began to hover.

After a year my girlfriend and I had to admit our New England experiment was a failure. We moved back to New York. Away from the predetermined doom of our Updikeian stage set of a life, we felt our sense of possibility recharge. We began cooking and taking dance classes. We trained for a marathon. I decided to propose, which meant I needed a ring. For the last time, I turned to Updike. I had gone through periodic purges of my shelves, attacking my bibliophilia like a cancer that required repeated radical surgeries. But it always came back, often more aggressive and pernicious. This time, however, I performed the most radical operation—my entire Updike collection. It took three cab rides, but in a few hours I'd managed to transport all three shelves to a New York dealer. Traveling down Park Avenue in a cab a week later, a little red leather box nestled in my lap, I felt purged and absolved. All the heartache and the wisdom and the weakness I'd absorbed through those books had been boiled down to something eternal, and pure: a wedding ring. No longer would the spines of those books stare out in judgment and gloom. I was free to become the husband I wanted to be, the writer I was meant to be— whatever that meant. I had swallowed Updike whole and spat out the bones.

I was surprised by how quickly things fell apart. A year after we were married, my wife moved out. When times were bad with her, I had fantasized about living alone, like a young Updike, writing in my garret. Only Updike had never lived alone. And now I had the place all to myself and I filled it with cigarette butts. As I looked out the window and smoked, I often thought about all the Updike books I had read in the past ten years and how witnessing his fictional marital breakdowns seemed to have done me so little good.

My wife and I divorced in the autumn. She had moved to California, and the laws of Maine—where we had married—required one of us to be present during the final proceedings. I drove up from New York alone, and spent the night with my soon-to-be ex-in-laws in their house on the beach, eating the saddest lobster dinner I've ever had. The next morning I drove to the court with my mother-in-law, who waited outside the empty chambers while I cut the thin legal string that still connected me to her daughter.

I didn't drive directly home. That afternoon, by a fluke of scheduling, I had arranged to interview John Updike at the Museum of Fine Arts in Boston. He had just published a collection of essays on art called *Still Looking*, and the interview conceit was that we'd wander among the paintings so he could riff on art in real time. It was not my first time interviewing him. Four months after my wedding, I'd interviewed him about his twentieth novel, *Seek My Face*. I'd been dazzled by his gentle but colossal intelligence, relieved to be able to treat him as an interview subject rather than the living embodiment of an abandoned dream.

I got lost on my way to the museum and arrived late. I found Updike waiting by the foyer, dressed in khaki slacks and a sports coat. Just over seventy years old, he had a full head of hair and the easy physical presence of a man at home in the world. We passed through a few galleries, Updike dispatching prose poems of appreciation with chummy good humor—as if surprised by how easily his mind created felicities with language. At some point I must have begun to flag, however, because he turned to me and asked, "Is this enough? I mean, you look pretty tired. I understand you are coming from Vermont?"

I told him it was not Vermont but Maine, and in response to his question about what I was doing up there I said I was getting divorced. The museum tour came to a dead halt. Updike faced me with real feeling, his ironic pose collapsing.

"I'm really sorry," he said. He would not allow me to make light of my newly minted divorce, and said that he had gone through this once before, too, which I knew, and that it was hell. His advice continued, briefly, but it was so surreal to hear him reference his private life that I can hardly remember what he said.

Apparently, though, he remembered. When *Terrorist*, his twenty-second novel, approached publication, a newspaper editor asked me if I could once again speak to John Updike. I called his publisher and was put on a junket schedule, then bumped, and bumped again. Finally I got through to his publicist. He switched from speakerphone to handset.

"We got some mixed feedback from John on the last conversation," the publicist explained. My ripped jeans and two-day stubble might have been noted, my mid-interview explosion of personal detail—which I remembered as more of a leak—had possibly made John feel uncomfortable. I had to understand, "John was of the old school."

I didn't know what to say. If I hadn't known before, I knew now: It was a breach of everyone's privacy when a reader turns to a writer, or a writer's books, for vicariously learned solutions to his own life problems. This is the fallacy behind every interview or biographical sketch, to tether a writer's life too literally to his work, or to insist that a novel function as a substitute for actually living through the mistakes a person must live through in order to learn how to properly, maybe even happily, survive.

I convinced the publicist to let me go ahead with the assignment. We sat in a conference room so high up over midtown Manhattan it felt like riding in a helicopter. In between bites of a turkey sandwich, Updike described what he saw on 9/11. I wore my nicest suit, in fact the one I got married in. I did not mention this detail to Updike, and just once did I interrupt the snowfall of his verbal prose poems: to ask him if he had read the Koran. He had, and then described it with beauty and grace. It was a perfect Updike moment—powerful and contained, only the littlest bit strange. He would have nothing to do with its shaping or its meaning, in either my fiction or my life. That would be up to me.

I have always felt there is something electrifying about meeting novelists. It isn't like running into a celebrity, where your eye readjusts to the true physical contours of someone seen primarily on-screen. It has to do with grasping that the creator of a fictional world, a universe that lives inside you as a reader while also feeling strangely disembodied, is not as interior as that world but alive: flesh and blood.

In this fashion, I wanted the pieces I wrote about novelists to describe an encounter, to show to the reader what the writer revealed to me, at their own choosing, over an hour or two or three, sometimes more, of talk. An interview, though, is not an actual conversation, but rather a form of conversation that has the same relationship to talking as fiction does to life. In order to work, fiction must abide by a set of rules it defines for itself, even if invisibly, and if an interview is to flow like a chat between two people it, too, must follow a set of conventions, some of them quite contradictory to how we are taught to interact naturally. Namely, that the interviewer asks all of the questions, offers pieces of information only for the purpose of stimulating more from the subject, and, primarily, that neither party calls attention to the artificiality of what is happening. My mid-interview explosion with Updike broke all three rules.

Novelists haven't always been representatives of their work, it's important to note. Yes, Charles Dickens bundled himself onto a train to travel across fifty cities in as many days when his books were released. But he was the exception. He was famous. So were Mark Twain, Oscar Wilde, Gertrude Stein, and, to a different degree, Ernest Hemingway. And through their fame they extended the power of the nineteenth-century novel into the public sphere, speaking and writing on all manner of things, even as the readership of the literary novel was about to begin its steady decline.

In the eighties, as bookstore chains expanded and the U.K. festival circuit began to develop, public readings became popular. Around this time Kazuo Ishiguro, whom I interview here, recalled going to an event for his hundredth or so time at the podium. He was reading with William Golding, who had won the Booker and the Nobel Prize but had yet to give a public reading. Ishiguro remembers Golding shaking with anxiety.

Some novelists, like J. D. Salinger and Thomas Pynchon, decided to sit out this expansion in their public role. Others have leapt to it. A great many, Updike included, were or are equivocal about it, even if they enjoy the attention, since the work that has brought them into the light—sitting at home in a room alone—is diametrically opposed to the task of talking about it in public with readers, journalists, or fans. When I started out in these assignments, arriving over-prepared, with twenty questions, often written out, I thought this was at least the most respectful place to begin. I quickly realized, though, that prepared questions lead to prepared answers. Gradually my list of questions decreased until I began arriving at interviews having read the books but without a single question in hand. This forced me to listen to people's answers, and it meant we could have an actual conversation, with all the unpredictability and freshness of a good one.

True storytellers write, I believe, not because they can but because they have to. There is something they want to say about the world that can only be said in a story. When it came to selecting the pieces I wanted to include in this book, my immediate preference was for those on subjects who felt that sense of urgency, and necessity, and whose work was important, beautiful, and enjoyable at the same time. In our interview, Robert Pirsig used the word *compelled*; he was *compelled* to write *Zen and the Art of Motorcycle Maintenance*, partly for his own sanity. It was a way of making the disparate parts of the world, and his experience, whole.

This theme—the consolations of narrative—kept coming up in interviews. Edwidge Danticat, Aleksandar Hemon, Peter Carey, and several other novelists I talk to here come from two places, and have distinct before and after periods in their lives. They spoke of their books as works of literature but also as a way to fathom the distance between these two worlds. To keep memory alive. An interviewer's job, I found, was not to close that gap—between here and there, between what was broken and what was whole—but to make it more mysterious.

For some novelists, like Toni Morrison or Ngũgĩ wa Thiong'o or Louise Erdrich, this task of telling stories about a place has a political dimension; it is about making visible a history, a sensibility, which history has repressed or occluded. For other writers, like David Foster Wallace, the need to write grew from an obsession with language, and further dimensions of their work all developed from that originating fire. Some of these novelists, like Mark Danielewski or Susanna Clarke, were so new to publishing that what haunted them was still developing and they spoke of it warily, revising and thinking aloud. Others were so near the end of their career—such as Philip Roth or Norman Mailer—they had already begun to try to curate how their work was read after they stopped writing or living.

All of these pieces were written on deadline for newspapers or magazines, with the exception of those I have included from 2013. Even if I hadn't been writing for newspapers and magazines, which at least in the United States are not terribly interested in the first person, it would have felt grandiose to include much of myself in these pieces. I am there, I suppose, in the questions I ask and in the things I note. I am there in the tack I take through their books, and the quotes I chose to give the narrative of our encounter sail, as all interviewers must do, but the self I live in, the one made by factors accidental and chosen, remains, I hope, discrete. I have done this with the goal of making it easier for readers to step into the frame and imagine themselves there. A handful of these novelists, Aleksandar Hemon, Peter Carey, and Edwidge Danticat, are friends of mine, and to write about them I had to re-estrange myself from them as people. With other novelists, like Robert Pirsig, who hadn't given an interview in twenty years, or Imre Kertész and Mo Yan, who give so few, to insert myself into the arc of the interview would have been, frankly, preposterous.

I haven't focused very much on craft, either. The problem with craft as concept is that it can become, like the idea of a novel itself when it lodges in a writer's mind, too much of an ideal. Wood carves differently in different environments. So does narrative. And thus my other hope, with these profiles, has been to reinstate some atmospheric context into the legend of a writer's life and work. A shelf of books has an inevitable feel, being of weight and mass; every writer I've ever spoken to, though, has mentioned how provisional their work seemed as they constructed it, how tentative and fearful they recall being about the prospect of achieving it, and especially how terrifying it is when the result of so much solitary thinking and chance and failure enters the world and leaves their hands.

The only thing an interviewer can do to capture what a novelist truly does is to make them talk and tell stories, and think aloud. These are not meant to be definitive life profiles but rather glimpses spied through a moving window. Writers are always evolving, publishing, and they are also in constant direct or indirect dialogue with one another. Jonathan Franzen and Jeffrey Eugenides, who lived in New York City in the early 1990s, each talked to me about their shared effort to bring back the sweep of the nineteenth-century novel in American fiction. The scale of their achievement in doing so meant both of them have reached the level of visibility Dickens once had in America and England in his time. Eugenides must be the only literary writer ever to be depicted on a Times Square billboard; Franzen was the first novelist since Updike to appear on the cover of *Time* magazine.

For the most part the connections that emerged from assembling these interviews were literary rather than personal. Mo Yan was influenced by Günter Grass, and they were both inspired by William Faulkner, who is clearly a beacon to Toni Morrison and Joyce Carol Oates, the latter of whom taught Jonathan Safran Foer, who it is often said borrows from David Foster Wallace—although Foer did not read him until recently—and Wallace himself pointed his compass to Don DeLillo, who on the subject of inspiration keeps his own counsel. And around it goes.

This fellowship—the deep connection of writer to writer as readers—is a hopeful thing, because it means that it is open to anyone who is a reader and who plans to be a writer. In the thirteen years of writing these profiles, this has been one of the main constants of my discussions: It is a pleasure—sometimes a challenge, but there is pleasure in the challenge—to read, but the best writing is always difficult to do. Whether they have a Nobel or a Pulitzer, or a first novel ten years in the making, all of these novelists are still shocked, each time they finish, that it gets done at all. Perhaps that is why chance remains, aside from sheer effort, the most cited factor in how they discovered their voices.

In the end, it becomes impossible to separate the two forces from one another, just as it is so difficult, but necessary, to separate writers from their work. Their bodies are their bodies of work, and even the most prolific of them, like Updike, are driven against a dying of the light. As he wrote in his memoirs, *Self-Consciousness*, "The idea that we sleep for centuries and centuries without a flicker of dream, while our bodies rot and turn to dust and the very stone marking our graves crumbles to nothing, is virtually as terrifying as annihilation." And as he said to me in 2004: "I've written a lot. I must have somewhere touched on almost every aspect of my life and experience. Nevertheless, there's this haunting fear that the thing you left out isn't going to be finally captured." Here then are fifty-five different writers trying to explain what it is they don't want left out.

Toni Morrison

Toni Morrison *is the footbridge between the past and present in American letters. In her novels* Sula *(1973) and* Beloved *(1987) she brilliantly conjured America's terrible history with slavery, and in* Song of Solomon *(1977) and* Jazz *(1992) she spun stories about the bargains of forced labor and its effect on African Americans today: the call of the past, and the need to improvise the future. These are the pillars of her body of work, and they illuminate a submerged part of America's past. Early this century, she began publishing a series of short, elliptical novels, including* Love *in 2003, when this interview took place, and* Home *in 2012. In all of her books the language is precise and poetic, a direct descendant of William Faulkner's lyrical modernism. No one alive in the United States knows the rasp and music of the American vernacular so well. Her writing on race and America—as collected in books such as* Playing in the Dark *(1992)—was instrumental to understanding the way race is a construct, not a genetic condition. Born Chloe Ardelia Wofford in Lorain, Ohio, in 1931, she won the Nobel Prize in Literature in 1993.*

Every day, Toni Morrison rises when the garbage trucks in New York are still collecting rubbish, when the ink from the morning newspaper still smudges on the fingers. If at work on a book, America's most fabulously praised literary novelist sits down with a pencil and yellow legal pad, and writes until her hand hurts.

"I don't like the act of writing for long periods of time," the seventy-three-year-old says, half-reclining on a divan in her lofty Manhattan pied-à-terre, dressed in a white T-shirt, black cardigan, and flowing black trousers.

"Some people think, 'Oh she's so virtuous to get up that early,'" Morrison says, letting loose a smoker's cackle. "It has nothing to do with that. I get up because a) the sun's up, and b) I'm smart in the morning. I just can't get it together in the evening."

This spartan routine has not changed since Morrison began writing. A single mother working in an editorial job in midtown Manhattan, she would wake at five—or sometimes earlier—and compose for a while before rousing her children and readying them for school. Morrison has been a literary fixture for so long that it's easy to forget she lived this way for almost twenty years. The steeliness necessary for this double life is still evident in her gait and the fierceness of her gaze when it has returned to a resting point after one of her noisy laughs.

Morrison has reason to kick up her feet and chuckle a little. When she published her debut novel in 1970, *The Bluest Eye*, she was an unknown thirty-seven-year-old writer. Since then, she has released six other novels, a study of blackness (*Playing in the Dark*), and several children's books; edited a number of anthologies; written the book for a musical, *New Orleans*, as well as a play, *Dreaming Emmett*; and held a teaching post at Princeton University since 1989. She has been a finalist for the National Book Award twice, won a Pulitzer for *Beloved*, and in 1993 became the first African American to win the Nobel Prize in Literature.

Thanks to this phenomenal acclaim, the financial urgency of those days is long gone. Located in a converted municipal building once famous for its models and celebrities, Morrison's apartment seems less like a writer's grotto than an exclusive getaway. Nestled between SoHo and Tribeca, hers is the kind of building one lives in when security and discretion are important. The rest of her time is spent in a converted boathouse up the Hudson River. It is not the kind of life often enjoyed by a writer.

All this does not stop Morrison from continuing to restlessly search and write. Just prior to our conversation, she delivered one of her best novels yet, *Love*, a slim but powerful story of five women and the charming man who possesses them from beyond his grave. As with William Faulkner's infamous epigraph, "The past is not dead. It is not even past," these women marinate in memories of old slights, recriminations, and sexual imbroglios.

"They are just entangled," says Morrison, flashing the wicked grin of a puppet master who enjoys putting her cast through hell. "They are totally entangled in this man who helped them or hurt them, whom they permitted some of these outrages because of the largesse accompanying it."

Speaking about her work, Morrison becomes nearly academic in her language. She leaves no doubt that she is the master of this text, and she holds its keys. The effect in person is slightly disjunctive. Short of stature, with a grandmotherly softness, Morrison appears nearly sweet, but when fixed with an intellectual question her speech slows, her voice dips to a whispery gravity. She wears her hair in long, somewhat knotty braids, which sprout from her head.

Love, too, sprung entirely out of Morrison's head, which is unusual. Most of her past four or five novels grew out of news stories. The germ of *Beloved* was a newspaper item about Margaret Garner in Cincinnati, a black slave who murdered her own daughter. *Paradise* emerged from the old black newspapers in Oklahoma that encouraged freed blacks to settle there in the nineteenth century. And *Jazz* was inspired by a photograph that Morrison saw of an eighteen-year-old woman murdered at a party by her lover out of jealousy.

This life-and-death brand of jealousy is everywhere in *Love*, the title of which grows more layered as one reads deeper. The love Morrison writes of both warms and devours, and her characters have yet to find the balance between the two. As a result, the language is taut but passionate, full of spoken idioms and the whirl and whoosh of hurricane weather, which ravages the part of Florida where the novel unfolds.

Morrison takes great pains to achieve this quality in her prose, working in longhand, then typing the manuscript on her computer, and then endlessly revising.

A former editor who spent two decades at Random House (until the mid-eighties), she professes to know the value of editing and relies on hers to achieve polish. "The language has to have its own music—I don't mean ornate because I want it to work with no sound, while you read it. Still, it also has to have that spoken quality: It's oral— a blend of standard English and the vernacular street language."

Rife with flashbacks and L's teeth-sucking voiceovers, *Love* has a structure to match its complex language. Information leaks out like clues in a homicide case; it's not until some time into the book that the characters' precise roles become clear, a deliberate strategy. This "deep structure" is where Morrison finds the art in novel-writing. "Plots are interesting, characters are fascinating, scenery can be totally enveloping," Morrison says, "but the real art is the deep structure, the way that information is revealed and withheld so that the reader gets to find out things appropriately, or in a time frame that makes it an intimate experience."

In this sense, Morrison's hide-and-seek game with key information forces a reader into an atmosphere where people think they know about one another, where envy and passion mix but find no release. In small towns, Morrison says, "the hatreds are severe, ancient, the passions and extraordinary silences are deeper, because they matter so much because you can't get away."

Morrison knows something of such communities. She was born Chloe Ardelia Wofford in Lorain, Ohio, in 1931. And to write about it she had to leave it. She moved to Washington, D.C., to attend Howard University, and later to Cornell in New York, where she studied English. During this time, she met her future husband, the architect

Harold Morrison, whom she later divorced. For a number of years she made her living as an instructor in English at Texas Southern University and then back at Howard before she wound up at Random House. She later retired to go back to writing—and teaching—full time.

While she writes much of enclosed communities, Morrison's community of readers has been expanding, especially since Oprah Winfrey chose a book of Morrison's not once, not twice, but four times for her book club. Each selection is believed to have increased sales by up to one million copies.

Add to that the Nobel Prize, college course adoptions, movie tie-ins (*Beloved* starred Danny Glover, a young Thandie Newton, and Oprah Winfrey), and the general avidity of Morrison's fans, and you have an author whose footprint in the dream life of Americans is enormous. She never questions whether the size of her audience is at odds with the rigor of her work. She is most impressed by Winfrey's transformation of a down-market show into America's most powerful bookselling tool. "I think her impact has been positive, really powerfully positive, just lassoing people," she says. "It's just amazing to me that here's a television personality who says, in effect, turn off the television and read a book."

Morrison is touchy on the subject of her Nobel Prize, not because she didn't feel it was deserved ("I never thought that my work didn't deserve it") but because she wishes critics would stop measuring her work on the before-and-after timeline of a prize that she won nearly a decade ago. "It can't authenticate me; it can simply say that they thought that my work was extremely good, that's all it can say. And then there's the fact that there will be another one next year. It's important, the money is fabulous, but let's go on."

Morrison says that twenty-five years ago she would have felt that such sales and prize visibility would have compelled her to remain in the spotlight and speak for the black community. She doesn't feel that way anymore. "They pretty much speak for themselves now," she says. "As an editor I felt that responsibility—to go out and find new writers that the agents didn't have—and I wanted to help publish and acquire books by activists so that their voices, their opinions, their narratives, their analyses could be distributed, unfiltered."

Now, at her level of publishing, Morrison seems eager to throw off some of the attention, and looks hopefully to the future of American literature, which she regards as promising.

She talks eagerly of the work of writers who are expanding the notion of the American novel: writers such as Chang-Rae Lee, Jhumpa Lahiri, and Colson Whitehead. While she stops short of calling them multicultural, she does applaud their broadening of the palate of American life represented in fiction. Listening to her speak, you get the sense that part of Morrison knows she made this possible. More important, her life as a reader has not abated. Even though she receives them by the box "with strings attached," Morrison still goes out and buys loads of books. It's her first love. As always, what she loves most comes back to language.

"English is a polyglot language, that's what makes it

exciting to write in; there are so many other languages in it, so many levels. When you get novels that pull from that or another tradition, for me it's a delight, an absolute delight."

August 2004

Jonathan Safran Foer

Jonathan Safran Foer made his literary debut at age twenty-four with Everything Is Illuminated *(2002), a manic and moving novel about a character named Jonathan Safran Foer on a visit to Ukraine in search of the woman who saved his grandfather's life during the Holocaust. In the book, Foer is guided by Alexander "Alex" Perchov, who mangles language and waxes poetic about girls and Lamborghini Countachs and cappuccinos. Foer's work often combines comic and tragic elements in the same breath, and explores the limits of language when faced with immense losses.*

I spoke to Foer upon the publication of Extremely Loud and Incredibly Close, *his 2005 novel, which imagines the tale of a boy whose father dies in the World Trade Center attacks.*

*In the decade that followed, Foer transposed this search for meaning into a nonfiction exploration on the morality of what we eat (*Eating Animals, *2009) and a retelling of the Jewish text that chronicles the Israelites' exodus from Egypt and sets forth the order of the Passover Seder (*The New American Haggadah, *2012). Born* *in 1977 in Washington, D.C., Foer lives in Brooklyn with his wife, the novelist Nicole Krauss.*

It's ten-fifteen on a Friday morning at Stuyvesant High School in Manhattan, and the seniors of the third-period English class are restless. As they file into the classroom, they glance at a small, tidy man wearing a black sweater and jeans sitting at the front. The bell rings and he introduces himself.

"Hi, I am Jonathan Safran Foer, and I am not a dead author but a living one." Sniggers, but once they stop it gets quiet. The students have been reading Foer's first novel, *Everything Is Illuminated*, and having the real writer here is a bit like having *Catcher in the Rye*'s Holden Caulfield in as a guest. And then discovering that he is really J. D. Salinger in disguise.

But there is something else making Foer's appearance especially loaded today. The novel he is here to speak about, *Extremely Loud and Incredibly Close*, revolves around a nine-year-old boy whose father dies during the terrorist attacks of September 11, 2001. Three and a half years ago, the students in this room had just begun their first year of high school when two planes slammed into the World Trade Center, roughly four hundred yards away. Close enough that when the towers collapsed, the school windows blew out.

On the day Foer visits, the Ground Zero site is an empty construction pit. In the classroom, the subject of That Day remains an empty pit as well. Sensing their nervousness, Foer reads the opening pages of his two books back-to-back and begins talking about their similarities. Hands go up and eager students kick off a wide-ranging discussion about literature.

In this sense, Foer makes for an unlikely literary hero. He wants to be accessible; he wants the class to believe they, too, can project their voices across centuries. Across tragedies if they wish.

It is exactly what Foer has done in *Extremely Loud and Incredibly Close*, which writes its way into the still-bruised heart of 9/11. The novel is driven by a precocious young New Yorker named Oskar Schell, who searches for the lock that will fit a key he believes was left by his father, who died because he attended a meeting at the Windows on the World restaurant.

Oskar copes with his grief by keeping his mind running at full tilt. He invents kettles that talk and writes letters to his heroes, such as Stephen Hawking, and talks to everyone he meets. "You get the sense that, were his mind to stop churning," Foer says later, sitting in a diner in Brooklyn, "he would self-destruct, like beavers whose teeth grow into their brain if they stop chewing."

Once again, Foer is writing about loss and how, under its duress, language becomes a leaky vessel for meaning. Oskar's grandmother and grandfather, survivors of Dresden, whose stories unfold alongside Oskar's, invent a language that fences off things they will not speak about. When that fails, they write letters. When that fails, they are no longer a couple.

Foer cannot help but dramatize this worry in person. He answers questions so deliberately and enigmatically—

often with metaphors or stories—that he resembles a human Magic 8 Ball.

Sitting in the garden of the town house where he lives with his wife, Foer tries to explain his fascination with erasure. "I remember, as a kid, I used to read the phone book and think that in one hundred years, all these people would be dead."

I ask him if he finds that morbid. "I don't know. I write about things I am afraid of now because sometimes they turn out to be the same things everyone else is afraid of."

Such fears aside, Foer grew up like a lot of middle-class Jewish boys of a certain time: Achievement was expected. The Holocaust was two generations ago. All three children in his family attended Ivy League universities. They were not rich but comfortably middle class. The brothers are all writers.

Still, despite this support and privilege, something had been lost. This is why, during college, Foer took a trip to Ukraine and imagined his way into his grandfather's shtetl, or village, then imagined himself imagining his way into that past. The interplay between these two activities became *Everything Is Illuminated*.

Though the world now knows this book as a runaway hit, it didn't feel that way for Foer, who until four years ago was a receptionist making $12,000 a year. "I was turned down by six agents; one finally said yes. She submitted it to every publisher in New York. All of them turned it down. I would have just been happy if it was published at all." Instead, after some revisions and a new agent, the novel became a bestseller and one of the most talked-about debuts of 2002.

However, if *Everything Is Illuminated* received some of the most laudatory reviews of any first novel in the past decade, *Extremely Loud and Incredibly Close* received decidedly rougher treatment in New York, before the rest of the country chimed in positively.

I ask Foer now what he makes of these early barbs. "I feel we are at a really destructive point in American culture where we don't just have to criticize something; we have to kill it."

Either way, the response to Foer's book shows he has touched a nerve. Long lines greeted him at readings, and letters arrived from people whose loved ones had died.

Take the train back into Manhattan from Foer's house and—ironically, briefly—you can wind up at the scoured-out foundation hole, visible from the windows of the skeleton of a station that was crushed when the towers fell. It is dusty and brown and empty in there.

July 2005

Haruki Murakami

 *Haruki Murakami is a Japanese novelist, short-story writer, translator, journalist, and former jazz club owner. He gave up his nightlife when he sat down to write his first novel,* Hear the Wind Sing *(1979). He spent the next three decades exploring the dark, strange corners of human imagination. Then he began running, the topic of his 2008 book,* What I Talk About When I Talk About Running, *the entry point for this interview. His books—which range from surrealistic fantasies such as* A Wild Sheep Chase *(1982) and* Hard-Boiled Wonderland and the End of the World *(1985) to amusing and sexy treatments on the anomie of youth such as* Norwegian Wood *(1987) and* Sputnik Sweetheart *(1999)—are full of cats, jazz, pasta, alien interventions, and portals to other universes. His most ambitious work—*The Wind-Up Bird Chronicle *(1997)—combines all of his storytelling modes: It is playful, yet also drenched in horror at the violence from which modern Japan was born. The 2011 publication of* IQ84, *a massive three-volume project written partly in response to George Orwell's book, was a worldwide phenomenon.*

Some people have epiphanies in church, others atop mountains. Haruki Murakami's came on April 1, 1978, on the grassy knoll behind Jingu Baseball Stadium in Tokyo. What if he tried to write a novel?

Thirty years and nearly three dozen books later, it's clear that Murakami answered the right call. His peculiar, beautiful, poignant novels, from *A Wild Sheep Chase* to *After Dark*, are cult hits the world over, translated into forty-eight languages.

But as he describes in his memoir, *What I Talk About When I Talk About Running*, this burst of productivity would have been impossible were it not for the simultaneous arrival—those many years ago—of another epiphany, an unlikely one for a three-packs-a-day smoker: What if he went for a jog?

Sitting in the dimly lit lobby of a midtown Manhattan hotel, having already woken, gone for a run, written, and conducted another interview, the energetic fifty-nine-year-old novelist explains how what started as a hunch became the organizing principle of his life.

"I have a theory," he says in a deep baritone. "If you lead a very repetitive life, your imagination works very well. It's very active. So I get up early in the morning, every day, and I sit down at my desk, and I am ready to write."

When he talks about his writing, Murakami sounds like an odd mixture of existentialist, professional athlete, and motivational speaker. "It's like going into a dark room," he says, his voice slowing. "I enter that room, open that door, and it's dark, completely dark. But I can see something, and I can touch something and come back to this world, this side, and write it."

He gives a long, Quaker-silence-like pause and then adds a caveat: "You have to be strong. You have to be tough. You have to be confident of what you are doing if you want to enter that dark room."

Even when he is not in Japan, Murakami follows a rigid routine. He wakes early, writes for several hours, runs, and spends his afternoon translating literature. He has translated *The Great Gatsby*, *Catcher in the Rye*, and, most recently, Raymond Chandler's *Farewell, My Lovely*.

The patterned nature of his days could not be more different from those of his characters, however. Murakami writes of people blown sideways through life by chance or freak circumstance. *Kafka on the Shore* features talking cats; *after the quake* includes a story about a man who believes a giant frog is taking over Tokyo.

Even though he lives by a strict set of habits and patterns, Murakami knows how fate can change a life. Two events outside himself have made a large difference to his own. The first came in the late eighties. Tired of what he called "the drinking and back scratching" of Tokyo literary society, of which he considered himself an outsider, he left the country and wrote a novel, *Norwegian Wood*.

"It sold very, very well—too much," Murakami says, laughing. "Two million copies in two years. So some people hated me more. Intellectual people don't like a bestseller." Murakami stayed away more, moved to America; and then 1995 came.

During that year, Japan suffered a financial meltdown

and a terrorist gas attack on its subways. Murakami went home and spent a year listening to the voices of the survivors. He ultimately channeled them into the oral history *Underground*. The experience changed him and how he wrote characters. "You know, many people don't listen to the other person's story," he says. "Most of them think other people's stories are boring. But if you try to listen hard, their story is fascinating."

Since then, Murakami has not only written characters differently—he opens the window, as he puts it, now and again. For two months of the year, he answers readers' e-mails. "I just wanted to talk to my readers," he says, "listen to their voices."

And then he shuts it. His determination to write still vibrates off him in sound waves. He wants each book to be different, better than what came before. Still, he doubts another epiphany will come. "I can remember what it felt [like]," he says about writing his first book. "It's a very special feeling. But I guess once is enough. I think everybody gets that epiphany once in a lifetime. And I am afraid many people will miss it."

December 2008

Richard Ford

Richard Ford was born in Mississippi, studied in Michigan, and has lived across the United States, from Montana to New Jersey, Louisiana to Maine. His writing is full of drifters (A Piece of My Heart, 1976), independent thinkers (his trilogy of novels about Frank Bascombe, an ex-sportswriter living in suburban New Jersey), and men troubled by marriage (any number of his short stories).

Ford began working on stories when he was encouraged by his friend the writer Raymond Carver. Rock Springs (1987), the resulting collection, might be Ford's best book. It has a high, lonesome clarity that allows him to peer into the lives of desperate and violent men with uncanny power.

The Lay of the Land (2006), the last in the Bascombe books, was the reason for this interview. Several years later, in 2012, Ford returned to the world of the wild plains and the north with Canada, the tale of a boy who is spirited away to Saskatchewan when his parents are arrested for robbing a bank.

Richard Ford isn't writing. At all. In fact, since he finished *The Lay of the Land*, his third novel about Frank Bascombe, the Pulitzer Prize–winning novelist has been doing just about anything but write.

Ford and his wife, Kristina, spent last winter rebuilding houses in their former hometown of New Orleans, still struggling to recover after Hurricane Katrina. When we sit down to speak, Ford tells me he has been watching college basketball finals. He plays squash in New York City. As for writing, he's spent.

"It completely took my measure," says Ford, sixty-three, of *The Lay of the Land*, sitting in the living room of their Riverdale home, surrounded by antiques and furnishings that used to ornament their Garden District house in New Orleans. The windows look out on the Hudson River, which glides slowly past.

"At the end of it I was physically ill, and I stayed physically ill for many months."

Tall and rangy, dressed in a purple shirt and Levi's, Ford doesn't exactly look ravaged. But that's not quite what he is talking about.

"I really use up every resource that I have in writing a book, so not only do I need to go around and find other things I might write about but I have to sort of reinstitute the whole vocation."

Ford has been enjoying what he once described in a piece for *The New York Times* as "a lavish period away from writing."

In the somewhat workaholic landscape of literary America, where gaps between books become legendary when they stretch over seven years, Ford's approach is unusual. Some might even argue it's bad for business.

But Ford has never enjoyed or followed the path of writer as careerist. His first novel was a neo-Southern gothic of sorts; his second could be categorized as a thriller. He started writing stories later in life, in part because Raymond Carver encouraged him to.

"I remember showing him my first story," Ford says about "Rock Springs." "And he didn't like it at first. I told him he was wrong. I can still see him, mumbling, smoking a cigarette. 'Maybe so, maybe so.'"

When Ford's early work got him pegged as a Southern writer, he pulled up shop and moved elsewhere, and wrote novels like *Wildlife*, story collections like *Rock Springs*. When he was pegged as a Western writer, along came the first Bascombe novel, *The Sportswriter*, set in New Jersey, a novel about the suburbs.

"New Jersey, the one place that I wish would claim me, never has," Ford says, laughing, looking out the window across the Hudson at the state, his face screwed up with an ironic expression of pained neglect. "I sit here looking longingly over there, waiting for the call."

Ford can joke about this because New Jersey is not exactly where he's calling from, as Carver might have put it. In addition to New Jersey, Ford has called from California, Chicago, and the Mississippi Delta, where he bought a plantation house and lived for a time. "I really liked it there," he says, "but I was worried I would stop becoming, which I thought was not a good thing as a young writer." He has also lived in Paris, Massachusetts, Michigan, and

Montana, and still keeps a house in Maine, where he lives most of the time now.

Some of this itchy-footedness is just a search for new stimuli; other times it has involved the career of his wife of almost forty years, Kristina. Ford brings her up often, and during the interview she sits in the kitchen reading Martin Amis's novel *Money*. Every one of Ford's books is dedicated to her.

"Kristina has had sort of a wonderful professional life," he says. "She has been the head of city planning in Missoula; she has been a professor at New York University; she has been the head of city planning in New Orleans. So we've traipsed around after those jobs."

The result of all this moving—besides a storeroom in Montana that Ford doubts they will ever open—is that he has developed a tone, a texture, and a flavor of Americana in his prose that is unexpectedly his own, and deeply American.

Next to John Updike's Rabbit Angstrom, there are few Everymen in postwar American fiction who have captured the reading public's imagination quite like Frank Bascombe. Haunted by the early loss of his child, a career change, a divorce, and then illness, Bascombe limps into *The Lay of the Land* and takes a big gulping look at America.

Ford says he has enjoyed being with Bascombe for so long, but disagrees with the idea that these three books have shown his hero develop in any sort of way. "That's just kind of a trope where some people think our life is continuous. It's probably something we just make up to console ourselves."

In *The Lay of the Land*, Frank enters what Ford calls the "permanent period." Where any illusion of personal becoming stops, all forks in the road—or most—have been stared down, and what remains is just, as the title suggests, the lay of the land.

The thing Ford is measuring is not only Bascombe's inner life, though, but the landscape of America, too. In *The Sportswriter*, which is set in the eighties, there is the whiff of promise and money of Reagan-era America. In *Independence Day*, which is set during the nineties, there is a deep nostalgia and pastoral flowering. *The Lay of the Land*, set during the anxiety-ridden late 2000s, lingers on strip malls and SUVs, the fungus of fast-food joints and brand-name retail shops.

Ford purposely put those details in the novel, he says. "That was one of the great freedoms of writing that book. I've got a pretty retentive memory, and I've got a pretty good ear for the weirdness of language. And I could just get it all in there. All this stuff I haul around with me."

But he says it would be a mistake to assume the novel should be read as a dirge about America's decline. "It's kind of a rhapsody, all that nomenclature. But I don't think it's a rhapsody in a passive way. You could, and many of us do, drive around America, and say, 'Oh, what a mess, look what we've done to the environment, look at what a wreckage this is.' If you decide you are going to be more of an affirming agent, one of the things you can do is take responsibility for it. You accept it as something you in some way or other have willed."

This idea that America could be reaching a permanent

period, for better or worse, is not, for Ford, an excuse to give in to a narrative of decay.

"You know that great line that was quoted in Kurt Vonnegut's obituary?" Ford says. "'You must conclude that they didn't like it here.' My thought is, no, I'm not going to conclude that, because this is what I've got to work with . . . and even though there are parts of America I'd rather were different, this is the life I have. I'm not going to continuously, mindlessly, reflexively disparage it."

Nor will he reflexively, mindlessly keep on with Bascombe. Ford is done with him, for now and forever, he claims. "I don't know if I have anything interesting to say about the period of life which is ahead of him."

So for now Ford will finish up the master class he conducts at Columbia, go to a few parties, recharge his muse. He has a novel in mind, but he is not rushing to start it. "I've never been sixty-three before," he says. "I sort of like being sixty-three. I think I'm just going to do that for a while."

May 2007

Ngũgĩ wa Thiong'o

 Ngũgĩ wa Thiong'o is a Kenyan novelist, essayist, and playwright. Born in 1938 and baptized James Ngũgĩ, he graduated from Makerere University College, Kampala, in 1962. His first novel, Weep Not, Child, appeared in 1964 when he was studying in England. It was the first novel published in English by an East African writer. The River Between, which takes as its backdrop the Mau Mau rebellion, was published the next year. Following the release of his third novel, Ngũgĩ returned to Africa, renounced his colonialist past, took on the name Ngũgĩ wa Thiong'o, and began writing in Swahili and Gĩkũyũ. In 1977, a play he was producing attracted the attention of the Kenyan government and he was imprisoned for more than a year. During this time he wrote the first modern novel in Gĩkũyũ on scraps of prison-issued toilet paper.

In Decolonising the Mind: The Politics of Language in African Literature (1986), Ngũgĩ argued that African writers needed to return to their native languages lest they enable their extinction. Ngũgĩ's later works of fiction include Petals of Blood (1977), which has become a foundational classic of modern African literature, and

Wizard of the Crow (2006), the book that coincided with his return to Kenya and this interview. In 2010, he began a trilogy of memoirs.

Forces within Kenya have tried to silence Ngũgĩ wa Thiong'o's voice twice. In 1977, the future president Daniel arap Moi—at the time the country's vice president—threw him into a maximum-security prison without trial for coauthoring a play critical of the government. Ngũgĩ was released one year later, only to discover that his teaching job had disappeared. Fearing for his safety, he left the country in 1982.

For a while, it looked like he would never return. "Moi used to say, 'I can forgive anybody but Ngũgĩ,' " says the sixty-eight-year-old novelist at his home in Irvine, where he is a professor of English at the University of California. At just over five feet tall, with a ready giggle, he is hardly the portrait of a steely revolutionary. When Moi agreed to abide by term limits, and his handpicked successor lost in the presidential elections, Ngũgĩ realized that he had a chance to return home. It was good timing. Ngũgĩ had just completed a six-volume novel called *Murogi wa Kagogo*, or *Wizard of the Crow*, a ribald satire of a fictional African dictator. It was also the longest novel ever written in his native Gĩkũyũ language.

He decided to turn his homecoming into a book tour. He and his second wife, Njeeri—they considered themselves husband and wife although they had never been married in the traditional sense—had never been to Kenya together as a family. "At the airport the crowds were there," he recalls, "some weeping, some holding on to books."

"Some of the books were covered in dirt," Njeeri chimes in, "because they had to bury them—to hide them—when his books were banned."

And then things went horribly awry. On August 11, 2004, intruders broke into their apartment. "We felt that this was no ordinary robbery," Ngũgĩ recalls, "because they didn't take anything first; they just sort of hung around, waiting for something to happen. Quite frankly, I thought we were going to be eliminated."

They managed to escape that fate but had to live through a nightmare. Ngũgĩ's wife was stabbed and raped in front of him. "I kept calling for help," she remembers, "and they kept trying to hush me." When Ngũgĩ tried to intervene, he was burned with cigarettes on his forehead and arms. "He is so dark," Njeeri says, her eyes welling with tears, "my husband was literally branded."

The couple emerged from the hospital a day later, and Ngũgĩ issued a profoundly sad but generous statement. "We have to keep rising up," he said. "The Kenyans who attacked me do not represent the spirit of the new Kenya."

Messengers from the attackers came to the hospital to warn his wife against speaking out. "We do not speak of that," she remembers being told.

Neither Ngũgĩ nor Njeeri have complied. While the robbery and rape trial drags on, Njeeri has spoken out about her experience. Meanwhile, Ngũgĩ has labored to bring his magnum opus from Gĩkũyũ into English—no small feat when the book runs to 766 pages. "The first time you are mapping the terrain," he says, "the second time, translating it, you are merely following it."

Sitting on his back patio next to a garden of mango and avocado trees grown by his wife, water trickling from a fountain, Ngũgĩ explains why he felt compelled to write the novel in Gĩkũyũ. "If I had published this book first," he says, holding up the English edition, "this book"—he pats the Kenyan edition—"would not exist."

Set in the fictional African republic of Aburĩria, the novel pokes fun at a ruler who has surrounded himself with comically sycophantic cabinet ministers. One has surgically enlarged his ears to prove he hears everything the people say; another has had plastic surgery on his eyes to show that he keeps watch on the public. For the ruler's birthday, this group suggests building a tower up to heaven so that the ruler can speak directly to God.

For funding, Aburĩria's majestically self-important ruler turns to the Global Bank for cash, but he must constantly fight against the mockery of the public. An underground resistance called Movement for the Voice of the People protests against his ceremonies, while long lines of unemployed workers betray his failure to provide for his people.

"When people talk about Africa," Ngũgĩ says, "they often only talk about it through one lens—so they blame its lack of progress on its people, or its landscape. In this book I wanted to show everything—the influence of aid, the neocolonialism of capital, and how this affects things for the people."

At the crux of the resistance are a young beggar named Kamĩtĩ and a revolutionary he falls in love with,

Nyawĩra. Kamĩtĩ discovers he has the capabilities of a seer when he sets up shop as a fictional wizard, dispensing advice to people who want to crush their enemies. Nyawĩra occasionally sits in for him when he cannot make his engagements.

"The trickster character is very important in this book," Ngũgĩ says. "All the characters perform themselves; they are inventing themselves, all the time." This is especially true of the ruler, whose sense of self-importance is so large that he literally becomes the body politic. When the state becomes buoyant with the possibility of improvement, he swells up like a hot air balloon, causing speculation that a curse has been put on him.

"The playfulness with language you find in the novel is very much to do with the language it was written in," the author explains. " 'Pregnancy' is a phrase as well as a term in Gĩkũyũ. So when there are strange things happening, you say, 'She is pregnant'—as with possibilities. So it's a kind of warning."

Although the leader's Westernized suits recall Moi's jackal dapperness, Ngũgĩ insists that this is not just a novel about Kenya and the failures of aid. "I was drawing from lots of Third World dictatorships: I was thinking of Moi, but also of Mobutu, Idi Amin, and Pinochet. They were all on my mind . . . In 1982, when I was exiled, I was based in London, and I worked on the committee for the release of political prisoners in Kenya. I worked closely with people from Chile, from the Philippines."

One thing Ngũgĩ shared with them was the colonial experience. He was born in a rural village north of Nairobi with the name James Thiong'o Ngũgĩ and raised a

Christian. He attended mission schools, where he read Robert Louis Stevenson. Like Wole Soyinka and Chinua Achebe, he left Africa and went to England for further study, earning a degree from the University of Leeds.

Returning to Kenya, he successfully petitioned the University of Nairobi to turn its English department into the Department of African Languages and Literature, soon after renouncing his birth name and taking on the Gĩkũyũ form of nomenclature. As he once explained, "language is a carrier of a people's culture; culture is a carrier of a people's values; values are the basis of a people's self-definition."

Ngũgĩ lived with *Wizard of the Crow* for ten years. The book has been his only constant during his life in America, as he moved from one teaching post to another. Now that it is done, his wife jokes, they can go to the cinema—she hopes—and he can play a game of chess.

Ngũgĩ says that living in sunny Southern California occasionally makes the events of the past feel a bit surreal. "Yes, the horror!" he says ironically, sweeping his hand at their lush gardens.

Njeeri breaks up laughing at this, too. "It is surreal," she says. But it is now their home.

And there is serious work to be done here, even if the prancing cheerleaders and frozen yogurt stalls on the Irvine campus do not suggest it. Since 2003 Ngũgĩ has been a distinguished professor of the humanities and director of the International Center for Writing and Translation at Irvine. "What is so devastating in a dictatorship is the taking away of a voice," he says. And the prevalence of

English in the world, he argues, has only sharpened that blade against the larynx of indigenous peoples. "It is not a balanced equation if all languages must come to English to mean something."

August 2006

Günter Grass

 Günter Grass is Germany's most famous living writer. A playwright, poet, and visual artist, he was born in 1927 in the city of Danzig—in what was then Poland— where his parents owned a grocery store. As a teenager, he volunteered for submarine service, and in 1944, not long after his seventeenth birthday, was conscripted into the Waffen-SS, an experience he finally wrote about in his memoir Peeling the Onion, published in 2006, which is when I interviewed him. The revelation that Grass was involved in the Waffen-SS was explosive in Germany, where he has been a celebrated novelist since he published his beguiling and beloved first novel, The Tin Drum (1959), the tale of a man in a mental institution remembering his decision never to grow up. The novel is the first part of Grass's Danzig Trilogy, about the war and interwar period in his native city. His books are full of satirical broadsides at the abuse of power and the pieties of righteous thinking, such as Local Anaesthetic (1969). The Flounder (1977), an allegorical novel that points to the German fairy tale "The Fisherman and His Wife," is one of the first Grass tales to veer away from World War II. Other novels include The Rat (1986); Too

Far Afield *(1995), an enormous epic about unification; and* My Century *(1999), published the year he won the Nobel Prize. In 2009, he released his third, much less controversial volume of memoirs,* From Germany to Germany.

In half a century of writing fiction, Günter Grass has shown a predilection for unusually compelling characters. His masterpiece debut, *The Tin Drum*, is narrated by a three-year-old genius; *The Rat* is populated by more rodents than the New York City subway in July. But of all his heroes, human and otherwise, the protagonist who gave Grass the most trouble is the man at the center of *Peeling the Onion*—himself.

"Looking back from my age at a boy of fourteen, fifteen, that is a long way—it's like looking at a strange person," says Grass, nearly eighty, sucking on a pipe in a New York hotel suite.

Indeed, it is odd. The Grass we meet in *Peeling the Onion* feels a distant relative to the "conscience of a nation" whose Danzig Trilogy of novels has inspired writers from W. G. Sebald to John Irving. This Grass was—as a boy and late teenager—an ardent believer in Nazism. He signed up for the Jungfolk at ten and, at seventeen, was drafted into the Waffen-SS, a notoriously brutal elite corps.

Grass served several weeks on the front, never fired a shot, and was captured and held prisoner in American POW camps. When he began to talk of this experience in interviews in the summer of 2006, the German press erupted in outrage at the nation's conscience admitting he, too, was part of its dark past. "I'm deeply disappointed," said Grass's biographer Michael Jürgs at the time. "If he had come clean earlier and said he was in the SS at seventeen, no one would have cared, but now it puts in doubt, from a moral point of view, anything he has ever told us."

Grass says he did in fact speak of being in the Waffen-SS in the sixties and "no one paid it any heed," and that "gradually, as I learned more about the crimes that were committed, I spoke less and less of it out of shame."

Now Grass calls the furor of the summer of 2006 "a campaign," lamenting the way it obscured more complex discussions about Germany's past sparked by *Peeling the Onion*.

"There is always the reaction of the critic," Grass says, betraying no obvious irritation, "but the readers are different—this book got so many letters from my generation, old people, and also young people—people saying to me, 'I was finally at last able to say I can talk to my children about my time during the war.'"

Grass thinks that's because *Peeling the Onion* revolves less around his service in the Waffen-SS than it does around the private domestic silences that have plagued him since 1945 and that—even after writing the book—he cannot understand.

In *Peeling the Onion*, Grass says he never asked what happened to an uncle who was shot down as a pilot and summarily executed by the Nazis. He did not ask after a teacher who vanished. He did not inquire as to the fate of a fellow soldier who would not carry his rifle.

"I actually got a letter from a woman with a picture,"

he says now, "and she said, 'I knew that man in a concentration camp.' It was indeed him and he had survived until the eighties."

Grass says he wrote *Peeling the Onion* to try to understand these boyhood silences, to ask his younger self why he didn't have the courage to ask these questions. In the end, he says, he found that memory would betray him.

"From my youth time I was a liar," he says. "My mother, she liked this kind of storytelling, my promises of where I would take her and what I would do—this was the basis for my writing, for telling stories. So you have to mistrust your memory. Because memory likes to make things look nice, it likes to make complicated things simplified—and I wanted to write down this mistrust. It's one of the reasons why I tell stories which begin this way and then I make a correction, a variation."

Of all Grass's books, *Peeling the Onion* is the loosest in form. It winds toward a story, investigates it, and in some cases imagines what could have happened—acknowledging that the truth may in fact not be retrievable.

Critics troubled by Grass's service will probably find in this forgetfulness a damning self-protection. At the 92nd Street Y in Manhattan, the Viennese-born writer Amos Elon spent most of an onstage interview grilling Grass. "Why did you wait sixty years?" he asked, to loud applause. Grass's answer to this question—that he had written them into his books, and that he had never hidden this experience but rather written through it—also earned applause.

At eighty, sitting in a hotel suite, Grass wears the burden of such scrutiny philosophically. Throughout the interview he sucks on his pipe and squints into the smoke as if the answers to his questions about his younger self, his younger "stupidity," as he calls it, will be just as ethereal.

"I wrote this book to come nearer to this young boy," Grass says wearily, "to come into discussion with him— but he was defending himself, with lies sometimes, as I did when I was a boy. This book, it is like two strangers are coming nearer and nearer, and sometimes they meet."

August 2007

Nadine Gordimer

Nadine Gordimer was born in 1923 outside Johannesburg to a British mother and a Jewish Lithuanian father. She began publishing short stories in 1951, and after 1960 participated in South Africa's anti-apartheid movement. Nelson Mandela read her 1979 novel, Burger's Daughter, *while in jail on Robben Island; she was one of the first people invited to visit him on his release. She has written fifteen novels—including* The Conservationist *(1974), which won the Booker Prize—as well as plays, essays, and short stories. In 1991, she won the Nobel Prize in Literature. In addition to these two novels, the Swedish Academy also cited* July's People *(1981), which is set during a fictional civil war after the fall of apartheid. She lives in Johannesburg, works as a UN Goodwill Ambassador, and was a judge of the inaugural Man Booker International Prize, on the eve of which I spoke to her.*

Nadine Gordimer has been doing some rereading. Six months before I meet her, the eighty-three-year-old Nobel laureate convened with Colm Tóibín and Elaine

Showalter, her fellow judges on the Man Booker International Prize committee. Since then she has read through a small library of work by the fifteen finalists, from Don DeLillo and Doris Lessing to Carlos Fuentes and Alice Munro. "I made a plan to read, say, the first two books by each author, one a bit further on, and then the book I thought was *the* work," says Gordimer of her judging strategy. "Then I'd catch up to the modern day. So I could see a progression." It was a labor of love, she says, but it led to a minor discovery.

"In two cases, the book I thought was *the* book turned out to be even more extraordinary than I remembered, because I had changed," says Gordimer, sitting in a hotel room in New York City, where she has traveled from South Africa for the PEN World Voices Festival. "I had lived more," she continues, "I had experienced more. And there were things in those books that I understood now, that I didn't then. If you read a book at your age now, read it again in twenty years, and you'll get something else."

At Gordimer's age, many writers have stopped writing, or at least reassessing older books. But, stubbornly, Gordimer has refused to stop evolving. Born in 1923 in Springs, Transvaal, she read her way into political awareness. Not much later, she wrote her way into antiracist activism, winning the Booker Prize for her 1974 novel, *The Conservationist*. When apartheid fell apart, it was speculated that her work would lose a certain vitality. Yet since 1994, the year South Africa had its first free elections, she has published ten books, adapting her focus, again, as the country's problems shifted to the AIDS epidemic, poverty, and crime.

Sitting on a sofa in her hotel suite, dressed in elegant shades of cream and gray, her hair expertly coiffed, she hardly presents the portrait of such a flexible artist. She has perfect posture and a sharp ear. To hear her speak is to experience a powerful generational dissonance: The clipped diction and perfect sentence structure have become things of the past, but her concerns—guns, the Virginia Tech shooting, the war in Iraq, South Africa's creaking move forward—could not be more contemporary.

"Graham Greene said, 'Wherever you live, whatever the form of violence is there, it becomes simply part of your life and the way you live,'" says Gordimer. And so it has been with her and the gun. She was spooked to discover resonances between the Virginia Tech shooting and her 1998 novel, *The House Gun*, in which a young man is driven to a crime of passion. What she omits is that in other fiction—*Get a Life*, in 2005—she predicted something else. In the fall of 2006, she was attacked in her home by three unarmed intruders, who robbed her of cash. "These men should have something better to do than to rob two old ladies," she said at the time.

Gordimer seems to take this event in her stride, refusing to allow it to spoil her notion of her country. "I think we were a little surprised by how much would have to happen after the change," she says of life after apartheid. "We had the apartheid walls coming down, and we had parties, and then we had to face each other—and I must say it was with a lot of courage and determination. Many things are wrong, but a great many things have been done to overcome the past in South Africa. But we now have the headache of the morning after."

There have been less painful adaptations, however, like the emergence of voices that were almost silenced by apartheid. At the PEN festival, she repeatedly championed the work of her friend the Johannesburg-born poet and novelist Mongane Wally Serote. During his youth, besides writing poetry and fiction, he was active in the militant arm of the African National Congress. According to Gordimer, he was nearly assassinated on several occasions. Serote spent some time in the United States and then returned to South Africa to become part of the first freely elected government. "You know, from the bush into parliament," Gordimer says. "Nothing could be more different."

Recently Serote instituted another change. He resigned from his position and went into Zululand to become a *sangoma*, a traditional healer—or witch doctor. Gordimer caught up with him not long ago and received a brief reeducation. "I said, 'Do you mean you are making love potions and hate potions?' And he said, 'No, no, no.' I said, 'If someone seems to be really sick, if they've got symptoms of HIV, do you give them holy water?' He said, 'No, no, no.' He said, 'Nadine! You are so ignorant!' So I said, 'Okay, Wally, I want to be informed.' So he did."

One subject on which Gordimer refuses to be reeducated is Günter Grass. The controversy over revelations last year in his autobiography that he was a teenage soldier in the SS has not moved her to reassess her friend or his work. In fact, she finds the media flap symptomatic of a culture addicted to scandal but lacking context. "If Günter Grass, in 1944, when Hitler knew he was losing the war, if he said 'I won't go,' he simply would have been killed," she says, her eyes fierce. "And why did he keep quiet about it? Well, he didn't keep quiet . . . If you read his books, the wonderful knowledge of what happened to people—he never would have had it if he hadn't gone through that experience . . . I cannot feel any blame is due to him for what circumstance unavoidably pressed upon him. He could not refuse."

Unlike fellow Nobel laureates such as Grass, Wole Soyinka, and Dario Fo, all of whom have published memoirs that revisit their political education, Gordimer will not be following suit. "I don't like to talk of things that my husband and I did as activists," she says, her face crinkling into a frown. "As a writer, three of my books were banned. But I lacked that final courage to go to the front line. So for me, to write such a book, it would require examining my private life and revealing it, and I feel that has got nothing to do with anybody else. And to me, all that could be of any interest of my existence in this world to other people is my books."

Aside from this difference, it's clear that in Grass, Gordimer sees something of a kinsman, a man who warned that reunification in Germany would be harder than admitted. Gordimer recognizes her country as dealing with a similar problem. Soldiers out of work after the fall of apartheid found new employment in military contracting, so a large number of mercenaries in Iraq come from South Africa. The country is also awash with guns left over from surrounding wars. It is easy to get an AK-47 in Johannesburg. "I say, a gun is now like the house cat," says Gordimer. "It's sitting there on a shelf somewhere. And it can't be locked up, since if someone comes into your home, you have to get it quickly. So it becomes an ordinary object. And you get cases, we had one recently—a pupil, angry with his teacher, took the house gun and shot the teacher."

Questions of race remain, too, and they will be part of her collection of stories, *Beethoven Was One-Sixteenth Black*. The title comes from something she heard on the radio. "Sometimes the ravens feed you," she says, flashing a smile. "I was listening to a classical music station, and there are these people who do that old disc-jockey thing and explain. Introducing one of his works, the announcer said, 'By the way, Beethoven was one-sixteenth black.' This fact, this DNA fact, really intrigued me."

So as she approaches eighty-four, Gordimer will be publishing yet another new work of fiction, a neat seventy years after she made her debut in the Sunday pages of a newspaper in South Africa with a short story. She's hardly celebrating. Right now, all of her focus is on pushing another writer forward for the Man Booker International. "We've got one more meeting. It will be in Dublin, where it'll really come down to the nitty-gritty. There will be each of us three judges, and each of us will have a particular favorite. One of the good things about this is it's been a monumental task of reading. We had to do our homework."

David Foster Wallace

 David Foster Wallace was an American novelist, short-story writer, essayist, and teacher. His suicide, in 2008, after a life-long battle with depression, remains one of the greatest blows to modern writing. Though admired for his 1996 novel, Infinite Jest, *it is Wallace's style in general—its finely tuned matrix of references and humor and self-deprecating neurosis, all layered atop linguistically perfect sentences— which is fast making him the Jack Kerouac of his time, his books likely to be stolen and displayed as hipster signifiers. Wallace was born in Ithaca, New York, in 1962, the child of two professors, and grew up in Illinois. In his teenage years Wallace was a nationally ranked tennis player. He attended Amherst College to study philosophy and English, with a focus on mathematics, and experienced the first of several breakdowns. His debut novel,* The Broom of the System *(1987), a philosophical exploration into the nature of reality, reflects the influence of Jonathan Swift and Thomas Pynchon. Wallace followed it up with the story collection* Girl with Curious Hair *(1989) and then* Infinite Jest, *a sprawling masterpiece about the toxicity of contemporary America, a world in*

which it was not illness but addiction that had become the defining metaphor of daily life. In the early nineties, as Wallace was working on this book, editors began to approach him to write journalism, a tremendous idea given how Wallace brought to seemingly innocuous activities—a tennis match, a state fair—the same rigorous skepticism with which he viewed any presented narrative. This interview occurred in early 2006, shortly after his second nonfiction collection, Consider the Lobster, *was published. A third collection of essays,* Both Flesh and Not *(2012), and an unfinished novel,* The Pale King *(2011), were released after his death, but he did not publish another new book in his lifetime.*

David Foster Wallace cares deeply about how Americans are using language, but he couldn't really give two cents about utensils. In a Manhattan sushi bar, the fast-talking forty-four-year-old novelist starts off a meal with chopsticks but soon trades them in for a fork. For a while this works fine, but something goes wrong. There's just something too *forky* about it. So Wallace starts picking up pieces, popping them into his mouth like tater tots.

Many readers would be inclined to forgive this culinary lapse because of Wallace's genius. Indeed, in a city not often cowed by literary reputations, the air flickers when he blows into town.

These gusts began with Wallace's ambitious *Infinite Jest*, an eleven-hundred-page reworking of *The Brothers Karamazov* set on the campus of an American tennis academy. The novel arrived in bookstores a decade ago to extravagant praise, even from critics not prone to over-statement. "With *Infinite Jest*," Walter Kirn raved in *Time*, "the competition has been obliterated. It's as though Paul Bunyan had joined the NFL or Wittgenstein had gone on *Jeopardy!* The novel is that colossally disruptive. And that spectacularly good."

While Wallace has released two short works of fiction since, not to mention a short book on the mathematical concept of infinity, there has been no follow-up novel to date. But there has been a very welcome development: his emergence as a popular—and essential—non-journalist journalist.

"I really kept saying to the *Harper's* people, 'You un-derstand I'm not a journalist,'" says Wallace. "And they'd say, 'Ooh-hoo, good, we don't want that.'"

He is referring to his earliest gig, when the storied monthly magazine sent him to cover the Illinois State Fair. Wallace returned with a gigantic riff on the kitsch of small-town life and the tyranny of cotton candy. A cruise for elderly passengers gave him a chance to zero in on the denial of death that undergirds so much of Amer-ican life.

Over the years, the assignments have expanded to in-clude more serious work. For a glimpse, one can turn to *Consider the Lobster*, which features, among other things, a long piece on the mechanics of talk radio, a bristling portrait of the American political system, and a brutal takedown of John Updike.

"For me, the hardest time of it is the note-taking," says Wallace. "There is so much. And so little that appears to me that is of interest. It's very anxiety producing. [With] fiction, you are in your head, so you are building the reality of what you are talking about. Which doesn't mean that it's not hard. It just doesn't feel like standing and watching while a tsunami is bearing down on you, which is how the nonfiction feels to me."

Wallace is supposedly a very difficult person to get to talk to. Over the years, the word *reclusive* has been used in interviews and profiles, including one in which Wallace was not, actually, interviewed. In person, however, Wallace is funny and charming and a little baffled by the reputation he earned for Pynchon-esque ghostmanship. Now that he has written some profile-style pieces himself, Wallace finds the reports of his shyness bogus.

"In the early nineties, one or two guys from magazines came to my house and met my dog. There was one guy who was very interesting—it was part of the whole flurry of publicity after *Infinite Jest*. He would ask a question, and I would give a fairly curt answer like, 'In fact, I think my life isn't really that interesting.' And he would stop the tape recorder and say, 'You captured that so well. What a brilliant tactical response—of course, that is to capture a history of your life, but also to represent yourself as humble.'"

Wallace maintains that the assumption that all public appearances are scripted has eroded our sense of what is real and what is not. As if on cue, Emma Thompson—or someone who looks just like the actress—walks by, and Wallace breaks into one of his typical expository riffs. "Are we not interested in celebrities partly because it is always fascinating? I mean, are we even the same *species*?"

Wallace's wife, Karen, begins to snicker, which sends Wallace into an endearing paroxysm of self-consciousness.

"Really," he says, "say you are doing a profile. The whole idea is to give the reader some slightly accurate sense of what it is to be this person, right? Or do you write about how the person seems to you, and then convince the reader to feel the same way? And how would you do this with Emma Thompson?"

This kind of mental gymnastics leads to fresh writing. For instance, the title piece in Wallace's new book, commissioned by a gourmet food magazine, describes a Maine lobster festival in terms of how the creatures are killed. On a junket to the Adult Video News Awards, Wallace spends most of his time recounting the infighting between rival pornographers and less on the flesh itself.

The approach turns subversive when Wallace addresses politics. "Up, Simba!," the collection's gem, describes a week of the 2000 Republican presidential primary race. Unlike the political-beat reporters he traveled with, Wallace got most of his information from the tech-support crew, who spent years watching moments get stage-managed and had a knowing sense of how the whole drama would play out.

"One of the reasons why I ended up talking to the techs was because they weren't like, 'Who are you?'" Wallace explains, dipping into the California Valley-talk that makes it virtually impossible to approach him with academic questions, even though he holds an endowed chair at Pomona College in California. "The first thing [the beat reporters] did was find out what organ you are writing for; then you wind up on some totem pole, where you are very low. They were just execrable."

On the job, Wallace's approach to reporting resembles an offshoot of former *New York Times* editor Howell Raines's "flood the zone" approach—send an overwhelming number of reporters to a scene. Wallace is such an astute and intelligent observer that he acts like a one-man press corps.

About his first assignment, Wallace says, "I must have really looked strange to people." He went without a notebook but with eyes wide open, grabbing at anything to write about. "I wasn't experiencing the fair; I was kind of locking it down in memory."

His sensitivity to texture and style, as well as story, makes it hard for Wallace to edit his own work.

"What runs is usually, at most, forty percent of what I send them," he says, but it's worth noting that Wallace knows he takes a certain liberty with assignments.

One piece in *Consider the Lobster* began as a profile of a conservative talk-radio host in California and evolved into a multi-tiered exegesis of the entire talk-radio industry. Wallace—a famous user of footnotes in his fiction—used boxes to reflect the ways that any attempt to write about this charged political material in a fair and balanced way fractured normal modes of storytelling.

"If you try to do that in footnote form, you start getting six-point type," he says, wincing at the compromise, as if it happened an hour ago, "which is just impossible. Footnotes are very much a call-and-response thing—you basically have two voices."

His great love of complexity makes it hard for him to

go back to straightforward narrative. Everything has complications and context, and, before long, Wallace has a manuscript that looks like it belongs on a PowerPoint slide.

Wallace enjoys moonlighting as a reporter in disguise, but he feels that fiction is far more powerful at helping us develop a sense of empathy for one another.

"If fiction has any value, it's that it lets us in. You and I can be pleasant to each other, but I will never know what you really think, and you will never know what I am thinking. I know nothing about what it's like to be you. As far as I can tell, whether it is avant-garde or realistic, the basic engine of narrative art is how it punctures those membranes a little."

March 2006

Doris Lessing

*For twenty-five years, Doris Lessing has lived in a small row house in a North London neighborhood that abuts Hampstead cemetery, where Sigmund Freud is buried. Each morning, the tiny, elderly author of the feminist blockbuster* The Golden Notebook *(1962) rises at five and feeds several hundred birds out on the heath. She then returns home, makes breakfast, and is usually at her desk by nine, where she writes because, as she puts it in her plain and simple terms, "it is what I do."*

Lessing's journey to this perch could not have been more circuitous. Born in 1919 in Persia (now Iran), where her parents met after her father had his leg amputated in a hospital where her mother was working, she grew up in Southern Rhodesia (now Zimbabwe). Her father moved the family there to grow maize. Lessing went to a Roman Catholic all-girls convent school, left home at fifteen, and was married with two children by her twenties. She left these children—and a second husband—behind when she fled to London in 1949 to pursue communism and writing.

On a bitterly cold afternoon in January 2006, a year before she won the Nobel Prize, Lessing agreed to sit down and speak about her latest novel, The Story of General Dann and Mara's Daughter, Griot and the Snow Dog. *The book is set in a future ice age and carries its hero forward from* Mara and Dann *(1999), in which Dann and his sister join a great migration north in search of a habitable climate.*

It's tempting to read this novel—as with all speculative fiction—as a parable of our times. But you have resisted this instinct in the past. Do you still feel that way?

Yes. You see, I wrote a book called *Mara and Dann* and I really became concerned with poor Dann. Some people hated him. He instigated such violence. But I was interested in Dann, so I wanted to write a sequel. I realized it would have to be in that semi-drowned world. I don't find it hard to imagine landscapes. See, the whole of *Mara and Dann* takes place during a drought, which I had just been watching in Africa. My son John had been there. Have you ever been in a drought?

No.

Well, it's hard. People are dying and their water is drying up and the trees are dead, and it's absolutely horrible. I didn't have to imagine that.

The descriptions of the refugees Dann encounters reminded me of your book about visiting Afghanistan in the eighties, seeing the refugees fleeing into Peshawar.

You know, it never occurred to me until afterward that everybody in these books is a refugee. But everyone is running from drought or flood or civil war. I do think a lot about them. You know, not far from here is a road where refugees of all kinds line the roads, and people go there to pick up a plumber or carpenter or something. This isn't an official thing, you know, but there they are. A friend of mine goes there when she wants anything. They are all very skilled people.

When you first came to London, in 1949, was it like that?

No, what was happening then was everyone I met had been a soldier or in the navy or something like that, so people talked about war all the time. And they talked about the war until somewhere in the mid-fifties. Then what happened, there was a new generation popping up. They were a new generation and they weren't interested. Suddenly, nobody talked about the war. I found that painful in a way. Now I think you can't spend all your life possessed by a terrible past, can you?

It seems like back then some people responded to this devastation by believing in an idea: communism. But now no one has any ideology outside religion.

No one believes in anything anymore. You know, we've seen several television films now about the ferment over the Vietnam War. And we look at this and think, this is America. What's happened to it now?

Have you ever wanted to write a romance?

Well, you know you can't write them cynically. I know a man who did it. He happened to be a very committed socialist. And he said, "You have to remember, Doris, you can't write these things laughing. Thank God I've got this vein of sentimentality." He did very well out of them.

When you began publishing, in the fifties, switching between naturalistic fiction and so-called genre fiction wasn't very common, was it?

No, and now all the boundaries are blurred. When I was starting out, science fiction was a little genre over there, which only a few people read. But now—where are you going to put, for example, Salman Rushdie? Or any of the South American writers? Most people get by calling them magical realists.

You've written many novels. Are there any you wish people would read more?

My science-fiction books. Canopus in Argos had a great readership way back when, and it even started a religion. *Shikasta* [the first in the series] was taken literally and they started up a commune in America. They wrote to me and said, "When are we going to be visited by the gods?" And I wrote back, and said, "Look, this is not a cosmology; this is an invention." And they wrote back and said, "Ah, you are just testing us."

I can't imagine that happening today.

Well, it was different back then. I used to go to San Francisco quite a lot. I was there before a big audience once, and a man gets up and says, "Doris, I hope you are not going to write any of your dreary realistic novels," and then another person got up and said, "Doris, I hope you aren't going to waste any more time with those silly science-fiction novels." And they got the whole crowd arguing. I can't imagine that happening today.

Do you believe that the cultural revolution of the sixties went too far?

Well, the hard drugs didn't reach here then. It was just marijuana. Also, the so-called sexual revolution I always have great difficulty in understanding—because it sounds like there wasn't a sexual revolution before that. In wartime, people screw! So I find what's wrong about the sixties is it's an aftermath of [World War II]. I think there were so many screwed-up kids. Why were they? They never had it so good. Ever. I remember one of their leaders sort of spoke up and said, rather bravely: "You think you have something special going. But you don't. You're the first market of young people in the world. That's why you are so privileged." He took a lot of abuse for saying that, but I think he was right.

Why do you think The Golden Notebook *was so popular?*

I think in part because it was the first book that had feminist ideas in it, but also I was writing out of enormous energy at the time. It was the late fifties, and my whole personal life was in turmoil, and communism was shredding before your eyes, and all that went into my book. The energy in that book is, I'm sure, why it goes on.

Well, The Story of General Dann *has quite a bit of energy in it, and you are eighty-six.*

But I'm not challenging any ideas in it. Nobody is going to believe this, but when I wrote *The Golden Notebook*, I had no idea I was writing a feminist book. Because I had been putting into it the sort of thing women had been saying in their kitchens. But something said doesn't have the effect of something written. People behaved as if I had done something amazing, yet I just wrote down what women were saying.

Speaking of that—in one of your previous interviews you described the fact that the threat of another ice age would make a nuclear threat seem like a puppy. Is this novel a warning?

Well, I do think about that, because we've had many ice ages, and we are certainly going to have another one. What pains me is that everything the human race has created has happened in the last ten thousand years, you know, and most of it in the recent years. An ice age would just wipe that out. It would. Then we have to begin again, don't we, which is what we always do.

January 2006

Hisham Matar

Hisham Matar is a poet, an ex–architecture student, and the author of two novels about the human costs of Mu'ammar Gadhafi's brutal regime in Libya: In the Country of Men *(2006) and* Anatomy of a Disappearance *(2011). Matar was born in New York City in 1970, but his family returned to Tripoli when he was three. His father's political activities forced the family into exile in Cairo in 1979. In 1990, while Matar was living in London, Egyptian security agents kidnapped his father. Matar's father smuggled out a letter in 1992, and aside from word that he was seen alive in 2002, little has been heard of him since. In 2014, Matar will publish the nonfiction story of his search for answers. His novels are poetic and elliptical studies of memory's warp, and the pain of a life defined by caesura—be it abduction or the silences that cluster around moments of shame. I spoke to him shortly after his first novel was published in America, years before the revolution that toppled Gadhafi from power.*

Proust had his madeleines, Studs Terkel his afternoon Scotch, and, judging by the shroud he creates over just one cup of coffee, cigarettes seem to jog Hisham Matar's memory. Sitting in a café in London's leafy Holland Park neighborhood, the thirty-seven-year-old novelist quickly burns through half a pack, his thoughts rising in cozy plumes. "I remember New York," says Matar, who was born in Manhattan, his father then an employee of the United Nations. "I remember driving downtown in a car and looking up at the tops of buildings. I must have been very young."

As with so much else Matar says, the memory materializes from the past, gauzily lit and more than a little poignant. A similar feeling hangs over the writer's prize-winning debut, *In the Country of Men*, the story of a young boy named Suleiman who comes of age in Libya in the seventies, a time when men were disappeared for speaking their minds.

Over the course of the novel, Suleiman's loyalties are wrenched to breaking point. His mother is a secret drinker, and his father is involved in something dangerous, something maybe even recklessly political. The book was published in Britain in 2006, where it was a finalist for the Man Booker Prize and the *Guardian* First Book Award. Matar was endlessly profiled, and nearly all of the interviewers made one key assumption—that the book was autobiographical.

"At first it made me angry, it felt like a very crude way to read this book, but I gradually began to feel more detached," Matar says calmly. A part of him understands why the assumption is made. Matar returned to Libya at age three and lived there until he was nearly nine. The Matars left the country when his father's name appeared on a list of dissidents. The family almost didn't make it out safely.

They eventually immigrated to Kenya, and from there, like Suleiman's family, to Cairo, where all was fine until one day in 1990, when Matar was a student in England, and a knock came at his family's door in Cairo. Matar's father left with Egyptian security agents and has not been seen since.

The cliché here would be that this experience made Matar a writer—but, as he explains, he was a writer from a very young age. "I was always entertaining people with my little poems and stories," he says. An uncle was a poet. Matar's father was something of an intellectual.

Although he hasn't lived in the Middle East for two decades, Matar seems to be a traveling example of its café culture. He often answers a question by darting sideways into memory or backwards into the literary labyrinths of the Argentine writer Jorge Luis Borges. A conversation with him almost always outlasts the warmth of the coffee.

Matar began *In the Country of Men* nearly ten years ago as a poem, and as he speaks, it's clear he still thinks of poetry as the higher form. "In the Middle East, poets are revered," he says. "There are Libyan poets who have sold millions of copies but who aren't even heard of elsewhere." Matar has maintained this affinity for poets. During the final stretch of writing the book, he and his wife, an American artist and writer, moved to Paris, where he was befriended by Pulitzer Prize winners C. K. Williams and Mark Strand. "I went to a reading and both of them were there, and I liked Strand's poetry so much I just decided to ask him for an interview. Strand said to the person beside him, 'He wants to interview me for an Arabic newspaper!'"

Although Matar grew up speaking Arabic, he writes in English now—not quite an exile from language but still not entirely at home. "It's sort of like a suit you put on that fits you—it's not quite your body but it feels right." Matar feels similarly about England. Born in New York, raised in Tripoli and Egypt, and married to an American, he has been exiled many times over.

When he goes back to visit his family in Cairo, he watches as his adopted culture infiltrates the one he left behind. "It's funny, you can see how certain words are often used in English. Words like *quality* or *efficiency* or *accountability*." He lets out a laugh. "All things you find missing from the Middle East!"

This world-weary humor is characteristic of Matar's approach to politics. When we met he would rather talk about the work of Javier Marías than fulminate over Gadhafi, who, in spite of the deep gouges he left in the lives of families like Matar's, has been resurrected in the West as a friend in the war on terror.

"I sometimes wonder if someone like me can be an artist," Matar says. "It's a serious question. Is it possible for me to write outside the political?" Matar believes there is enough mystery in writing to assure he'll never know the answer to this question. He is comfortable with this, as he is with so many other open-ended questions.

"My father loved New York and Rome. He used to say, 'Rome is for people who know what they want and are comfortable with it. New York is for those who have no idea what they want.' I've always aspired to be a Roman," he says with a smile that shows he knows the chances of that occurring are quite small, especially when the territory of memory remains so rich, so large, so dark, and, as yet, so unexplored.

March 2007

Mark Z. Danielewski

 Mark Z. Danielewski is one of the most innovative and impossible to categorize writers in America today. Born to a concentration-camp-surviving Polish American film director, he grew up in New York City, trading stories with his sister, Anne, who later became the rock singer Poe. He studied at Yale and Berkeley and the University of Southern California School of Cinema-Television, and poured his considerable interest in theories of language and narration into his 2000 debut novel, House of Leaves, *a multilayered, footnoted maze of a book about obsession and horror. Danielewski followed this up in 2006 with* Only Revolutions, *a two-sided flip book about two teenagers traveling across America. Along the way, each side of the story shows the evolution of language, from early Americana to the slang of today. It was a finalist for the National Book Award. In the thirteen years since his debut, Danielewski has become a cult figure for young readers for his ability to straddle the high theory of post-structuralists with the language of the film and screen culture of today.* House of Leaves *has sold hundreds of thousands of copies in paperback, and first edition copies sell for as much as*

$3,000. In 2014, he plans to begin publishing a twenty-seven-volume serial novel called The Familiar.

We met at a bistro over brunch at the time of the publication of House of Leaves. *It was his first interview.*

When e-tailers started touting the e-book as the next big thing, bibliophiles cried out in alarm. How dare technology invade our cozy relationship with text? As the first book to be simultaneously available online (at iuniverse .com) and in book form, Mark Danielewski's *House of Leaves* straddles these traditional and digital loyalties with a coy smirk. Have it either way, it says. It's a fitting strategy for Danielewski's doorstop-size novel, which melds the zeitgeist of postmodern point-and-click interactivity with the oldest fictional trick in the book—the found manuscript.

Ten years in the making, *House of Leaves* recounts how Johnny Truant, a Los Angeles tattoo-parlor employee, becomes obsessed with a manuscript he finds strewn across the apartment of a recently deceased man named Zampanò. In it, Zampanò deconstructs a film called *The Navidson Record*, a documentary of filmmaker Will Navidson's retreat to the countryside that becomes a descent into hell. Navidson has discovered that his country house is a quarter inch bigger on the inside than on the outside. Matters get weirder when a doorway appears out of nowhere, beckoning the curious Navidson inside. Always trawling for potential film material, he walks through, camera in hand. After that, all hell breaks loose for Navidson and his family, and in reading about it, for Truant, too.

House of Leaves will most likely either madden or electrify you. Thirty-three-year-old Danielewski himself admits that "there will be a few readers out there who will be thrown into a murderous rage." But there is no denying it is a work of genius. Zampanò's close reading of the film references everyone from Heidegger to Mary Shelley to Camille Paglia, who later appears in the book. When Danielewski, who studied literature at Yale and worked as a plumber and short-order cook to keep himself afloat, is asked how he pulled off such a complex first novel, he responds with a laughing, ironic dodge. "I faked it all, man."

Over brunch, the author buzzes with excitement, talking a blue streak about Derrida, Quark design software capabilities, and his book's elaborate layout, flipping open a galley copy to refer to a scene. It's not just his blue hair giving off sparks—Danielewski comes across like a true believer, a visionary. What he's pushing seems like not so much a circus sideshow but the real deal—a literary act of infinite seriousness.

House of Leaves takes David Foster Wallace–style self-referentiality to extremes. It has footnotes that run vertically and horizontally and even backward in half a dozen different fonts and voices. At some points the text is modeled after SOS patterns, the word *house* appears in blue throughout, and there are appendices totaling almost two hundred pages, some of which include poetry and photo collages.

Even though Danielewski first posted portions of the novel on the Internet, he says he believes deeply in the untapped potential of the old-fashioned book. "I see these guys—Wallace, Pynchon, and Gaddis—heading out toward this huge break, saying, Look, we can do it, we can ride that wave. I hope more people push books to new limits. I believe books are like analog computers with a great deal in them that hasn't been discovered."

Still, without computer processing this book may never have existed. Writing the novel, Danielewski burned up three Macs. He spent several weeks at the office of his publisher, Pantheon, formatting the book. It was almost as though he became Navidson. "One chapter took about nine months to map out," he explains. "It was a bit like shooting a movie. The preproduction took a long time."

It's fitting that Danielewski, who is the son of avant-garde filmmaker Tad Z. Danielewski, should describe things that way. Among his first writing projects were screenplays, and in his novel he uses typography to comment on the celluloid image: "I want to play with how the screen changes. Facing these gaps and silence [on the page], you ask, do you want to put something there?" But as much as he draws from (and spoofs) film culture, Danielewski won't sell the film rights. "I believe [movies] rob something from books," he says. Still, his screenwriting helped when it came to the novel. "It was great training for drawing blueprints. And then it was time to build the house."

To complicate the book's plot, the author uses Navidson's discovery to double as a metaphor for the growing gap between Navidson and his companion, Karen. Even though they share a house and a life, the emotional gap between them grows as unbridgeable and unknowable as the fateful quarter inch between the walls and beyond.

A love story by a semiotician? In the end, it turns out that Danielewski, like his sister, a rock singer named Poe, has a songwriter's heart, as attuned to heartache as he is to Derrida's theory on the sign. But at the end of our talk, Danielewski is back on technology, talking about surveillance equipment that can read text through heat sensors placed on keyboards. One imagines that if such a thing had been used on Danielewski as he was writing *House of Leaves*, the meter would have shot off the board, reading electric-blue flames and revealing that even in the Internet age, there's a little fire in the novel yet.

March 2000

John Irving

 John Irving made his literary debut at the young age of twenty-six, and has remained boyish into his seventies. His first three novels received mixed reviews and modest sales. His fourth, however, The World According to Garp (1978), was a massive bestseller and National Book Award winner. It combines a number of tropes—wrestling, sex, and writing fiction—that occur and recur throughout his work, with the freshness, however, of their being deployed for the first time all at once. Irving novels also often feature novels within novels, bears, prep schools, and older women deflowering younger men. He has remained in the top rung of literary bestsellers for almost forty years, a remarkable feat for a writer without the prop of a genre writer's series. Five of his novels—Garp, The Hotel New Hampshire (1981), The Cider House Rules (1985), A Prayer for Owen Meany (1989), and A Widow for One Year (1998)—have been made into films. I met Irving at his home in Vermont, where he was nursing a hamstring injury.

To get to the inner sanctum of John Irving's huge mountaintop home in Dorset, a visitor must walk past a long row of shelves of the author's books, seemingly printed in as many languages as there are countries. At the end of the hall is the heart of the home, a long, cozy room that stretches toward the horizon like the prow of a ship. And at its center sits Irving, the sixty-three-year-old author best known for his much-loved 1978 novel, *The World According to Garp*, as well as his near fanatical passion for wrestling.

Irving, who was born in Exeter, New Hampshire, and his second wife have lived in the six-thousand-square-foot home for the past fourteen years, during which time he has been a regular on the bestseller lists and picked up a screenwriting Academy Award. "You know when it's really great up here?" he says as I enter the room he calls an office, swiveling in his chair toward the panorama. "The winter. It's just all white treetops."

Our meeting is in late June, though, so the hills are shrouded in haze. And at nine o'clock in the morning, Irving is dressed for hot weather—shorts and an athletic T-shirt. No AC for him. There is a locker-room pulse to the air about him, as if he had just completed the literary equivalent of a hundred one-armed push-ups. In a sense, he has: The reason for our interview is the book he has just released, the 848-page tome *Until I Find You*.

Physically, however, Irving is under doctor's orders to steer clear of the weight room; he suffered a hernia after challenging the youngest of his three sons, Everett, to a quarter-mile foot race. "Let's just say I won't be doing that again," he says with a shake of his leonine head.

Irving admits he should know better. The days when he could take down men half his age on the wrestling mat are behind him. Nor does he need to drop full nelsons on America's literary heavyweights; the magnitude of his sales make grappling with onetime rival Tom Wolfe almost unseemly, like beating up on old folk.

Indeed, as if we needed any reminder, the walls around him are proof positive: In the battle among America's literary crossover artists, Irving has won, and by a knockout. Just inside the doorway on a bookshelf is the Oscar he won in 2000 for his adaptation of his 1985 novel, *The Cider House Rules*; on the wall behind his desk are three framed bestseller lists, all with John Irving at number one. Two of them are from the past decade.

Irving reckons he would have had a fourth number one in 1989, for his Vietnam War–influenced *A Prayer for Owen Meany*, were it not for the fatwa-boosted sales of Salman Rushdie's *Satanic Verses* that year. "I called Salman briefly after he went into hiding back then," says Irving, boasting only a little. "I told him congratulations, since we were one-two on bestseller lists all over the world. Rushdie laughed and came right back at me. 'You want to switch places?'"

Sixteen years later, Rushdie is back in the public eye; Irving has never left it. And the latest reason for limelight is his controversial eleventh novel. *Until I Find You* has a backstory so long and tortured it nearly eclipses the actual book. Like *Garp* and *Meany*, the new novel spins a picaresque yarn about a fatherless boy's journey into the world. This, of course, is Irving's core story:

He was born out of wedlock and his mother, from a distinguished New England family, refused to reveal his father's identity.

Until I Find You starts with a long and entertaining sojourn through northern Europe, where the central character, Jack Burns—who is four as the action begins—and his mother are searching for his wayward father, an organ player who is gradually tattooing Bach sonatas across his body.

The man proves elusive, and Jack and his mother return home and settle in Toronto—a city that has been Irving's second home over the years. Jack is enrolled in an otherwise all-girl school (a typical Irving touch), and his mother sets up shop as a tattoo artist. An unusual childhood, adolescence, and young adulthood unfold, replete with sexual escapades.

Then, suddenly, Jack is living in Los Angeles, a successful actor and international sex symbol who has everything but the one thing he truly wants: a dad. And so his real quest begins.

Although the novel reprises themes Irving has touched on before—the ache of growing up without a father, the sadness and hilarity of sex—he says they struck closest to the bone in this book. For once, the author is willing to dig into these themes in person.

"The principal event of my childhood was that no adult in my family would tell me who my father was," he says, his handsome face turning suddenly fragile. "I was born John Wallace Blunt, Jr., and my name was changed when my mum married my stepfather, Colin Irving, in

1948. I was six. I loved this guy, I loved my stepfather. I named my first son Colin after him. And my life just got so much better when he came into it that I thought it would be a betrayal of him if I had gone looking for my real father. I felt this way even in my twenties and thirties."

Instead of obsessing over this issue in life, Irving exorcised it on the page, plowing into the literary world with the head-down thrust of a man who is a little bit on the short side but determined to succeed anyway.

After graduating from Exeter Academy, the elite New Hampshire preparatory school where his mother and stepfather were teachers, Irving briefly went to college in Pittsburgh, where his love of wrestling was overtaken by a desire to write. After his freshman year, he traveled to Vienna to study. There he met and married the painter Shyla Leary, who was studying art. Their first son, Colin, was born in Austria.

In 1970, the couple had a second son, Brendan, but the marriage broke up painfully in 1981. Six years later, Irving married Canadian literary agent Janet Turnbull, who now represents his work. Their only child, Everett, is thirteen.

Irving seems exceptionally proud of being a father, or perhaps he's just fond of photographs. His home is plastered with dozens of shots of Colin and Brendan, often in wrestling gear, which is not surprising since Irving coached them in the sport as teenagers. Both are good-looking and beetle-browed like their dad. There are dozens more pictures in the full-size wrestling arena Irving had built onto one side of the house.

Irving seems relieved that Everett did not fall for wrestling, but this is a marked shift from his previous involvement in the sport. He used to drive up from New York to New Hampshire, where his older boys were in school, to give them personal instruction. When *The World According to Garp* was released as a movie, Irving appeared in one scene as a wrestling official. Now, hernia aside, he seems to be slowly giving up the idea that he is one of the boys. "I don't need to try and keep up with the young kids anymore," he says.

Although he has avoided the subject in the past, Irving has finally come to admit that he had a sort of prolonged adolescence. And he also knows why. Like Jack Burns, Irving had his first experience with sex at an improbably young age.

"She was a young woman, in her early twenties, when I was eleven," he says, swerving abruptly back into the past, "but she was someone that was sort of known and trusted by all the adults around me."

Irving is hesitant to call the experience molestation, but he admits that it was far too early for Mrs. Robinson–like thrills. "I was of such an age that I wasn't even aware we were having sex, until later, when I was old enough to have it on my own initiation [and] I thought, 'Shit, this isn't the first time.'"

Although previous Irving novels, such as *The Hotel New Hampshire*, have depicted sex between an older woman and a younger man with a wink and a nod and a backwash of sadness, in this one it seems terribly empty. The sex Jack has comes out a little weird, and deeply sad.

It also sets up the novel's central theme—innocence not lost but *taken*. This rises like a recrimination from the omniscient narrator in one scene, in which a friend's mother reveals herself to Jack:

> In this way, in increments both measurable and not, our childhood is stolen from us—not always in one momentous event but often in a series of small robberies, which add up to the same loss. For surely Mrs. Oastler was one of the thieves of Jack's childhood—not that she necessarily meant to hurt him, or that she gave the matter any thought one way or another. Leslie Oastler was simply someone who disliked innocence, or she held innocence in contempt for reasons that weren't even clear to her.

According to Irving, time has allowed him to escape the older-woman complex that grew out of his early introduction to sex. But it took a few accidents to force him to come to grips with his father fixation. The first came in 1981, the year he published *The Hotel New Hampshire.*

"It wasn't until I was thirty-nine and divorcing my first wife that my mother deposited a package of letters on my dining-room table," he says. "They were all written to her from my father from an air base in India, and from hospitals in China in 1943."

And so Irving discovered that his father was a pilot during World War II who had been shot down and held as a prisoner of war in Burma and China. The letters did not depict a deadbeat, but a man who had become a father too young.

The second epiphany came twenty years later, in the form of an even greater shock. In 2001, after appearing in a television documentary, Irving got a call from a man named Christopher Blunt, who had seen the program. "He said, 'I think I am your brother,'" Irving recalls. After a few hours of conversation, the two men discovered they were half brothers; Irving also learned from Blunt that their father had been dead for five years.

It was a crushing blow, after so many years of pining. Blunt filled Irving in on the man their father had become: the manager of a well-to-do investment firm who married three times, and who suffered from bipolar disorder.

"I began to think a lot about what I inherited from him," Irving says. He had started writing *Until I Find You* by this point, and in an uncanny twist had already given Jack Burns's father a mental disorder similar to the one he now knew had afflicted his father. Irving went into a tailspin, experiencing his first real bout with depression. He was prescribed antidepressants, but gave them up when it became difficult to write under their influence.

Irving eventually completed the novel in 2004. But that was not the end of the saga. He had written the book in the first person, but at the last moment, he pulled it back from his publisher and rewrote it from scratch in the third person. That took another nine months, but Irving is adamant that he didn't do it just to put some distance between himself and Jack Burns. It was to get more control of the story.

"It's the same reason why I didn't write this as a memoir," he says, his voice almost rising. "I've only written one memoir [*The Imaginary Girlfriend*, in 1997, about the writers and wrestlers who have influenced him], and it's very small. You just have so much more control over a story when it's portrayed from the third person."

The quest for control is one of the reasons why Irving has had such an adversarial relationship with journalists. A precondition of this interview was that I had to have read *Until I Find You* in its entirety. If it became clear I had not, I was warned, Irving would terminate the discussion.

He may be able to control his narrator and whom he lets into his home, but Irving has never been able to control his critics. And they came out swinging at this new novel. The weekend before its release in mid-July it was panned by many American newspapers, including many of the ones that count.

Writing in *The Washington Post*, the novelist Marianne Wiggins expressed bafflement: "He's too good a journeyman to have written anything this bad on purpose." On publication day, legendary slash-and-burn *New York Times* critic Michiko Kakutani delivered her verdict: "Jack's 'melancholic logorrhea' might yield some useful therapeutic results, but in terms of storytelling, it makes for a tedious, self-indulgent and cruelly eye-glazing read." The Sunday *Times* was a bit more positive, but by that point the damage was done.

Irving has gotten used to this drubbing over the years, but, as usual, he finds much to quibble with in the reviews of *Until I Find You*. And not just, as he explains to me later by e-mail, because Wiggins had a conflict of interest. ("A significant ex in her life is an old friend of mine," he writes, referring to Salman Rushdie.) No, he suggests, the reviewers' inability to appreciate his novels—especially this one—has something to do with reviewing itself.

"This is a long novel, and the theme of Jack's abuse as a child, which renders him a childish, acquiescent adult, makes the sexual explicitness germane," says Irving. "Both the content of this novel, which is not for the prudish, and its purposeful length—a solid sixty percent or more of book reviewers dislike long, plotted novels—make *Until I Find You* an easy target for lazy, impatient readers.

"My readers are neither lazy nor impatient," Irving continues. "Readers who relish long, plotted novels like me, and readers who have liked my other long novels will like this one."

It is possible that the best review Irving will receive for *Until I Find You* will come from his old friend and one-time mentor, Kurt Vonnegut. The iconoclastic American writer taught Irving how to craft and tell stories three decades ago at the Iowa Writers' Workshop. On the day of our meeting at his house, with those negative reviews yet unpublished, Irving tosses me a postcard he has received from Vonnegut. On the front is the slogan, "Life Is No Way to Treat an Animal." On the back is a carefully scrawled message: "What a perfectly tremendous piece of work, and so humane. You deserve to be richly rewarded. Proud to know you, Kurt Vonnegut. May 30, 2005."

And that's one certainty about the world according to John Irving: Despite what the critics say, Vonnegut's command—that he be rewarded—always comes true.

July 2005

Kazuo Ishiguro

 *Kazuo Ishiguro was born in Nagasaki, Japan, in 1954, and moved to England at age six. He studied at Kent and later in the creative writing course at the University of East Anglia under Malcolm Bradbury and Angela Carter. On the basis of his 1982 debut,* A Pale View of Hills, Granta *magazine put him on their inaugural list of the Best of Young British Novelists, alongside his contemporaries Pat Barker, Julian Barnes, Ian McEwan, Graham Swift, and Salman Rushdie, all of whom have won the Booker Prize. Ishiguro earned his own Booker for* The Remains of the Day *(1989), his classic and mournful tale of a butler who has given his life's work in service to an English lord in the final days of the British Empire. Ishiguro's novels are exquisite, rivetless creations, books so seamless in their execution that his range has yet to be fully appreciated. Some are suffused in the memory of a lost Japan and its former influence, like* An Artist of the Floating World *(1986) and* When We Were Orphans *(2000), both shortlisted for the Booker, while others, such as* The Unconsoled *(1995) and* Never Let Me Go *(2005)—the publication*

of which formed the timing of this interview—reflect the
mind of a more silken Kafka.

Kazuo Ishiguro looks at my plate of scones with dis-
may. "You're making quite a mess of it, aren't you?" It's
afternoon teatime at Richoux in Piccadilly, London.
Somehow I have managed to scatter crumbs on Ishiguro's side of the table. With mock irritation, he studies
my plate and has another go at instruction. "First spread
the cream down, and then place the preserves on top like
so," he says. "Just think of it like putting blood on fresh
snow."

It's hard to tell if this display of fastidiousness is a
performance, a strategy for our interview—the first, he
later reveals, of hundreds he will give about his novel
Never Let Me Go.

If that is truly the case, it would be hard to blame
him. Ishiguro turned fifty last November, and most of his
adult life has been spent writing novels (five to date),
then talking about them publicly. From *A Pale View of
Hills* to his Booker winner, *The Remains of the Day*,
about a repressed butler, Ishiguro has taken the "reliably
unreliable" narrator to its artistic zenith and stood at
the summit. But while his mastery brought him the
Booker and Whitbread prizes, among others, Ishiguro
admits there is a danger of being too good at this deli-
cate art.

"There's a certain way of telling a story," he says.
His eyes are kind but his tone is clipped. "There is a

certain texture in your scenes that you become addicted to: the texture of memory. I have to become careful that I don't continue to use the same devices as I did in the past."

Never Let Me Go is Ishiguro's most radical stylistic departure to date. Set in England in the late nineties, the novel is essentially a love story dressed in the garb of alternative history. But whereas Philip Roth's *The Plot Against America* used a slight alteration in American political history as its foundation, *Never Let Me Go* turns to science: It imagines a world in which genetic engineering—not nuclear technology—turned out to be the defining development of World War II.

Never Let Me Go is free of gadgetry and technology. The story exists in a parallel world whose contours we must infer. Ishiguro, dressed smartly in black sweater and crisp trousers, bristles when the term sci-fi crops up. "When I am writing fiction I don't think in terms of genre at all. I write a completely different way. It starts with ideas."

Although *Never Let Me Go* takes Ishiguro beyond his normal bounds, it circles the same thematic territory of memory. As the book unfolds, Ishiguro's protagonist, Kathy H., looks back on her childhood growing up in a rural English boarding school called Hailsham. Instead of hearing about students who have become famous politicians or society mavens, though, Kathy's pantheon of alumni involves "carers" and "donors."

It takes a while to work out just what this means, but one thing is clear: At the age of thirty-one, Kathy does not have much time to live, and telling her story is a way to make sense of all the miniature crises and spectacles of her pre-shortened life.

"I guess it was a useful kind of metaphor for how we all live," Ishiguro says. "I just concertinaed the time span through this device. These people basically face the same questions we all face."

The gap between donors and carers and the relative immaturity of their day-to-day concerns gives *Never Let Me Go* a spooky poignancy. Ishiguro's adolescent cast is hormone-crazy, hell-bent on being cool, but know as little of the world outside the school as readers do. Only Kathy, her friend Tommy, and Tommy's girlfriend, Ruth, have the intellectual curiosity to figure out what fate has in store.

"What really matters if you know that this is going to happen to you?" Ishiguro says of the death that awaits them. "What are the things you hold on to, what are the things you want to set right? What do you regret? What are the consolations? And what is all the education and culture for if you are going to check out?"

The novel's title comes from a jazz standard by Jay Livingston that recurs throughout the book, as Kathy recalls her friendship with and love for Tommy. Initially, Ishiguro began writing a novel set in fifties America about lounge singers trying to make it to Broadway. "The book would both be about that world and resemble its songs," Ishiguro says, "but then a friend came over for dinner and he asked me what I was writing. And I didn't want to tell him what I was writing, because I don't like to do that. So I told him one of my other projects, just in two sentences: I said, maybe I'll write this book about cloning."

A year later Ishiguro had given up on his original *Never Let Me Go* and was polishing the book he's just released.

The fact that Ishiguro has talked about it makes it seem unlikely he will go back to his jazz-themed book. In a way, he's already lived it: Lyrics were his first literary effort. When pressed for a description of his student days, wooing girls with guitar ballads, he steers the conversation back to writing. "You write about the things you've experienced. I basically did that with songwriting."

Many critics attempted to read Nagasaki-born Ishiguro's early work as veiled autobiography, and he concedes there was some truth in this view, but also a downside. "People kept asking me if I was trying to be a bridge between East and West. It was a real burden, and I also felt like a complete charlatan. I wasn't in a position to be an expert."

Ever since *The Remains of the Day* was made into a movie, he has been increasingly involved in films. In 2003, his screenplay *The Saddest Music in the World* was filmed starring Isabella Rossellini. In 2005, *The White Countess*, with Ralph Fiennes and Vanessa Redgrave, was released. Like Richard Russo, he tends to alternate novel projects with filmscripts. Not long after we speak he will begin working on the film adaptation of *Never Let Me Go*.

More screenplays are in the pipeline, along with novels. In the meantime, he will continue telling the story of his life over and over, refining its delivery to a sheen as perfect as his prose. And you can be sure he'll be in control of every minute of it.

February 2005

Charles Frazier

Charles Frazier was born and educated and lives in North Carolina, a state he has written about in three elegant works of historical fiction. Cold Mountain, *his 1997 debut, published when he was forty-six years old, tells of a wounded Confederate soldier who deserts and makes his way home through the North Carolina mountains. The book, coaxed on through word of mouth by Southern booksellers, became a colossal bestseller and flushed its private, soft-spoken author into a limelight he seemed equivocal about, at best. Not surprisingly, it took him nearly a decade to finish his second novel,* Thirteen Moons *(2007). It was on the eve of this book's publication that I spoke to him. In 2011, he published his third novel,* Nightwoods, *a thriller.*

There are many things that Charles Frazier would like to preserve in his home state of North Carolina, but right now two loom large in his mind: independent bookstores and the Cherokee language. The chances are that *Thirteen Moons*, his new novel, could make a difference with both. Sitting in Quail Ridge Books in Raleigh, North

Carolina, Frazier has begun to set this plan in motion. Rather than hit the road and barnstorm the big U.S. cities and morning talk shows, he has chosen to unveil *Thirteen Moons*—perhaps the most anticipated novel in America in the last decade—at this tiny independent store.

The mood in the back room is jubilant, as Frazier methodically signs his way through a stack of books the width and density of a Land Rover. Clerks stand around handing books to create a human conveyor belt. A publicist offers to spell him with whiskey, but he says no thanks, it being just after nine in the morning.

"They took a chance on me when I was just some first-time novelist," says the author of *Cold Mountain*, as the store's owner beams like a proud mother. Frazier has the sheepish expression of an easily embarrassed son. He wears acid-washed jeans and a black silk shirt. His beard is white and trimmed close.

Frazier's gratitude could seem forced, were it not so real. This is, after all, a man who quit his job as a university professor in his mid-forties to write a first novel about a soldier coming through the American Civil War. "I remember when this place used to be on the other side of town," he continues later in a small office, surrounded by purchase orders. "I know, because I helped them carry the boxes when they moved."

Thirteen Moons draws back the region's history even further. It tells the story of the destruction of the Cherokee Nation—once a country within a country in the United States, stretching from present-day North Carolina across Appalachia to Tennessee—through the eyes of Will Cooper, a ninety-year-old man adopted at twelve by a Cherokee chief. At the same age he meets a girl with whom he falls in love and pursues for the rest of his life. When not pining for his one true love, Cooper fights against the tide of unfair treaties and westward expansion unleashed by President Andrew Jackson through the Indian Removal Act of 1830 and carried out by the army in 1838. Cooper ultimately helps to secure a small piece of ancestral land for a group of Cherokee. It still exists today: the Eastern Band.

Frazier has done a lot of work trying to re-create the texture and feel of the time on Cherokee lands. He learned recipes for bear soup and yellow-jacket stew. In one brief scene, Will plays a kind of Cherokee ball game, which Frazier spent several days researching without getting a clear idea how it was played. Finally, one day in a stroke of good luck, he stumbled on some local Cherokee playing it at dusk. "The ball is so little—the size of a Ping-Pong ball," Frazier says. After watching the game played he had no trouble writing it into the novel.

For all their original culture, the Cherokee had begun to assimilate by the time the Indian Removal Act was passed. "They had a council house, a Supreme Court building; they were starting a museum," says Frazier. "It was indistinguishable from how people were living on white plantations in Georgia."

The son of a high-school principal and a school librarian, Frazier grew up within spitting distance of this region, when it was not uncommon to see farmers plowing by mule, and went to school with some of its residents. "I still remember when there were people farming

the old way," he says. In this part of the state, where
vending machines sell fried pork rinds and train conduc-
tors call people ma'am, these things count. "He's just a
country boy," one local leader said of him. When Frazier
first got reader's copies of the new book, he didn't send
them to writer friends but brought them over to the Eastern Band to see what the tribal council thought.

"I gave them to some of the elders . . . and Chief
Hicks and other people in the community to read. Then
we had a lunch just to talk about it," Frazier says. "One
of the things I said that day is, 'What I'm trying to do in
this book is not tell your story. I'm trying to tell our
story—of this land that we've all occupied together.' "

The significance of this gesture has not been lost on
the Eastern Band. Frazier's relatives were among the
white settlers who displaced many nearby Cherokee. "My
ancestors came [to North Carolina] soon after one of
those treaties after the Revolutionary War opened up land
west of Asheville to white occupancy . . . What happened
is what usually happened: Some well-to-do people came
in and bought big chunks of land, and leased them to less
well-to-do people."

Thirteen Moons was in many ways born out of this
legacy. Frazier initially planned to follow the life of William Holland Thomas, a white Confederate adopted by
the Cherokee who went on to represent them before
Congress. Thomas later died in a psychiatric hospital.

As he began to study Thomas, Frazier started turning
up documents that showed he was not an anomaly, that
settlers' and Indians' lives were more intertwined. "When
the army came to throw out the Cherokee," Frazier says,

"they kept ledgers of possessions because the Cherokee were going to be reimbursed when they got out West. So you can go through farmstead after farmstead and see what they all owned. Over and over, the lists would have been exactly what my ancestors had back then: a little cabin, some fields, a few animals, a plow."

In some ways, Frazier is trying to make reparations of a sort with this book. Not only is he telling the Cherokees' story, he has also started a fund to funnel some proceeds of the book into preserving the Cherokee language. "At the rate that it's going, it will be a dead language in twenty or thirty years," Frazier laments.

The first project in their translation experiment will be the "Removal" section of this novel, which chronicles the ejection of Cherokee—some only one-eighth Indian—from their land. Frazier is looking at it just as a beginning, to "learn what the problems are for publishing in Cherokee." Ultimately he hopes to move on to books for younger readers so that children who come out of a Cherokee day-care program will have something to read in their own language.

This sort of generosity does not jive with the perception of Frazier created by his enormous payday. The novel was sold to Random House for a briefly infamous sum of eight million dollars on the basis of a few pages and an outline. But those who know him say that he was embarrassed by the attention the deal created. Frazier still lives in Raleigh, while keeping a horse farm nearby and a house in Florida. He says that his life has hardly changed. "Somebody asked me the other day what I do for fun," Frazier says, breaking into another big, sheepish smile. "I do the same things I did when I was twelve years old: I ride bikes, I read books, I walk in the woods. And I listen to music."

These were the only activities Frazier allowed himself in the past ten years as he tried to finish *Thirteen Moons*. The first chunk of time was spent researching, but once he began writing things went very slowly. "I'd say a paragraph or two was a good day," he says. For several years, he hardly spoke to either his agent or his publishers. "I just kept trying to tell myself, 'I want to finish this book without having rewritten *Cold Mountain.*'"

Reception in the U.S. literary community has been pretty unanimous on that. "Whereas the narrative in *Cold Mountain* was rich and dense as a fruitcake," wrote Michiko Kakutani in *The New York Times*, "*Thirteen Moons*—despite its often somber subject matter—is a considerably airier production . . . a lot closer to Larry McMurtry than to Cormac McCarthy." The book has received its share of knocks, but they have not slowed it down. *Thirteen Moons* debuted at number two on the *New York Times* fiction bestseller list just as Frazier hit the road for his driving tour of Southern cities. He seems to know what people want from a storyteller and how to give it to them. Most of all, he knows the woods will be waiting when he comes back home.

November 2006

Edmund White

Edmund White began writing at age fifteen and has not stopped since. The story of his life, from his childhood in Cincinnati and early years in New York City before the AIDS crisis to a decade abroad in Paris, is beautifully spun in his memoirs and novels, including the semiautobiographical quartet that started with A Boy's Own Story *(1982), the first coming-out novel, and ended with* The Married Man *(2000), an elegiac tale of the death of a man's lover from AIDS. White helped to found Gay Men's Health Crisis in New York City in 1982, to battle the silence over the spreading AIDS epidemic. He is as virtuosic as he is prolific.* Skinned Alive *(1995), a collection of linked stories, is one of the best works of short fiction of the last quarter century. A biographer of Proust, Genet, and Rimbaud, an essayist, and an anthologist, White has made gay writing visible around the world and also created the possibility for a period of post-gay fiction to exist.*

By some accident of real-estate karma, a single street in Manhattan is home to three of America's most illustrious figures in gay arts and letters. At the end lies the apartment of the poet John Ashbery; farther along one will find Martin Duberman, the essayist and historian who unyoked scores of gay men from self-hating therapy with his memoir, *Cures*. Finally, near Eighth Avenue, where on Saturdays muscle heads can be found promenading like peacocks, spitting distance from the cafés and leather shops of the gayest corner of arguably the gayest neighborhood in America, lives Edmund White. Right next to a church.

To appreciate the irony of this juxtaposition a few numbers might be useful: one hundred, for instance, is roughly how many men White says he had seduced by age sixteen. Another important number, twenty, captures how many years he has been HIV positive and healthy.

So far, White is one of the lucky few in whom the virus does not progress, leaving him stranded in the so-called post-AIDS world with a legion of memories and a sense of carpe diem. "In spite of what my doctor says, I have never been able to refuse a second piece of cake," says the portly sixty-five-year-old. "Even when I know it's bad for me."

White's triumph over self-censure has been a beacon for many, but it also makes for a difficult interview.

We are speaking about his memoir *My Lives*, but what exactly does one ask a man who has admitted to lacing up his mother's corset and picking her blackheads? How do you get someone to open up when he has already devoted page after page of lyrical writing to being tied up in a dungeon?

"I am very exhibitionist in my writing," says White,

almost by way of apology for one of the awkward silences that yawn in these moments. "But I'm actually quite shy about my life in person."

This is true. Sitting in his living room White is somewhat bashful and, surrounded by the pungent fug of a soft-cheese dip, the author of *A Boy's Own Story* and other novels proves an excellent source of gossip, literary conversation, and good humor. He talks quickly and fluently, and will follow a debate down any rabbit hole. He is not, however, such a terrific expert on being Edmund White.

That knowledge has been funneled into his books, and *My Lives* appears to be the one he has built toward for the past thirty years. "Alan Hollinghurst said he thinks it is my best yet," White blurts out at one point. His puppyish glee makes the boast forgivable. You almost want to buy him an ice cream in congratulation.

Part of the book's luminosity comes from the structure. *My Lives* proceeds in long, set-piece chapters with titles like "My Mother," "My Europe," and "My Genet." The result is an even more personal, lyrical glimpse of his life and times.

If his autobiographical novels were a blueprint of his memory, this book is its scale model. For White the two projects are connected, even if nonfiction labors more greatly under the pressure to be, somehow, complete and, of course, accurate. "I could have written a whole other book like this about entirely different subjects," says White. But he did not want to fall prey to the confessional. "I felt if I went chronologically, I'd get bogged down in childhood and that's part of our culture of complaint in America. This endless wailing about your childhood."

White would have had plenty of reasons to gripe. As *My Lives* reveals, he grew up in the heartland of America long before casual bigotry against homosexuals became a Republican reelection tool.

White has more claims to being Texan than President George W. Bush. Both sides of his family hail from the Lone Star State, where one grandfather was a member of the Ku Klux Klan and the other a one-legged misfit.

Some of the details found their way into *A Boy's Own Story*, but not all. *My Lives* makes apparent how much he toned things down. In *A Boy's Own Story*, White says, "I tried to make the boy more normal than I was—in real life I was precocious both intellectually and sexually . . . I had tried to normalize him a little bit."

Over time, White's fiction caught up with the frantic way he was living. After two formative decades in New York, he moved to Paris, and his novels followed him. *A Boy's Own Story* led to *The Beautiful Room Is Empty*, and *The Farewell Symphony* in 1997, which White thought would be his last. He made this series a quartet in 2000 with a mournful novel about his lover Hubert Sorin's death from AIDS: *The Married Man*.

It says something about the power of the first person that even though White has published three collections of essays, an award-winning biography of Genet, a short life of Proust, a memoir of life in Paris, three collections of short stories, a book of travel, and a historical novel, he remains known for his semiautobiographical quartet.

One reason for readers' great love of these books is

White's ability to isolate memory from history. He is careful not to romanticize the gradual closing of this gap between how he lived and what he could write.

A lot of self-hatred and self-doubt had to be demolished, and these elements of his persona are evident in *My Lives*. "I think most people have a tendency to rewrite the past in light of what happened later," he says. "So, for instance, if let's say you were a Stalinist in the fifties, now you'd say you were a socialist. I run into that a lot—where people just don't own up to what they fervently believed."

Although he merely hinted at homosexuality in his coded and mandarin first two novels, *Forgetting Elena* and *Nocturnes for the King of Naples*, White has been relatively stalwart in his advocacy in print—and person— since. His second book was *The Joy of Gay Sex*, which he wrote with his therapist. After that came *States of Desire: Travels in Gay America*.

My Lives does not dish up quite as much dirt as it could, but there is some. Susan Sontag makes a brief appearance at a dinner party, as does French philosopher Michel Foucault, whom White rescued from a bathhouse where the professor was having a bad LSD trip.

White knows (and fears) that his incontinent sense of humor will probably "earn him a lot of teasing." The English critic Mark Simpson has attacked White for his "gayist" ideology. He also blames White for the exportation of "gayism—an American invention and export," which he describes as "not the antithesis of the American quest for self-revelation and perfection but the gym-buffed embodiment of it."

Since White's partner of more than a dozen years screens such attacks, he does not often hear them directly. But that does not mean he has become out of touch or fossilized. "I think Alan Hollinghurst's novel [*The Line of Beauty*] is a perfect example of a post-gay novel," he says, speaking to the idea that in the future there may not be such a thing as gay fiction. "I think he would have written the same book were he straight."

For White, a similar swap seems unlikely—in fact, after *My Lives*, it seems entirely beyond the realm of possibility.

March 2005

Geraldine Brooks

Geraldine Brooks was born in Australia in 1955 and grew up in the Sydney suburb of Ashfield. She began her career as a rookie reporter at the Sydney Morning Herald, and later covered wars in Africa, the Middle East, and the Balkans for The Wall Street Journal, where she worked alongside her husband, the writer Tony Horwitz.

Her first book, Nine Parts of Desire (1995), explored the cloistered lives of some women in Muslim countries. Foreign Correspondence (1998) celebrated and remembered her childhood pen-pal relationships with people around the globe. As a novelist, Brooks's interests have been equally global and hint at the prodigious amount of research that has gone into them. Year of Wonders (2001) takes place in a small Derbyshire village stricken by the bubonic plague; March (2005), her best novel to date and winner of the Pulitzer Prize, reimagined the American Civil War through the lives of characters from Louisa May Alcott's American classic. People of the Book (2008)—the novel I traveled to Martha's Vineyard to talk to her about—begins with the Sarajevo Haggadah, one of the world's oldest Sephardic texts.

Geraldine Brooks may have hung up her press pass, but the foreign correspondent turned novelist has retained a journalist's knack for blending in.

Exhibit no. 1: her decision about where to lunch on Martha's Vineyard in late December. Beside the Atlantic Ocean, the wind is slicing, the sky high and bright, but the apple-cheeked, Volvo-driving, Australian-born author thinks this is the perfect place to find a good lobster roll.

Brooks, fifty-two years old, settles on a bench and begins eating her sandwich with the ruminative silence that befalls New Englanders whenever they contemplate nature's awesome cold shoulder.

"These are the days the tourists miss," shouts a local walking toward the water. Brooks agrees the joke is on those outsiders.

Back in the car with her three dogs, driving to the large Greek Revival house she shares with her husband, the Pulitzer Prize–winning journalist Tony Horwitz, Brooks admits she doesn't fool the true-blue locals. "Some of them would say I've blown ashore recently."

Chances are that won't stop her. It didn't stop her, as an immigrant to the United States, from daring to borrow from one of America's most beloved books, Louisa May Alcott's *Little Women*, to re-create Civil War–era America in her novel *March*, which won the 2006 Pulitzer Prize for Fiction.

And she has gone out on a limb again in *People of the Book*. It tells the story of the Sarajevo Haggadah—a rare, illuminated fourteenth-century Jewish religious book— which disappeared from the city's library during the Balkan War. Brooks, neither a believer nor a religious scholar, follows the Haggadah backward through time, through its close calls with Nazis and other occupiers, all the way back to its creator.

Simultaneously, in a near-present-day thread, the novel tells the story of Hanna, a brisk, cool Australian book conservator, who is called to Sarajevo and charged with bringing the damaged codex back to life. These two strands make for a kind of literary *Da Vinci Code*, a book less about the occult mysteries of faith than it is about the power books have to bind people together.

"Let's cut to the chase," wrote a critic in the *San Francisco Chronicle*. "*People of the Book* . . . is a tour de force that delivers a reverberating lesson gleaned from history."

When asked what that lesson would be, Brooks responds, "That our societies are at our best and strongest when they do appreciate difference."

She didn't learn this lesson from history, but first-hand. As a reporter for *The Wall Street Journal*, she was sent into war zones and famines from Somalia to Iraq, often with Horwitz reporting alongside her, and watched societies suffer by not observing this lesson.

It was during the end of this period that she crossed paths with the Sarajevo Haggadah. "I was covering the UN peacekeeping mission over there," she says, sitting in her kitchen a world away from any combat zone.

The city's library had burned and the Haggadah was missing. "There were all kinds of rumors: that it had been sold and the money used to buy arms, or the Israelis had sent a commando team in to rescue it," she says. "And then it was disclosed it had been rescued by a

Muslim librarian who had gone in during the first days of the war to try to do what he could to save some of the things in the collection that he thought would just be destroyed if the Serbs managed to take the building. He had taken it to the bank and put it in a safe-deposit box."

That's where the book was when Brooks was allowed to sit in on its conservation. "It gave me a great insight into how a conservator actually works, her tools and her training."

Brooks heard the book had been rescued in similar fashion from the Nazis in World War II. She went back to Sarajevo and learned by chance that the widow of the librarian who saved the book from the Nazis some fifty years earlier was still alive. Brooks's storytelling antennae stood up. She knew she had a story.

Early this year, Brooks was on the road explaining why the Sarajevo Haggadah is so significant. She gives a little taste of that pitch when she takes me upstairs to show me two replicas.

The book is smaller than one would expect and extraordinarily beautiful. A hush falls over Brooks, and then she gives a little laugh, as if we're looking at a treasure.

February 2008

E. L. Doctorow

 *Edgar Lawrence Doctorow, better known as E. L. Doctorow, was born in the Bronx in 1931 to second-generation Russian Jewish emigrant parents. He attended Kenyon College and spent a year in the army in Allied-occupied Germany, before returning to the United States and, following a brief stint reading scripts for the movies, entering book publishing. His own fiction began to appear in 1960 with* Welcome to Hard Times, *which he started as a parody of the Western. He is best known, however, for having written his way into history, from his vigorous reimagining of the trial of Julius and Ethel Rosenberg (*The Book of Daniel, *1971), to his portrait of America in the early twentieth century (*Ragtime, *1975), to his gangster saga based partly on the life of Dutch Schultz (*Billy Bathgate, *1989). Doctorow has won most of America's major literary prizes, many of them twice.* World's Fair *(1985), which took home the National Book Award, melded his interest in history with a first-person narrative about a boy named Edgar who is growing up in the Bronx in the thirties. His short stories, collected in* All the Time in the World *(2011), often appear in* The New Yorker. *I spoke*

114 HOW TO READ A NOVELIST

to him in 2005 on the release of his first Civil War–era novel, The March.

E. L. Doctorow may not cotton to the term "historical novelist," but it is startling how tangible the past is to him. "Sherman was a wonderful writer," says the seventy-four-year-old novelist, as if the Civil War general sent him a postcard just yesterday. The moment is even odder because Doctorow is sitting in his publisher's glass-and-steel Manhattan office tower, traffic murmuring by nineteen stories below. "He was almost as good a writer as Grant. They were the best writing generals in American history. They were incredible writers. He got a lot of detail, the value of specific detail."

Over the past three decades, Doctorow has proven himself a master at tuning out the modern world, and, like Grant and Sherman, channeling the details of American history onto the page. He did it in his breakout bestseller, *Ragtime*, and he does it again with his latest novel, *The March*, which tracks the Union Army's march of destruction from Atlanta to the Carolinas in 1865. "The march was actually Sherman's idea," says Doctorow, making a typical interjection—not so much to elucidate as to correct the record. "But he didn't invent the idea of total war—that is, living off the land and pillaging. That was actually done in Mississippi by Grant. But Sherman made it epic in size."

Doctorow knows this because he reads history, but he is not what they call a Civil War buff. In fact, as with his other novels about history, from *Billy Bathgate* to *Rag-*

time, he composed *The March* in an improvisational style and did the research later. Asked once by the novelist Russell Banks how much research he did for a novel, Doctorow replied, "Just enough." And yet to sit with him for an hour feels like speaking with someone who stepped out of a time machine from the year 1865, fresh with eyewitness accounts. "I didn't think of napalm," says Doctorow, referring to what the destruction wrought by a column of soldiers a mile wide and several deep might look like. "I was thinking of a certain amount of pressure; if you see sixty thousand men tramping across the land, it creates its own weather system."

Caught within this storm are an array of men and women, running for their lives. In addition to Sherman, there is a recently freed slave masquerading as a white drummer boy and a doctor who later becomes the first surgeon general of the United States. Comic relief arrives occasionally at the expense of two bumbling soldiers who resemble Rosencrantz and Guildenstern—as Tom Stoppard imagined them.

This racial mix seems unlikely from a contemporary vantage point, but Doctorow says that the chaos of the movement put the country into a kind of fugue state of devastation, where unusual bargains were made out of necessity. "It wasn't only the troops but the freed slaves who attached themselves to the columns," says the novelist, who is known to friends as Edgar. "So their safety and movement came from attaching themselves to the army. Everything was transformed, including their identities."

This comet trail of slaves hoping to march with Sherman to the promised land pushed the general into the role of an emancipator, says Doctorow, and he correctly reflects the record by having his Sherman—the fictional one—being none too thrilled about this.

"I have marched an army intact for four hundred miles," says Doctorow's Sherman in one memorable scene. "I have gutted Johnny Reb's railroads. I have burned his cities, his forges, his armories, his machine shops, his cotton gins. I have eaten out his crops, I have consumed his livestock and appropriated ten thousand of his horses and mules . . . And that is not enough for the Secretary of War. I must abase myself to the slaves."

Another American writer may have blanched at the prospect of putting words into the mouth of so storied a historical figure, but not Doctorow. Ever since he published *Ragtime*, a historical montage of nineteenth-century Manhattan, Doctorow has entered a zone where boundaries don't seem to exist. His novels don't read like researched books but restored originals, recently redis-covered. *The Book of Daniel* revolved around the trial of Julius and Ethel Rosenberg, while *Billy Bathgate*, a final-ist for the Pulitzer Prize, unfolded in the shadow of the gangster Dutch Schultz.

As much as Doctorow admits that time—and the pas-sage of time—has been his key framing device, he has trouble with the term "historical novelist." "I don't think of myself as writing historical novels," he says, brow knit-ting. "There is such a genre, of course. But I don't think I participate in it. My idea of a historical novel is a novel that makes literary history."

This is something Doctorow knows a thing or two

about. For the past thirty years he has taught literature and writing, twenty-three of them spent at New York University. He often answers questions with examples from the work of great writers, delivered with the folksy charm of an afternoon radio host, whose ease with his role makes everything he says seem matter-of-fact. "You know," he says during one such interruption, "when Mark Twain wrote *Tom Sawyer* and *Huckleberry Finn*, he set those novels thirty, forty years before the time of the writing. *The Scarlet Letter* is set a hundred and fifty years before Hawthorne's own life. We don't think of it as a historical novel."

Growing up in the Bronx during the Depression, Doctorow came upon these writers early and often. Although Doctorow's father ran a music store, he was a reader and named his son after the poet Edgar Allan Poe. Doctorow's mother was a pianist. Doctorow once told an interviewer that by third grade he already knew he wanted to write for a living. First would come Kenyon College in Gambier, graduate study at Columbia University, service in the U.S. Army Signal Corps, and then a job reading filmscripts for Columbia Pictures.

His first book, *Welcome to the Hard Times*, grew out of the experience of reading so many bad scripts for Westerns. "It occurred to me that I could lie about the West in a much more interesting way than any of these people were lying," Doctorow once told the *Washington Post* critic Jonathan Yardley. For his second novel Doctorow switched to the science-fiction genre, telling the story of two human giants who show up nude in New York

Harbor. Needless to say, the book got poor reviews and Doctorow has not allowed it to be reprinted. "It took me three novels to figure out how to do it," he says now.

During this time Doctorow worked as an editor at Dial Press. "We were a feisty little house," he says modestly, perhaps excessively so given that this little press published big names like Norman Mailer, James Baldwin, and Margaret Mead. By assiduously acting as if he had nothing to lose, Doctorow was regularly promoted and wound up in the job of publisher between 1968 and 1969. "And then I walked away from the best job I'd ever have," he says, in order to finish work on his 1971 novel, *The Book of Daniel*. The move paid off—the book was a finalist for the National Book Award.

Since then Doctorow has taught and written, the latter coming more slowly than some of his contemporaries— but gradually with more and more critical acclaim. He was forty-four when *Ragtime* made him something of a household name. The book borrowed figures from real life and put them into fictional scenarios, all set to a ragtime beat.

With *Ragtime* Doctorow began a strategy he has followed for almost every book since. "Depending on the time, I've always gravitated toward the place where American life was being most vividly expressed," he says. "When the national identity flashed into being. So in 1910, it would have been New York and the music and changing of attitudes and the whole technological revolution. So *Ragtime* is set in New York and the suburbs. In the thirties, the city was feverish with gangsters, all the cities. So that's the city novel [*Billy Bathgate*]. In 1865, the hot spot was in Georgia, in the Carolinas, so that's where I was."

Although Doctorow hasn't radically overhauled his writing, his few vociferous detractors have raised a white flag at last after reading *The March*. Michiko Kakutani— who has given Doctorow a few broadsides over the years—wrote that *The March* highlights "the author's bravura storytelling talents and instinctive ability to empathize with his characters, while eschewing the self-conscious pyrotechnics and pretentious abstractions that have hobbled his recent books like *City of God*." Writing in *The New Yorker*, John Updike uncharacteristically put things more concisely by saying *The March* "pretty well cures my Doctorow problem."

Sitting in his khaki trousers and cardigan sweater, Doctorow appears very unruffled by this entire hullabaloo. It's not that he hasn't seen it before—he has also won a PEN/Faulkner Award, a National Book Award, two National Book Critics Circle Awards, and the William Dean Howells Medal, the highest honor given by the American Academy of Arts and Letters—but he also knows medals are beside the point. "I'll let someone else worry about all that," he says. For a moment his eyes grow dim and it's clear he's not thinking about the long-ago past but the more recent—and his own. Perhaps all those hours he spent at his desk alone, dialing in to a frequency he alone seems to hear so clearly. "You just have to do the work," he says enigmatically. "That's the most important thing. You have to do the work."

Imre Kertész

Imre Kertész was born in 1929 in Budapest and received the Nobel Prize in Literature in 2002. As a teenager, he was deported with many other Hungarian Jews, first to the Auschwitz concentration camp and then to Buchenwald. His experience of surviving formed the basis for his first novel, Fatelessness *(1975). Kertész's career as a playwright and novelist has closely tracked the fallout of post-Nazi-era Hungary, and the dissolution of this memory and collapse of communism. I spoke to Kertész through an interpreter upon the publication of his 2004 novel,* Liquidation, *which imagines the end point of Holocaust memories in a society much like his own.*

For a man who spent the better part of fifty years thinking about suicide, Imre Kertész wears an alarmingly broad smile. "Albert Camus once said that suicide is the only philosophical problem," says the seventy-five-year-old Hungarian writer, speaking through an interpreter at the offices of his American publisher. "I tend to agree."

One part of Kertész is playing a coy game here. After all, his latest novel, *Liquidation*, concerns a Holocaust survivor named B., who writes a play in which he is a character. At the end of the play, which is also called *Liquidation*, the character B. commits suicide. As Kertész's novel begins, the real B. commits suicide, leaving behind questions of his motivation.

This dizzying metaphysical paradox—the idea that survival in the conventional sense is conforming, and that true survival sometimes means taking matters into one's own hands—has been at the root of all Kertész's work. *Kaddish for an Unborn Child*, his fourth novel, examines this dilemma from the perspective of a Holocaust survivor who cannot bring a child into a world where mass murder occurs.

Fatelessness, the novel that was singled out by the Nobel committee as his masterwork, mirrors Kertész's own experience of being imprisoned in Buchenwald and Auschwitz as a teenager, of surviving and then realizing life in the world and life in the camps share the same philosophical problem: To live is to conform—so why live?

Kertész has been pondering this question ever since he was liberated from Buchenwald, but it took him almost thirty years to find the form to express it in a book. After being released he worked as a literary translator and from 1949 to 1951 as a journalist, but he was deemed unfit for the job.

"Whenever there was an article that we had to write about Mátyás Rákosi, who was basically Hungary's Stalin, there were three adjectives that you had to use," he says. "I remember actually dictating my last article to the typist, and I had these two adjectives that came to my mind, but I couldn't remember the third. So there she was, her fingers hanging in limbo; we were going to print, and there was nothing that came to my mind as the third adjective. And I just had to admit for a fact that I was unsuitable."

For the next three decades, Kertész wrote musical comedies to finance his literary works. "These were absolutely written for the purpose of making a living," Kertész says when I ask him if we will see these plays published anytime soon, "and I was actually very conscious of making sure they had absolutely no literary value."

Back then Kertész told no one about his real writing. "In Hungary at that time one had to distance oneself from the whole aura of success, because in that system success was a completely false path. Anyone who has experienced life under communism would write novels like *Kaddish* and *Fatelessness*."

Eventually, after having shorn more than a thousand pages from his manuscript, Kertész completed *Fatelessness* at the age of forty-four. It was published in 1975 and the response in Hungary was modest.

The book had a much greater impact in Germany. "I got stacks of letters from German readers—young people also," Kertész says without bitterness. He eventually moved to Berlin and has lived there for the last decade.

It has taken a long time for him to get letters from English-speaking readers. *Fatelessness* wasn't published in an English version until 1992, and even then it languished at a small university press. In 2004, in the wake of the Nobel Prize, Vintage Books published the novel along with *Kaddish for an Unborn Child* in new translations by Tim Wilkinson, who has also translated some of Kertész's essays.

In some way, Kertész seems to blame the book's failure in the English language on its previous translation. "I should say, really, that it was unfavorable circumstances. The novel was published here, a rather mistranslated version. These new ones are the ones that I really would adopt," he says.

Kertész will also have another shot at English readers when the film version of *Fatelessness* is released. After funding problems, the movie is finally under way. Kertész has written the screenplay.

"A professional is incapable of following this very slow, linear line of events in the movie," says Kertész, in one of his characteristically straightforward comments, "because they fear the movie will be boring if things don't happen. Analytical prose is actually not something you can transpose onto the screen. So what I was really striving to do was to write, if you wish, a version of the novel that actually works well on the screen."

In the meantime, Kertész's relationship with Hungarian readers has been positive, but strains do show from time to time. For example, at a reading on the day of our interview, while he received a standing ovation from most of the audience, some hard-line conservative Hungarians among them whistled and jeered. This is not an uncommon experience for Kertész, wherever he reads. His interpreter explained to me that a small minority believe Kertész's Nobel Prize is the result of "the Jewish lobby."

It is an ugly reminder that Hungary has had conflict-
ing feelings about the Holocaust. The country's pro-Nazi
government during World War II aided in the deporta-
tion and eventual death of six hundred thousand Hungarian Jews, and talk about Hungary's role during that
time still touches a nerve. Although he is not bitter about
this, Kertész believes there is a link between this period
of collaboration and the rise of communism. He has written about it in a novel called *Fiasco*.

Often labeled a Holocaust writer, Kertész says the influence of communism was equally powerful, and it was
through this second survival of sorts that he became the
writer he is today. "You constantly, constantly think about
the idea of suicide—especially if you live under a dictatorship," he says. "I believe I would have written very
different novels had I lived in a democracy."

When he talks of this period, Kertész gets a wistful,
almost faraway look in his eye, as if the lack of friction in
his world now has made him—or his work—obsolete.
It's a worry that B. struggles with in *Liquidation* as well.

"In retrospect, when I look back on these really dark
ages between the sixties and the nineties, when it comes
to suicides and the 'suicide game'—and when I use this
term I use it in the serious sense of Goethe—I do have a
sense of longing for it," says Kertész. "Back then it gave
me very fertile ground for my thoughts to develop."

Kertész explains that his novels form a quartet about
the Holocaust, with *Fatelessness* describing the camps,
Fiasco describing the aftermath in Hungary, *Kaddish for
an Unborn Child* delving into a survivor's metaphysical

grief, and *Liquidation* approaching the dissolution of Holocaust memories with the deaths of actual survivors.

Kertész says he wrote *Liquidation*, like all his other novels, out of a feeling of happiness. When I tell him that, once again, he seems to have formed a rather thorny paradox—novels about the Holocaust and suicide coming from a happy place—he laughs. "Well, I killed the character. I survived."

December 2004

Aleksandar Hemon

Aleksandar Hemon was born in Sarajevo and has lived in Chicago since 1992, just as war came to his home city. There are traces of this conflict in virtually every moment one spends with Hemon. His humor, which is black and laced with stories told to him by friends and family, is a frequent punctuation mark, even to the most somber of tales. When Hemon speaks he mumbles—"I come from a city of great mumblers," he repeats often—but the volume increases when he breaks into huge-mouthed laughter. His fiction, which he began writing in English in the mid-nineties while rereading a lot of Nabokov in English, is richly imagined, threaded with metaphor and simile, and beats like a heart with two ventricles, one of them Chicago, one of them Sarajevo. A Question for Bruno, *his debut collection, appeared in 2000, followed by* Nowhere Man *(2002), the tale of a young Bosnian man who is separated from his past and struggling with a coherent sense of self. On the basis of these two works, Hemon won a MacArthur Genius Grant, which enabled him to work on his astonishing debut novel,* The Lazarus Project *(2008), a two-pronged narrative about a Jewish émigré to Chicago who was*

murdered in cold blood by the police, and a Bosnian
writer in the present day who is trying to fathom how
such a crime could be committed. The book was a finalist
for the National Book Award. Hemon writes frequently
about soccer and politics, and in 2013 published a
memoir, The Book of My Lives, *which is when I went to*
see him.

An ice storm looms over Chicago and Aleksandar Hemon is going for a walk. Flat-capped, black-coated, his
stride reduced at the knee by old soccer injuries, he gives
the impression of a man older than he is. Two-story
North Side homes huddle in the falling light as we stroll
toward the lake. On days when he dons a suit jacket to
give a lecture, the Sarajevo-born writer can resemble a
bouncer with a dandy streak. Glasses, elbow patches. Hemon is tall and has a shaved head. Everyone who knows
him even a little bit calls him Sasa. Today, dressed for
winter Chicago weather, he is the sturdy flaneur.

"I walked a lot when I first moved here," Hemon says,
as we enter a small, nondescript storefront. For the past
year he has gone to this studio during the daytime to
write. He makes a coffee and leads us to a silent conference room; it is twenty-one years ago to the day that
Hemon landed in America. January 26, 1992. The Serbs'
terrible siege of Sarajevo had yet to begin, and Hemon
was just a young Bosnian journalist about to set off on a
tour of the United States. His plan was to return home
with the cultural loot of new experience.

He remembers his arrival acutely. "I landed in D.C.,

and an escort from the U.S. Information Agency and I went out to see his friends," Hemon recalls. "We parked in Georgetown, and I remember the street—it was one of those things. A nice town house in Georgetown, and I could see the light inside and the people inside moving, and whatever little bit of furniture, and I thought with that kind of pressing clarity: *I will never get inside this house.*

"And there was no basis for that. I did not intend to stay, I had no experience in the United States—I may have been here less than twenty-four hours—but I knew I would never get inside there. And 'there' not being America necessarily but that harmonious mode of living that some people are lucky enough to have in this country."

It was not an auspicious first feeling, and one he would have to live with for a while. Hemon wasn't able to return to Sarajevo for five years. Shortly after he arrived in the States, war descended on Bosnia, cutting him off from friends and family. On the rare phone call that got through he heard the news: Friends had been conscripted into the army, separated from their fathers and brothers. Killed. Snipers riddled his neighborhood with bullet holes. Dogs learned to anticipate shelling.

Many Sarajevans who escaped lost their whole families. Hemon was luckier. His parents, an engineer and an accountant, got out the day the siege began. His sister escaped a little earlier. Eventually they wound up in Canada, where they worked in grim jobs and his father was able to resurrect his love of beekeeping. Stuck in Chicago, no longer on a tour of any joyous kind, Hemon watched over the news as his city was destroyed.

The loss of Sarajevo was, to Hemon, a terrible one, as it removed him from his past. He has spent the last two decades trying to narrativize it back to wholeness. His work—from the 2000 debut collection, *The Question of Bruno*, with its eight, radically different tales, to his most recent work of fiction, *Love and Obstacles*—borrows heavily from the outlines of his life to tell tales not only about love and loyalty but also about the difficulty of living within a fractured self.

Now he has written a memoir, *The Book of My Lives*, collapsing all the ruptures his fiction describes into one book, which stretches from his early years in Sarajevo to his very recent life in Chicago. It is less an autobiography than a series of maps, inner and outer, which make up the planet that lives inside of his head. It begins in the Sarajevo apartment block where he grew up with his father, mother, and younger sister, and ends at his home in Andersonville, Chicago.

To understand Hemon's displacement, it is important to understand two things about him—his childhood, and the Proustian way in which he has always linked memory and the sensory experience of a place—both of which he lays bare in *The Book of My Lives*.

Hemon had a happy childhood. He played soccer, performed in League of Young Linguists competitions, became a reader, and learned to play chess from his charismatic, domineering father. His sister became a model and used some of her earnings to buy a dog, Mek, an Irish setter, who also made it to Canada later.

Like so many teenagers, Hemon fell in love with Salinger and Rimbaud, was sex-crazed, listened to the Sex Pistols, played in a band, and drove recklessly after he got his driver's license. His family curated their imagined noble past. Much of this is lost to them, as they left behind most of what they owned when they fled Sarajevo. "For people who are displaced, you can reconstruct the story of your life from the objects you have access to, but if you don't have the objects then there are holes in your life. This is why people in Bosnia—if anyone was running back into the burning house to salvage something, it was photos."

When he first arrived in Chicago, Hemon didn't just lack photographs. He barely had a change of shirt. So he roamed the city, haunting diners and coffee shops where chess was played and cigarettes were smoked and clothed himself in stories. In *The Book of My Lives* he described meeting Peter, an Armenian Iraqi who had lived in Europe and lost his family, winding up in Chicago alone. In another, more humorous piece, Hemon describes playing soccer with a ragtag bunch of immigrants from Italy, Cameroon, Nigeria, Tibet, and elsewhere.

It is tempting to see in Hemon's tale about Peter, whose trauma was greater than Hemon's, a young man seeking out people who were like him. People who had a before and after. Hemon insists this was not the case. He was looking, rather, for complication, and for Hemon complication is not just at the root of being human but is about the stories we tell about ourselves. "The privilege of a middle-class, stable, bourgeois life is that you can pretend that you are not complicated and project yourself as a solid, uncomplicated person, with refined life goals and achievements."

Hemon saw these things from the outside because he was, literally, tumbling down a ladder into the underclass. For the first time in his life he was poor. When the fellowship that brought him to the United States was over and the lies on his overqualified résumé—sure, he had been a salesman, yes, he had been a bartender!—caught up with him, he was nearly homeless. A smoker then, he remembers upending an armchair "like some kind of Hercules," to try to shake the change out of it so that he could buy cigarettes. He ate terrible food and gained weight. "My brother was so good-looking as a teenager," his sister told me. "Girls used to call constantly, 'Is Sasa there?'" For the first time in his life, he wasn't turning heads.

And he wasn't writing. For three years, from 1992 to 1995, Hemon simply couldn't write. "I couldn't write in Bosnian because I was cut off from that, and it was traumatic," he recalls. Friends asked him to file dispatches for their magazine from afar—their principle being that if the war led everyone to talk only about the war, then the war had won. Hemon couldn't do it. He walked and he listened, he smoked and he worked at jobs that made it hard to do nothing but think about what he had lost.

•

Finally he began to start over, first with deciding how to write. Hemon began rereading the books that mattered to him, this time entirely in English: Salinger, who held up, as did Danilo Kiš and Michael Ondaatje, others who did not. "I had to reevaluate my aesthetics," Hemon says, "because of the war and the siege, and the fact that my professor would have been at work had he not shot himself."

The man who taught Hemon to read and write critically, as he relates in *The Book of My Lives*, turned into a right-wing genocide-enabler during the war. Everything the man had planted in Hemon felt tainted. Hemon started over.

Most brutally, Hemon reread his own work. "I went back to things I had written, many of the things I had written in the nineties, and there was only one paragraph that I really liked." The paragraph was discrete, intense, and built from an array of associations that rose from the senses. Here, he realized, is what he wanted to do. Here is how he wanted to write.

From the very beginning, when he began to publish pieces in *Story* magazine and *Ploughshares*, and later in *Granta* and *The New Yorker*, Hemon's prose has been chiseled, direct, and saturated with similes. A boy remembers a trip to a family retreat, where he meets a relative whose lips were "soft like slugs." In a long short story about Jozef Pronek, a Bosnian man who is stranded in America on a trip not unlike Hemon's, the hero watches American sportscasters with bafflement. "Pronek would see them grinning at their microphones, as if they were delectable lollipops."

Hemon has been widely praised for the unexpected images this style creates, but it was not, he says, the hallmark of a writer trying to bridge here and there. It was deliberate, honed, and in some cases mapped out. "I wanted to write with intense sensory detail, to bring a heightened state." He is a sentence writer who counts beats as a poet does syllables.

At a certain point Hemon decided if he was to survive in Chicago, the city would have to become as intensely real to him as Sarajevo. He would have to be able to hear it and sense it and taste it. Simultaneously, he would have to retrieve and capture the Sarajevo that he had left behind, before memory, and his changing self, erased it. "Memory narrativizes itself," Hemon says, like a warning.

So he went back to Sarajevo, and stayed with his grandmother, and strolled the streets in a state of delirious confusion and déjà vu. In one chapter of *The Book of My Lives* he describes how a smell would trigger a backward glance to reveal not the movie theater that was once there but something else. People who had stayed behind were hollowed out, like the buildings around them. He began to go back more often.

Hemon also continued to write about people, like himself, who were caught between two worlds, looking skeptically at the new one while the old one remained fraught and internally present. In *Nowhere Man*, Hemon's second book, he wove an extended series of fragments about Pronek, who appeared in *The Question of Bruno*. "One of Pronek's problems is that he seeks a kind of moral continuity," Hemon says. "If I change suddenly and decide not to be who I am right now, what happens to all the other people that I'm connected with, and how do I sustain some kind of moral continuity?"

The Lazarus Project, Hemon's 2008 debut novel, attacked this question in a twinned narrative that shows how moral continuity can come from an unlikely connection with the past. The book portrays a confused Bosnian American writer named Vladimir Brik, who is living in Chicago and adrift in his life and work. He becomes obsessed with the story of another immigrant, Lazarus Averbuch, a Jewish man who escaped the pogroms in what is now Moldova and came to Chicago. Shortly after his arrival Averbuch was murdered by a police officer.

Moving elliptically from Chicago in the long-ago past to a trip Brik takes with a photographer friend, the novel circles the idea of memory and its moral component. What happens, it asks, when certain memories recede from American life, and how can a nation have any moral continuity if its culture is amnesiac? Hemon wrote the book at the height of the Bush years, when his attention began to shift away from Sarajevo to what his new nation was doing in the name of the war on terror. Throughout the book are photographs by Velibor Božović, which lend this meditation a documentary lyricism.

The novel was a critical hit. It was a finalist for the National Book Award, a literary prize only open to American citizens. In the run-up to the prize, Hemon was interviewed and profiled, and his story became a deeply American one: the war-stranded immigrant who arrived on these shores and made the language and a big multiethnic city his home by holding them up to the highest standards.

There was a lot of truth to this narrative, too. But this tale, the yarn of Hemon as heroic immigrant, planes down the contours of his journey to its destination. And even now that is a notion Hemon is extremely ambivalent about.

As he writes in *The Book of My Lives*, Hemon has always been fascinated by spies. The longer he remained in Chicago and wrote in his borrowed language, the more the obsession came back to him in a potent, emotional way.

"There was this gap, not so much a language or cultural gap but a kind of a metaphysical gap, that I was projecting someone that was not entirely me," Hemon explains, "and that I could never fully explain all the intricacies of myself. And therefore there was a difference between who I was on the outside and who I was on the inside. And with spies that gap is volitional. They construct it."

Spies, therefore, recur throughout Hemon's fiction, from his first collection, which features a forty-page story about Richard Sorge, the great Soviet spy who infiltrated Japanese intelligence, to a story in *Love and Obstacles* set in Zaire in the eighties, when Hemon visited with his family, and the African theater was part of the great game.

One of the other offshoots of Hemon's fixation with this gap is a flamboyant honesty. On stage or among acquaintances it can feel like frankness. Among friends Hemon closes this gap with constant physical comedy.

When he is tired he naps, whether people are talking to him or not, and when he is hungry, he will eat whatever is there in the house, even if it means spreading Nutella on a slice of mille-feuille, which I have seen him do. He is a hugger, a bum slapper, and if he doesn't like you, a glarer.

Not surprisingly, it took a while for some parts of Chicago to adapt to Hemon's style. In his early days he struggled to charm the opposite sex. There was another issue at hand, though, aside from his directness. He had never had to hit on a girl. Sarajevo life, as Hemon describes in *The Book of My Lives*, was different in many regards from the reality he came to in Chicago. If it was not communal, it was a shared space, with a fixed number of figures.

"There was a network of people you've known for twenty years and you've never spoken one word to each other," he says. "And then one day you might end up at a party and then you might start dating, or just become best friends. But there was no rush, and there was no need to impress anyone with your whatever."

Hemon found it easier to collect the casual yet close relationships that amount from mapping a place. A butcher, a barber, a baker, and a coffeehouse. Found acquaintances. A pick-up soccer team.

Twenty years after his arrival, Hemon is—and it is not an exaggeration to say so—beloved in Chicago. Not for what he represents but for the physical intensity of his affection, which travels in his frame the way a prizefighter contains a rage. He grasps an arm as you're walking with him, not unlike an Arab man. Still, he is a difficult man to interview, because while he's a phrasemaker, his stories take several minutes to tell. They are whole things, not easily clipped and cinched into a three-sentence nugget. To like Hemon requires the enjoyment of a slower pace, and a willingness to sit back and let him talk, which he admits he now does endlessly.

Eventually, in spite of his terrible memories and the anger he carried, Hemon did meet and marry a woman, Lisa Stodder, a writer. This provided some stability for his life when the publication of his first two books brought not just a doubled awareness of his project but also deepened, to some degree, a feeling of imposture. In a later chapter in *The Book of My Lives*, Hemon describes the slow, then sudden, breakdown of their relationship. He returns to the dumps, literally and financially, and nearly feels more at home there.

The Book of My Lives is full of such reversals of fortune. He experiences, again and again, the impossibility of retrieving Sarajevo, while what happens to him in Chicago seems to threaten any idea that it, too, will be a stable, safe place. After his split with Stodder, Hemon quickly met and married Teri Boyd, a photo editor from Florida. They elope and get married. They have a daughter, Ella, and two years later, they have another one, Isabel.

And here *The Book of My Lives* enters its sad, final chapter. Nine months into Isabel's life, a doctor's appointment reveals her head to be slightly larger than normal. A CAT scan shows that this is not a harmless aberration but the result of a golfball-size tumor on her brain.

Surgery is scheduled immediately, followed by two more. It is discovered that she has a rare form of cancer, one with very low survival rates. Still, for Hemon and Boyd there is no choice but to fight it.

Eight surgeries and several months of chemo later, Isabel dies.

In the piece, called "The Aquarium," Hemon describes the peculiar disembodiment of being in the middle of the worst imaginable thing. The way the world recedes and the laws and priorities around which the universe outside revolves cease to apply.

Language, the thing meant to help us connect, breaks down. Meanwhile, storytelling becomes essential. Hemon writes of how when he became a father he used to start to imagine something terrible happening but would stop himself. He knew, from imagining his own life in Chicago, and from flinging himself into experience that was not his own so that his language could catch up, that this was playing with fire.

In the meantime, his first daughter, Ella, began to tell stories about an imaginary brother called Mingus. He had his own siblings, Mingus, but he spoke in Isabel's voice. Hemon watched as his daughter used the facility he had relied on to survive in Chicago, to survive something she could only grasp through narrative.

We do not talk about Isabel in our interview. It is not a grief that needs to be explained any more than one needs to say that in winter Chicago is cold. Hemon carries the sadness in his bulk, which on some days weighs on him

and rests in his eyes like a man who carries something
heavy. He is not ashamed of his grief, and he will not forget his daughter. Pictures of her remain on display in
their apartment and *The Book of My Lives* is dedicated
to her, "For Isabel, forever breathing on my chest."

It's hard to read this line without thinking of another
one in the book. It appears in the essay on learning chess
with his father, where Hemon writes that the old board
he was given was "evidence that there once lived a boy
who used to be me." I ask him what this means, for it is a
remarkable sentence, and we wind up talking about spies
again. For Hemon, there will always be a before and after,
but it turns out, there will also always be the period in
between. The time when he had to make a choice about
who he was, where he pointed his compass.

"I was cut off," he says, emphatically, "the language
was cut off, all my friends were scattered, I had no access
to them. This was, among other things, before the Internet, and before I had any money. So I couldn't even call.
And so I had this sense that I could make up my life entirely and that no one would know. Because who could
say, 'No, no, no, he was not that, he was this'?" Book by
book, Hemon is making that impossible, it's all right
there on the page, especially with *The Book of My Lives*,
and it is formidable.

January 2013

Kiran Desai

Kiran Desai was born in Delhi and moved to the United States via England as a teenager. She has studied at Bennington College and Hollins and Columbia universities, but it is likely she learned as much about writing at home: her mother is the three-time Booker Prize finalist Anita Desai. Kiran Desai's first novel, Hullabaloo in the Guava Orchard, *was published in 1998. It tells the story of a young man in a small Indian village who convinces people he has become a seer. For her second novel, the vast and ambitious epic* The Inheritance of Loss, *she won the Booker Prize and the National Book Critics Circle Award. She was barely thirty-five years old. I spoke to her as the book was being released in paperback.*

Kiran Desai does not seem like an angry woman. Her voice is as high and quiet as a young girl's, and the first impression the novelist presents is of shyness—or humility.

And perhaps those are qualities she possesses. But listen to her closely, and a very different impression forms. Desai is not just troubled about the state of the world. She is enraged.

"Is it really such a brave new world?" she said during an interview in Manhattan. "I don't know if anybody would say so right now, but when I look at globalization right now, it seems like a very old story. And it seems pretty rotten."

Her sentiments are shared by the cast of her powerful second novel, *The Inheritance of Loss*, which won the Man Booker Prize.

Set in the eighties in a remote Himalayan village, the book is about a society for which leave-taking has been a way of life and arrival has almost always meant the shattering of a dream.

Take Jemubhai, a cantankerous, aging judge. Raised in a small Bengali village, he was sent off to Cambridge, all his family's hopes and dreams traveling with him. In flashbacks, Desai shows how he was ridiculed for his accent and became so shy he could barely visit the grocery store for tea and milk. He returns to India embittered and confused about his place in society.

As the book opens, Jemubhai takes in his wayward granddaughter Sai, while his last remaining servant has managed to send his own son Biju to the United Sates. In New York City, Biju bounces from one restaurant job to another, landing at an Indian café where he sleeps on tables at night, wrapped in a tablecloth.

"There is this incredible desire to say that India's past is a story of great hope," Desai says, "that we now have this enormous middle class. But at whose expense? The immigrant community here constantly tell you they are the most successful immigrants, economically, but we are also the poorest of immigrants, which of course is not talked about."

Through the story of Biju, the book re-creates this invisible scrum—adapted migrants taking advantage of new ones, the fight to stay alive. In one scene, Biju scrambles to be first to the visa counter at the U.S. embassy: "Biggest pusher, first place," Desai writes; "how self-contented and smiling he was; he dusted himself off, presenting himself with the exquisite manners of a cat. I'm civilized, sir, ready for the U.S., I'm civilized, mam."

In another scene, one of Biju's roommates evades calls from new immigrants from Zanzibar who have spoken to his parents back home and been assured he will provide shelter and jobs.

"Immigration is not this sunny thing where each day gets sunnier," Desai says. "A lot of times it's about throwing people overboard so you can stay."

Desai never had to struggle like that, but she has seen it up close.

"Part of the book started when I was living at 123rd Street in Harlem," she says. "I remember there was a bakery nearby very much like the one I write about, and a lot of the characters are from knowing the people up there—and talking to them."

Desai can relate to feeling trapped. She grew up in Delhi when it felt, as she describes it, more like a backwater than the heart of the globe's future, as it is today. "There was the feeling that books were the only thing that led you to the world," she says. "You read really *hard*—that was the only thing you could do."

She was taking after her mother.

"When my mother was writing, it was a very different world. There was no literary scene. There were no moneyed book tours. She just sent out the manuscripts to the addresses from the backs of books, even until the eighties. I remember we had to get money from the council."

Like Sai, Desai was packed off to a remote Himalayan village for a year—in her case, to live with an aunt—and it left an impression. "It's awful; it's isolating in the middle of the monsoon. You get reduced to nothing all over again—especially if you are poor."

In her book, the anger and resentment of being trapped this way spill over to a homegrown resistance movement for Kashmir, which draws Sai's well-educated, middle-class tutor away from her and into a much more dangerous endeavor. Today it would be called terrorism.

"Why is there so much violence?" Desai wonders. "Why is there so much anger? It's not surprising at all. The gap between the rich and the poor is greater than it's ever been, and sometimes the angriest people are the people who have seen both sides."

Again, Desai would fit this description. It took her eight years to write this novel, and along the way she learned the habit of solitude, moving around, living cheaply by herself and often around people who were poor.

Her first book, *Hullabaloo in the Guava Orchard*, made a splash, earning praise from Salman Rushdie and many reviewers. Yet rather than bask in the attention, Desai wanted to run away from it, she says.

"I was living in Latin America for a bit. I was working

in Brazil and Chile and Mexico. I think something very odd happens to you when you spend a lot of time alone. I barely talked to people. The mailman would come by, and I would hide."

She may now look the part of the glamorous young novelist, but she is distrustful of this particular kind of literary infamy because she knows it has nothing to do with the writing.

"Who is going to write an honest book? To look at something straight takes a lot of work. So who is going to do it? I don't know—no one is going to volunteer. It's much more fun to go to a literary festival and drink champagne or whatever, attend a conference and have a fantastic time. There's no better time to be a writer, in that sense. You get so many goodies thrown at your head. You are writing for *Travel & Leisure* and eating sushi for breakfast."

But for this writer, the real stories are those of the people serving the food.

October 2006

Philip Roth

Philip Roth is America's most revered novelist of the postwar period and living proof of the idea that American novelists are most vivid when they write of place. Roth was born in Newark, New Jersey, in 1933 to a homemaker and an insurance salesman, and he has returned over and over again to this period in his writing, from his National Book Award–winning debut, Goodbye, Columbus *(1959), to* Patrimony *(1991), a memoir of his father, and* American Pastoral *(1997), a Pulitzer Prize–winning tale of the generational conflicts that churned within families and communities during the countercultural revolution of the sixties. Roth's breakthrough,* Portnoy's Complaint *(1969), the mock confession to an analyst of a sex-obsessed young Jewish man, made him wealthy, a luminary, and a lightning rod for feminists. Roth continued publishing through the haze of this notoriety, and in 1979 introduced his most beloved alter ego, Nathan Zuckerman, with the perfect novel* The Ghost Writer. *Zuckerman narrates or plays a part in eight other Roth novels, from the postmodernist dazzler* The Counterlife *(1986) to the elegiac* Exit Ghost *(2007). Like Don DeLillo and Saul Bellow, Roth dedicated his*

seventies to developing a late style, which he carried into four novella-length fictions that focus on mortality, morality, and the persistence of desire in spite of both. During this period, he began speaking more publicly about his work. In 2012, as the Library of America neared the end of publishing his books in uniform editions, Roth announced his retirement from writing and said he would not give another interview.

No American novelist knows his craft better than Philip Roth. But in the past decade, as he turned out a series of strikingly vital novels about American history and became, at seventy, a bestseller all over again, Roth apprenticed himself to a form new to him: the eulogy. "It's not a genre I wanted to master," says the writer, dressed in a black sweater and blue Oxford shirt, at the Manhattan offices of his literary agent. "I've attended funerals of, let's say, four close friends, one of whom was a writer." He wasn't prepared for any.

"The plan goes like this," he explains. "Your grandparents die. And then in time your parents die. The truly startling thing is that your friends start to die. That's not in the plan." Roth says this experience prompted him to write *Everyman*. The action opens at the funeral of its unnamed hero and then backtracks to give us the man's life story. In many ways, Everyman is not a typical Roth character. He works in advertising and remains a faithful father and husband for long stretches of time. "I wanted a man who was in the mainstream," says Roth. "So [this guy] attempts to lead a life within the conventions, and the conventions fail him, as they do conventionally."

Over time, as his body breaks down, Roth's character leaves his marriage, falls out with his brother, and ultimately quits his job in advertising to spend his retirement painting. All the while his body clock is ticking away. In fact, the novel, which Roth once called "The Medical History," could be read like a fleshed-out physician's chart. "As people advance in age," says Roth, who turned seventy-three in March, "their biography narrows down to their medical biography. They spend time in the care of doctors and hospitals and pharmacies, and eventually, as happens here, they become almost identical to their medical biography."

In numbers alone, Roth has hit upon a winning conceit. The population of America is getting older, and questions of health—and mortality—are on their minds. Jerome Groopman, a medical columnist for *The New Yorker* and a professor at Harvard Medical School, says Roth "clearly did his homework when it came to many of the clinical aspects." Several operating scenes are described in detail, as are the technicalities of procedures. But Groopman believes there's much more to the novel than that. "The meat of the book, the heart of it, is the story of this man and the human condition, and the mistakes we make through life—how these then come back and are shown to fail to protect us from the fear and loneliness of facing mortality."

In this fashion, the novel draws upon the fifteenth-century morality play *Everyman*, in which a vigorous young man meets Death upon the road. "Everyman then utters what is perhaps as strong as any line written between the death of Chaucer and the birth of Shakespeare," says Roth, savoring the language. "Oh, Death, thou comest when I had thee least in mind." Roth's hero has a series of these moments. In his childhood, he nearly dies from a burst appendix. In his youth, he has an epiphany while standing on the beach. "The profusion of stars told him unambiguously that he was doomed to die," reads one passage.

Roth has written of mortality before. He addressed the topic with pathos in his National Book Critics Circle Award–winning memoir *Patrimony*, and with hysterical humor in his novel *Sabbath's Theater*, which won him a second National Book Award. The last line of that book read: "How could he leave? How could he go? Everything he hated was here." *Everyman*, however, has none of these hyperbolic flourishes. "It's extremely dark," says the poet Mark Strand, a friend of Roth's for more than forty years, "and really unalleviated by the usual high jinks and humor that Roth is able to inject into novels."

It will be interesting to see whether Roth's readers will follow him into this dark territory. His previous novel, *The Plot Against America*, reportedly sold ten times as many copies in hardcover as the books that preceded it. Grateful but chagrined, Roth refuses to let this fact buoy him. "Well, it doesn't change my opinion of the cultural facts," he says. "If it's this book or Joan Didion's book that strikes the fancy of people, it doesn't change the fact that reading is not a source of sustenance or pleasure for a group that used to read for both."

Roth's writing method has not changed in decades. "I write the piece from beginning to end," he says, explaining how he works, "in drafts, enlarging it from within, which means I tend not to work by adding on. I have the story, and what I find I need to develop is stuff within the story that gives it the punch, that thickens the interest."

When Roth reaches a point where he can do no more work, he takes the manuscript to a select group of early readers. "And then I'll go and sit down with them for three or four hours, however long it takes, and listen to what they have to say. For much of it I don't say anything. Whatever they say is useful. Because what I'm getting is somebody else's language about my book. That's what's useful. What they do is break the book open, they shatter it, and I can go back in for one last attack."

The novelist Paul Theroux, who read the book "in one sitting" and then again "with even more pleasure and admiration," says that Roth's careful consideration of his story's effect shines through. "Something I admire greatly is Roth's apparent casualness—in reality his effects are carefully built up." In this case, Roth's ability to work without his usual stunts is what makes the novel so impressive to Theroux. "Its power arises from . . . its persuasive detail, its fully realized and recognizable people, their weaknesses especially."

In the past, Roth has written autobiographically enough that it is tempting to confuse him with his characters— and their weaknesses. During the sixties, when *Portnoy's*

Complaint was racking up half a million copies in sales, even Jacqueline Susann, author of *Valley of the Dolls*, joked she would like to meet him but wasn't sure she'd like to shake his hand. *Everyman* has its share of Roth moments—Everyman is remarkably virile into his seventies, for example—but they tend to be of a tender biographical note. The opening scene alludes to the funeral of Roth's close friend and literary mentor, Saul Bellow. Later, after several operations, Roth's character calls his friends who are ill themselves to say goodbye.

Finally, the character visits the grave of his parents and meets the man who probably dug their grave. "That is almost certainly based on Roth's experience," says Strand. "Nothing is lost on Philip; whatever he can use, he'll use."

Still, it would be a mistake to think that Roth is contemplating the end with shaky hands. In person, the novelist appears fit and hale, arriving at the interview with a duffel bag like a man who has just returned from the gym. His gaze is powerful and intense. Death does not frighten him. The book "wasn't on my mind because of my own death, which I don't think is—I hope isn't—imminent," he says, laughing. Even when Roth had open-heart surgery in 1988, he didn't think twice about the end. "Well, I never believed I would expire. I was pretty sure these guys knew what they were doing, that they would fix me up, and they did."

"He's had physical setbacks," Strand says, "but he began much stronger and more athletic than the rest of us. When I met him he was a terrific baseball player: He could hit the ball a mile. And intellectually, he's one of the most alert people I've ever met. He serves up stories that are just mesmerizing and hilarious."

"When I was a kid," says Roth, "because my father was in the insurance business, he had actuarial booklets, and I knew women lived to be sixty-three, men to be sixty-one. Now I think it's seventy-three. It hasn't changed dramatically when you think of all the medical progress of the postwar era."

Groopman sees a certain sad truth in this. "There is a very prevalent illusion with all the technology we have . . . there is this sense that we should have control over our clinical outcome." But, as Roth's hero finds out, as we all do, that's not the case.

"The contract is a bad contract and we all have to sign it," Roth quips grimly. In nineteenth-century fiction like Tolstoy's *The Death of Ivan Ilyich*, awareness of life's end sent characters reaching to God. Not for Roth's *Everyman*. Or for its creator: "Nothing will force my hand," he says.

May 2006

Dave Eggers

 Dave Eggers is a publisher, activist, reporter, and fiction writer. He was born in Boston, Massachusetts, in 1970 and moved to the suburbs of Chicago when he was a child. In 1992, Eggers's parents died within months of each other, both of cancer, and he was left to raise his younger brother, Toph. This experience provided the germ of his debut work, A Heartbreaking Work of Staggering Genius *(2000), which is to the memoir what Donald Barthelme's stories were to short fiction: a neutron bomb that destroyed the form's most sacred pieties. At this point, Eggers had already failed with one magazine (*Might*) and started another,* McSweeney's, *which was on its way to cult status.*

In the dozen years after the publication of his first book, Eggers proved how much can be done with limitless energy. He turned McSweeney's *into a book publisher; opened a drop-in nonprofit tutoring organization with eight locations around the United States; started a literary book review (*The Believer*) and an oral history project, which has documented the lives of people from exonerated prisoners to Zimbabweans; wrote two screenplays that became major motion pictures; and un-*

leashed a torrent of his own work, which includes several collections of stories and four novels—among them the award-winning bestseller What Is the What *(2006), a nonfiction novel about a Sudanese refugee, and* A Hologram for the King *(2012), a swift and affecting tale of a salesman in Saudi Arabia attempting to make one final sale to earn back his dignity—as well as several works of nonfiction, including* Zeitoun *(2009), a book about a Syrian man made homeless by Hurricane Katrina. I met Eggers in Brooklyn upon the publication of* Teachers Have It Easy, *an argument for the importance of raising teachers' pay.*

It's one o'clock on a hand-chappingly cold afternoon at the Brooklyn Superhero Supply Co. in New York, and Dave Eggers has things to do. After concluding a meeting with the board members of his latest venture, a tutoring center called 826NYC, the young writer, book publisher, and founding editor of the literary journal *McSweeney's* collapses onto a ratty old sofa. He starts to lean back and then resists the respite. He cannot relax just yet.

After this interview Eggers is off to a meeting at two-thirty in midtown Manhattan. Then come more appointments and the following day a long drive to Pittsfield, Massachusetts, where he will fund-raise for Word Street, a tutoring center inspired by 826NYC. His black travel bag sits at my feet like a dog begging for a walk. "I'm trying to cut down on travel," Eggers says, when I ask him how he finds time to write. "But with things like this, I really don't want to say no."

As if his debut novel, *You Shall Know Our Velocity*, did not make it clear enough, perpetual motion is a key component to being Dave Eggers. In just ten years, the tall, curly-haired writer has gone from being a marginal editor of *Might*, a little-known spoof magazine, to America's most unpredictable literary star, humorist, serious novelist, and publisher wrapped into one.

And for all the press his unconventional live readings garnered—one of which involved Eggers quietly cutting hair—the real engine driving this rise was not a Warholian understanding of celebrity but a deep skepticism of the status quo and a desire to change it.

A Heartbreaking Work of Staggering Genius built a moat of irony around the loss of both of his parents to cancer in the space of three months, sealing out the memoir's sanctities in the process. Quick on its heels was the inventive *You Shall Know Our Velocity*, which told the story of two high-school friends who race around the globe trying to give away money only to discover how arbitrary their generosity is. Last fall there was a collection of short stories.

Add to that a few anthologies geared to reinvigorate the short story, a new journal (*The Believer*) aimed at bringing what Eggers describes as "a level of respect" back into book reviewing, a book on giraffes, the expansion of *McSweeney's* into book publishing, and two storefronts that sell, respectively, pirate supplies and (as this one does in Brooklyn) superhero gear, and it becomes clear that Eggers has grand, if quirky, ambitions.

But his biggest ambition is just beginning to become

apparent. As we talk about his recent book of short stories, *How We Are Hungry*, I realize that Eggers doesn't just want to make people laugh. He wants to push readers beyond their comfort zones culturally and stylistically. And he wants them to become activists, too.

For the past five years he's been leading by example. Back in San Francisco he teaches two free writing classes a week at 826 Valencia, the mother ship of his writing labs. One is about writing, the other reading. The latter is called "The Best American Nonrequired Reading," and it resulted in an annual anthology published by Houghton Mifflin (alongside *Best American Short Stories* and other literary institutions). As Eggers says, it "starts out as a reading class where [students] are reading everything in the U.S. they can get their hands on, then it sort of morphs into everything—counseling, creative writing. And it goes on for about eight months."

Thanks to Eggers's profile, the kinds of students who are showing up at 826 Valencia and 826NYC have changed slightly. Parents are becoming clued in to the caliber of talent teaching for free down the block. Daniel Handler, the brain behind Lemony Snicket, is active in the programs, as is the Pulitzer Prize winner Michael Chabon, who recently taught a horror class at the San Francisco branch.

"Great story," Eggers says excitedly. "[Michael Chabon] was talking to Stephen King. He said, 'Hey, I'm going to teach a writing class. I'm going to be teaching your work.' King said, 'If you teach that, I'll fly out.' And he did it. He flew out all the way from Maine to teach a two-hour class to thirty students."

·

What's so fascinating about Eggers as a public figure is
that he has found a way to take an existing concern about
how to give back to the world and made it both his life's
passion and his subject as a writer. Getting people to join
in the campaign seems almost easy for him. The New
York tutoring center reaches five hundred students. His
San Francisco center offered seven thousand workshop
sessions last semester alone. Together, they draw from a
pool of some eight hundred volunteers. A new chapter
was launched recently in Los Angeles, and more are on
the way in Chicago, Seattle, and Ann Arbor. The numbers might sound small now, but you can be sure they're
going to grow. Whereas once Eggers's book tours were
Dadaist art shows, now they're fund-raisers.

Eggers's initial response to the hype of his first book
did not predict the person he has become. After *A Heartbreaking Work of Staggering Genius* climbed the bestseller lists he fired his agent, turned down publishing
deals from mainstream houses, and put out his first novel
by himself, selling copies only via the Internet. Any rough-
ness is gone now. Over the course of an hour and a half,
Eggers is friendly and cheerful, coming back time and
again to his 826 projects, always deflecting credit to
colleagues, such as Nínive Calegari, a friend and longtime schoolteacher with whom he started the tutoring
enterprise.

Along with Daniel Moulthrop, whom Eggers is quick
to note did "the lion's share of the work," the three of
them have written a book about teachers' pay called

Teachers Have It Easy: The Big Sacrifices and Small Salaries of America's Teachers. The book uses teachers' first-person narratives to make a compelling case for why the only way American public schools will get better is through a huge increase in the salaries paid to teachers.

Although there has been so much written about teaching and why it isn't working, Eggers and his coauthors managed to drum up new stories and statistics. As they discovered in their research, being a teacher is no summer vacation. In fact, some forty-two percent of American schoolteachers work summer school or a nonteaching job to make ends meet. This leads to long days for people like Erik Benner, who arrives at Cross Timbers Middle School at six in the morning to open the gym for morning football practice, then ends his day close to ten at night, finishing a second job at Circuit City.

Teaching is something that is in Eggers's blood, and he is especially sensitive to those who are called to it. "My mum and sister and I were teachers, and one of my best friends who was on our board in San Francisco, named Casey Fuller, was a teacher in San Francisco. I'd known her since I was twelve and I just remember she got her certificate and her master's. She was teaching year one and then later on in high school. She was the most motivated and inspired and happy person I'd ever met in any field."

But, as is often the case, Fuller simply couldn't make the finances of her passion work. "As the years went by— she taught for five years—it became harder and harder to make ends meet. She was living with a roommate and she couldn't even live on her own unless she got married."

Until leadership at the top catches up with the problem, Eggers says, America's most talented graduates will continue to think twice before they teach. Seventy-eight percent of college graduates polled in one survey in 2000 said being "seriously underpaid" was a major deterrent to considering the field.

This is why Eggers and his coauthors are turning Reaganomics on its head to argue for higher salaries for teachers. "It's our theory that everything trickles down from there," says Eggers. "That if you have high salaries, good conditions, you have good support, you have a lot of communication between teachers, you pay for teachers' supplemental training, and the students learn."

This narrative-based approach is an appropriate model for the book—teachers are, after all, somewhat invisible in America—but it's also an appropriate metaphor for Eggers's own story. He suffered a great loss, and though narrative could not bring his parents back, it gave him a container for his grief. The power of story also got him out of Brooklyn and back to California, where he is happier, and lives with his wife, the novelist Vendela Vida.

The power of story brought *McSweeney's* out of the margins and into the mainstream. Story also gave Eggers the power to publish himself and the writers he believes in. And now the stories of teachers' struggles are going to power Eggers's message out into the world—to get people to give something back.

June 2005

Vikram Chandra

Vikram Chandra was born in New Delhi in 1961 and educated in America. After flirting with film school—his mother is a screenwriter and playwright, one sister a director, and another a film critic—he studied with the American postmodernists Donald Barthelme and John Barth at Johns Hopkins University in Baltimore. Their attention to language has left traces on his work, but Chandra's fiction has none of their corrugated inwardness. His 1995 debut novel, Red Earth and Pouring Rain, *is a sweeping epic based on the nineteenth-century Anglo-Indian soldier James Skinner. A collection of stories,* Love and Longing in Bombay, *appeared two years later, and in 2007 he published one of the most thrilling and perceptive novels about the so-called New India,* Sacred Games. *The book was one of the Booker Prize's most glaring omissions in its forty-year history.*

For the past seven years, the diminutive novelist Vikram Chandra has spent a lot of time with very bad people. He met men who killed for a living and others who simply extorted and tortured people. He's been driven around in circles and rushed to secret hideouts. "I remember one night I went out for beers with some of these shooters," said the forty-four-year-old novelist on a recent visit to New York, "and I thought, gosh, I could almost be friends with these guys. They're really nice guys. Then I realized they probably would go out later that night and maybe kill someone."

Chandra wasn't doing this for kicks. He has spent the last decade working on a major novel. *Sacred Games* tells the story of a crime boss and a Sikh police inspector, and the way their lives connect in Bombay (now Mumbai) and beyond during the eighties and nineties. It is a terrific, brilliant, earthmover of a book, *Crime and Punishment* crossed with *The Godfather*, with some *Sopranos*-inspired irony thrown in to boot, and it has made Chandra a bit famous back home in India. "Every time there is a shooting in Bombay now, I get a call and someone asks me to come on air and talk about it. Last time it happened, I said, 'Well, I'm not really an expert about this.' And the newscaster just said, 'That's okay. Can you come on anyway?'"

The idea of organized crime and Bombay might seem quaint, but Chandra says it's not the kind of thing people chuckle about. In the eighties the influence of organized crime became so great it could affect elections. Then in the nineties the bloodbaths moved into the public realm. "You would open the newspaper in the morning and there would be four dead in a shootout," Chandra says, "and the next day it would be six. It was like a cricket score every morning." Middle-class citizens were not just witnesses; they became targets, too. "People that I knew who were doctors would get a phone call saying, you know, we want this much money, more or less, to let you live."

Around the time that Chandra's brother-in-law, a film producer, hired bodyguards, Chandra figured it was time to start writing about the subject. He banged out a short story about a middle-aged lovelorn Sikh police inspector named Sartaj Singh that was published in his 1997 collection *Love and Longing in Bombay*, but that didn't satiate his interest. "I started to get to know a little about policing in India, more than I needed to know as a citizen. And I started to hang out with policemen, became friends with a couple of them, and the character in that story just wouldn't leave me alone. I felt like we had unfinished business."

So Chandra threw himself into the project, believing he was writing a very short book. "I thought of it as a two-hundred-page book. You know, one of those thrillers where you find a dead body in the water, and two hundred pages later it all gets explained." But each time he pulled a thread, another would unravel, and then another. What felt like a local phenomenon proved to cut across all of India, all of the subcontinent, encapsulating even the current geopolitical situation and the War on Terror.

"Intelligence agencies like to use these organizations for logistical support," Chandra explains. "These guys operate as an extraconstitutional arm, so the government can always deny responsibility if someone gets busted doing something that they shouldn't. But they become cyborgs of a sort that no one can control. The militant movements will sometimes obtain arms from these organized-crime gangs, who have business with gunrunning. And then these guys will get in Afghanistan and Pakistan heroin, which then gets them bringing in new revenue. It's a very incestuous, naughty triangle."

One of the most bizarre twists in all of this is that many of India's biggest crime bosses have a reach into the film world, where they can script their own mythologies. In *Sacred Games*, the book's key gangster, Gaitonde, works his way up and into the heart of Bollywood, where he runs dirty money into the film system. It sounds improbable, but as with much in this book, it's drawn from real life. "One of the movies that came out a few years back about the gang world actually won a big award," Chandra says. "The day the award was announced the guy walks onstage to accept and everyone realizes he's the brother of one of the biggest bosses, right, so his representation was basically about his life."

Chandra grew up in the Bollywood film world so it didn't take much research for him to imagine his way into it. Members of his family work across scriptwriting, producing, directing, and film criticism. Chandra himself has dabbled as well, cowriting *Mission Kashmir*, a drama about a police officer who adopts the son of a man he kills while pursuing a terrorist. The film was not a huge success, but it received a big boost in the United States when Shaquille O'Neal held it aloft in an episode of *MTV Cribs* and proclaimed it his favorite film. "The sales went way up," Chandra says.

As much as he seemed destined to flicker at the edge

of this world, Chandra never expected to be fully immersed in it. He attended film school at Columbia University in New York but dropped out to start writing his first novel, *Red Earth and Pouring Rain*, which was published in 1995, when he was thirty-four years old. Following this Chandra spent time working as a computer programmer and software consultant.

Sacred Games has pretty much put an end to any such moonlighting. The book sold for more than one million dollars in the United States and a hefty six figures in England. Now he lives a thoroughly global existence, dividing his time between India and Berkeley, California, where he teaches literature and lives with his wife, who is also a novelist.

Living in these two worlds doesn't create much friction for him, as Chandra has been observing where and when and how cultures overlap since he began writing. "One of the amazing things about the city of Bombay is how everything is so wrapped together and on top of each other," Chandra says, sounding every bit like the city's booster, even if his book might make some tourists think twice before going there.

"So you have an expensive posh suburb where it is extraordinarily expensive, but right next to it is a slum."

This clash is not seen from the outside, where India's growth rate is constantly described in glowing terms. Beneath it, though, lurks a harsher truth—that even for the middle class it's not enough. "A lot of the younger front-line shooters of the organized-crime people and these companies, they are actually not the poorest of the poor," Chandra says. "They are actually lower-middle-class boys who maybe have a bit of a college education. The gang guys are really smart—they come up to them and they say, 'Okay, I'm going to give you a motorcycle and I'm going to give you ten thousand rupees a month. And if you work hard and are loyal, you might one day own a fleet of Mercedes.' "

Chandra shakes his head as if to say he cannot even make this stuff up. "That's the narrative that actually attracts people," he continues. "What the young kid is thinking is, I could spend my whole life working in an office and, at the end of all that, I wouldn't even be able to afford a house in the city. So I think the abject quality that one thinks generates crime is not necessarily the only dynamic that's working there." As *Sacred Games* reveals, there is in fact much, much more at play.

January 2007

Tom Wolfe

Along with Joan Didion, Norman Mailer, and Hunter S. Thompson, Tom Wolfe is one of the early proponents of New Journalism. Born in Richmond, Virginia, in 1931, Wolfe began his career as an old-style journalist, banging out stories for the Springfield Union *in western Massachusetts, and later for* The Washington Post *and the now-defunct* New York Herald-Tribune. *During the 1962 newspaper strike, he asked Esquire if he could cover a hot-rod convention in Southern California. He struggled so much to write it straight that he sent his editor a long letter about what he couldn't put in the piece. The result was "There goes (VAROOM! VAROOM!) that Kandy Kolored (THPHHHHHH!) tangerine-flaked streamline baby (RAHGHHHH!) around the bend (BRUMMMMMMMMMMMMMMM-MMM)," the cornerstone piece for his first book of essays. Wolfe's interests in Americana are as vast as they are unexpected. The Black Panthers, astronauts, modern art, and American stock-car racing are among just a few of the things he has covered. In the mid-eighties, he responded to an offer by Jann Wenner, the publisher of* Rolling Stone, *to serialize a novel he had been meaning*

to write. Wolfe accepted and began publishing monthly installments of what would become The Bonfire of the Vanities *(1987), a runaway bestseller and a potent skewering of the haves and have-nots of the eighties Wall Street boom. Wolfe has since published three more novels—A* Man in Full *(1998),* I Am Charlotte Simmons *(2004), and* Back to Blood *(2012). I spoke to him upon the publication of* I Am Charlotte Simmons, *which deals with the sexualized world of university life in America.*

Sitting cross-legged on a plush gold couch in the library of his Upper East Side apartment, wearing the trademark white suit, navy tie, and spotless two-tone spats, Tom Wolfe is about as far from a college keg party as one can be in the United States.

On the table before him stands a small statuette of Chairman Mao. The walls around us support shelf after shelf of books on Flemish masters and folios of modern painters, along with portraits of Wolfe's daughter in full equestrian gear.

Visit Wolfe in this setting and it becomes easy to understand why life on American university campuses was a distant and shocking reality for him. Indeed, his seven-hundred-page novel, *I Am Charlotte Simmons*, reads like every father's worst nightmare. Set in the fictional Dupont University, it reaches down into America's deep-fried soul and returns with an inflammatory portrait of the pornographic hollowness of that $160,000 investment otherwise known as college: all the drinking and the partying, the video-game playing, test cheating, wanton fucking, and athlete worshipping.

Even Wolfe, who has traveled with the psychedelic novelist Ken Kesey, attended NASCAR races, hung out with Black Panthers, and made millions by telling us what the madding crowd is doing, acknowledges that America's youth may have slipped a little. "I'm glad I didn't know this before my kids went off to college," he says with an uneasy smile.

It's an odd statement for America's preeminent clocker of the zeitgeist. As if we needed a reminder of how, well, pre–September 11 such concerns over life on college campuses seem, the view out of Wolfe's library stretches all the way to the former site of the World Trade Center.

I ask him whether he may have mistimed his target, if, perhaps, the zeitgeist passed him by this time.

"I did pause and say, you know, wait a minute," says Wolfe with the languid cadence of a born Southerner. "This is supposedly changing everything. But look at New York today: real estate is out of control. Besides, I found on campuses that the reaction to September 11 was zero."

Why do they hate us? Who are they? Osama bin who? These are the questions Americans asked after September 11, and if you believe Wolfe's portrait in *I Am Charlotte Simmons*, even American college students didn't pause too long to ponder the answers. Using his brilliant interior monologues, Wolfe reveals that kids are ignorant and have remained so because they have one thing on their minds: sex.

•

Critics have already pointed out that Wolfe's decision to write a female lead might be a response to those who carped, among other things, that he could not make a woman come alive on the page. Wolfe disagrees.

"I finally decided on Charlotte because her simple naïveté is a good way to introduce the reader to this campus life, so every revelation to Charlotte Simmons is supposed to be a revelation to the reader. Also, from what I had seen, the changes in terms of sexuality are much harder on a woman than a man."

Tom Wolfe as a feminist? Indeed, the action that follows reads like a literary dramatization of the themes and observations contained in Wolfe's essay "Hooking Up," in which he noted that by the year 2000 sexual stimuli bombarded the young so incessantly and intensely that they were inflamed with a randy itch long before reaching puberty.

Life at Dupont reflects what happens when these hypersexed teens reach college age. Within a day of her arrival, Charlotte is "sexiled" from her room when her roommate brings a young man home for sex; fraternity brothers engage in stopwatched contests to see how quickly they can bed fresh meat.

All this could be written off as melodrama were Wolfe not so thorough about his research. He visited more than a dozen college campuses over four years. He talked to students and attended classes, and, just a few years after having quintuple bypass surgery, stayed out until four or five in the morning, standing in the corner of fraternity house basements with ears pricked. No notepads.

Although he never observed "sexual congress," as he puts it, Wolfe did see plenty of dirty dancing and became so fluent in what he called the fuck patois—in which the expletive is used as a noun, verb, and adjective—that he could speak it himself.

A novel by Wolfe has become a kind of once-a-decade event in American publishing and is greeted with the polarized fanfare characteristic of an industry fighting over fewer and fewer spoils.

If the sales of *The Bonfire of the Vanities* thrust Wolfe to the top of the heap of America's social novelists, *A Man in Full*, which was a finalist for the National Book Award, gave Wolfe's critics a thorn in their side. Reviewing the book in *The New Yorker*, John Updike wrote that it was entertainment, not literature.

The food fight over *Charlotte Simmons* was fierce. In *The New York Sun*, Adam Kirsch argued that Wolfe has never been able to discover the deeper, stranger, more elusive truths that fiction can bring. Charles McGrath responded in *The New York Times* with a profile that compared Wolfe to other American masters who graduated from the newsroom to the novel: John O'Hara and Stephen Crane.

Wolfe seems to have known *I Am Charlotte Simmons* would be greeted with a certain savagery, and he's started a new essay, his response, perhaps.

"I've begun working on a writers' Hippocratic oath," Wolfe says. "The first line of the doctors' Hippocratic oath is 'First, do no harm.' And I think for the writers it would be: 'First, entertain.' Entertain is a very simple word. I looked it up in the dictionary. Entertainment enables people to pass the time pleasantly. And any writing—I don't care if it's poetry or what—should first entertain. It's a very recent thing that there's a premium put on making writing so difficult that only a charmed aristocracy is capable of understanding it."

November 2004

Robert M. Pirsiġ

Robert M. Pirsig is a philosopher and the author of two novels, Zen and the Art of Motorcycle Maintenance *(1974) and* Lila: An Inquiry into Morals *(1991), both of which are concerned with knowing the meaning of the visible world and the way one lives morally within it. Both books trace a journey—in the former, a motorcycle trip with the author's son to California; in the latter, a journey on a boat traveling down the Hudson River with a woman in the wake of her mental breakdown. Pirsig's own life is a kind of meandering trip of its own. Born in Minnesota in 1928, he entered university to study biochemistry. He then began a period of wandering, from South Korea, where he was stationed during World War II, to Seattle for more study, to Bozeman, Montana, where he taught writing, and back to Minnesota, where he experienced the first of a series of breakdowns.* Zen and the Art of Motorcycle Maintenance *grew from the ashes of his dissolving family life and his attempts, post-breakdown, to find meaning and structure in the world. I spoke to him upon the rerelease of* Lila*—it was his first interview in more than twenty years.*

Robert Pirsig has a bone to pick with philosophers. As his era-defining novel *Zen and the Art of Motorcycle Maintenance* levitated up the bestseller lists in 1974, all he heard from them was grumbling.

This story of a father–son motorcycle trip across America was just a skeleton of a philosophy, they said. What exactly was this "metaphysics of quality" he kept talking about? And who was he to tell them about it? Seventeen years later, Pirsig gave his answer and it came in the form of a five-hundred-page novel, *Lila: An Inquiry into Morals*. Now, at last, the thinkers of the world had something to tinker with. Their response? "Silence. They have just given me zero support and great hostility," Pirsig says on the eve of the novel's reissue in Britain.

"It's just, they don't say anything." Now Pirsig believes he has one last shot at explaining his philosophy to the public, and if it means coming out of seclusion, so be it.

Sitting in a hotel room that overlooks the Charles River in Boston, a meditation mat at his feet, his wife, Wendy, at his side, America's second-most reclusive New England novelist does not appear to have sweated much over his public persona.

At the age of seventy-eight, Pirsig is a white-haired, bandy-legged old coot, as the phrase goes. Years at sea and on the road have given his face a sun-blasted quality. His voice is strong and clear, but when he takes out a pen and paper to demonstrate a concept, his hands shake.

"As I see these two books," Pirsig says, drawing an oval on a notepad, "there is a Zen circle. You start here with Zen," he says, marking an X, "and then you go here to enlightenment, that's what's called 180 Zen. Then you go back to where you started from—that's 360 Zen—and the world is exactly as it was when you left it." Pirsig sits back and lets that sink in, then adds, "Well, I felt that *Zen and the Art of Motorcycle Maintenance* was the journey out, and *Lila* was this trip back."

This might explain why *Lila* was not as universally adored as its predecessor. *Zen* was a serious feel-good book, a modern-day *Walden*, written by a man who had been through the wringer but emerged having found a better way to live.

It was also as picturesque a tour of western America as one could find between two covers. *Lila* is an almost noir-like novel about a writer who falls in love with a former prostitute. As they float down a brooding river toward New York City, the writer—whose name is Phaedrus, the name Pirsig gave his insane alter ego in *Zen*—muses on the woman's nature and on the Metaphysics of Quality (MOQ).

The novel is structured like a river with many locks—each stage a new level of Pirsig's philosophy. The mental work it takes to measure these ideas explains why *Lila* has sold six hundred thousand copies, hardly a failure but nowhere near the four to six million of his more famous book.

There are two types of quality, as Pirsig sees it: dynamic and static.

"Without dynamic quality, an organism cannot grow,"

he explained in an essay. "But without static quality, an organism cannot last."

While it has become a cultural cliché to say that we have moved beyond good and evil, Pirsig believes just the opposite—and he believes that the MOQ can be a useful tool in bringing order to a chaotic world.

"You know the structure of the MOQ," he says, bringing out the pad again. "Static quality can be divided into intellectual, social, biological, and inorganic realms. Any attempt by a lower order to overcome a higher order represents evil. So those forces which prohibit intellectual freedom are evil according to the MOQ, just as those biological forces which tend to prohibit social freedom are evil, and, at an even lower level, even the inorganic forces of death that try to destroy biology are evil."

Pirsig's insistence on the existence of evil has a painful personal note. In November 1979, his son Chris was stabbed to death in a robbery outside the San Francisco Zen Center. He was two weeks shy of his twenty-third birthday. Pirsig was living on a houseboat in England at the time. He came home for the funeral and wrote a moving eulogy about his son—the child at the heart of *Zen*—and it has been printed in every edition since. This loss can be felt in *Lila* and might explain why it took Pirsig almost two decades to write it. "One reviewer said, 'The shadow of Pirsig's son's death seems to hang over this entire book,'" Pirsig says, looking bewildered. "I had no idea that was true at the time, but now I see in retrospect that I was very gloomy."

.

Pirsig seems to have come into the world capable of thought—but less so of gloom. Born in 1928 in Minneapolis, Minnesota, he was a gifted child whose IQ was measured at 170 when he was nine years old. Pirsig was so young when he began grade school that he was picked on. He entered university at the age of fifteen, flunked out, then served in the Korean War, coming home with an interest in philosophy. He eventually finished his undergraduate studies and went on to get a graduate degree in Oriental philosophy from Banaras Hindu University in India. And here's where the drifting begins.

Pirsig returned to the United States in the fifties and studied journalism. To make a living, he began doing technical writing and some editing at a university newspaper, where he met his first wife. For twenty years they moved around, Pirsig doing odd jobs, occasionally teaching English composition, raising their two kids.

Without knowing it, he had begun a kind of internal philosophical quest, but the heat of his intellectual searching pushed him over the edge.

In 1960, he began the first of a series of hospital treatments for mental illness. Pirsig's father obtained a court order to commit him to a hospital, where he received electroconvulsive shock therapy. It seemed to work, but Pirsig maintains that he was not insane. "I never thought I was crazy. But I wasn't about to tell anybody that at the time."

Pirsig took to writing as if it were a life raft. In 1965 he bought a motorcycle, and in 1967 began what he thought would just be a few essays on motorcycle maintenance—he was, after all, a technical writer. But the book grew into a fully fledged project.

In 1968, he wrote to 122 publishers offering sample chapters. Only one wrote back. This was enough encouragement for him. He rented a room at a flophouse and would go there from midnight until 6:00 a.m. to write.

Then he would go to work. Each night he went to bed at 6:00 p.m. "When I talk about compulsion in that book," Pirsig says, "that's what I mean. I was *compelled* to write that book."

Pirsig admits that this regimen had as much to do with his ambitions as with "problems at home," as he calls them. When the book finally became a bestseller, Pirsig dealt with it as best he could then felt he needed to get away. He and his wife bought a yacht and planned to travel the world. Instead they divorced.

Pirsig's response was to keep moving, and it was in this fashion that he met his second wife, Wendy Kimball, on a boat in Florida. She was a freelance writer who wanted to interview him. He hung around for two years in Florida while she worked as a reporter, and then they started a life of travel together, down to the Bahamas, up to Maine, where they were married, and across the North Atlantic to England—a trip so rough that Pirsig thought they might not make it. "I saw this bank of icebergs moving towards us very fast, and I turned to Wendy and said, 'Well, hon, it's been nice knowing you.' "

Their joy at surviving the journey aboard their floating honeymoon was shattered that same year when Pirsig's son was murdered. Over time Pirsig has moved forward. He and Wendy had a daughter, Nell, in 1980.

•

There are other new beginnings brewing as we speak. In 2006, an academic philosopher named David A. Granger published a book called *John Dewey, Robert Pirsig, and the Art of Living*. Pirsig is overjoyed. "This really could be my white knight."

The ongoing sales of *Zen* have afforded Pirsig and his wife "a very nice life," he admits, and he doesn't want to appear ungrateful for this gift. But he adds that it is not for his sake that he wants *Lila* to be read. He truly believes it can help people. "I think this philosophy could address a lot of the problems we have in the world today," he says, leaning forward, tapping the pad of paper, "just so long as people know about it."

September 2006

Peter Carey

 Peter Carey was born in Melbourne, Australia, where his parents ran a General Motors dealership. In the early sixties he began a career in advertising that spanned nearly three decades, culminating with the launch of his own firm, McSpedden Carey, from which he divested in 1990. He started publishing stories in the early seventies, which were collected in The Fat Man in History (1974) and War Crimes (1979). In the eighties he published three extraordinary novels—Bliss (1981), Illywacker (1985), and Oscar and Lucinda (1988)—which established him as a major literary voice and laid out the themes that possessed his entire career: the chaos of family life, the fine line between hucksterism and ingenious improvisation, and the immutable stain of Australia's convict past. Carey moved to New York City in 1990 to teach at New York University and has lived there ever since. From 2000 to 2010, he unleashed a decade's worth of material that has few rivals, beginning with the barbarously poetic True History of the Kelly Gang (2000), a historical novel about the bushranger and resistance hero Ned Kelly, which won Carey his second Booker Prize, and ending with Parrot and Olivier in

*America (2009), a freewheeling, fabulous tale that re-
prises Alexis de Tocqueville's travels around America. In
the same decade Carey became the director of the Hunter
College creative writing program, and in less than five
years made it one of the top writing programs in the
United States according to a US News & World Report
ranking.*

The word *happy* does not come easily from Peter Carey's
mouth. Under normal circumstances, it dribbles off his
lips in a trickle of sarcasm. It is a word used about Americans, pets, and teenagers. But not long ago the two-time
Booker Prize–winning novelist began using the word about
himself without apology.

"I was miserable for a long time," says Carey, sixty-
four, sitting in his large, airy lower Manhattan loft. "I
just thought, the kids will grow up and I will die. Then I
turned sixty and I was suddenly amazingly happy."

Behind him are two striking paintings, one enormous,
the other quite small, both by painters who had lived in
Australia. The small one, which depicts the Santa Monica freeway, is titled *Study #3 "for Crossroads,"* by James
Doolin; the other is *Three Crossings* by David Rankin.

The choice of artworks could not be more apt. For, as
hard as it is to imagine, after two Bookers and numerous
bestsellers, Carey is passing through another crossroads.

Toward the end of our interview, one of the biggest
forces behind this shift walks through the door bearing
chocolate tortes the size of oven mitts. Frances Coady is a
publisher and the longtime editor of such writers as Paul

Auster, Alan Bennett, and the historian and activist Na-
omi Klein.

Carey and Coady have been together for nearly five
years and living in this apartment for two years. Their
paths first crossed in 1985, but they did not meet properly
until a dinner organized by the writers association PEN,
while Carey and his then wife, Alison Summers, were in
the process of getting divorced.

"It took me two years to call her," Carey remembers.
"She was always so full of life and energy, and with
somebody. And then she wasn't." They have been together
ever since, and they make an amusing pair: the diminutive, large-eyed, cackling-voiced Coady often goading
and scolding Carey, who skulks and grumbles under his
breath.

It's natural to wonder how much Carey's unbelievable
burst of productivity has to do with this newfound
domestic happiness. Since 2003 he has published three
books. When we meet he is releasing a fourth, *His Illegal
Self*, a road novel that culminates at a hippie commune in
Queensland. Along the way it tells the story of Che, a
seven-year-old boy raised by his wealthy grandmother in
New York.

As the story begins, Che is smuggled out of the country and becomes part of a manic quest through the outback to find his parents, famous outlaws wanted by
the FBI.

It is Carey's tenth novel and the latest in a string of
stories about a character divided between two places and
not entirely belonging in either. "If I think about it, every

single one of my novels deals with this idea of being in two places," Carey says.

Landscape, a portal in past works such as *Theft* and *Illywhacker*, plays a similar role again in his new novel. "I had such a good time writing *Theft*," he says, "because I was remembering a place I loved, north of Bacchus Marsh [in Victoria]. I just loved it beyond belief, and I couldn't believe how much of it I could remember."

But there was another place he wanted to revisit: the Queensland commune where he lived quite contentedly in the seventies after his first long stint in advertising. "No one asked me, 'What do you do?' People had simple needs," Carey remembers. "I used to write in the morning and read at night." It was an ideal life, except the police at the time were crooked and dangerous, and the hippies were likely to be Maoists.

"I remember this American guy turned up," Carey says. "And he kept planting dope plants. One night there was this big raid, helicopters and the whole bit, and the American had had to go into the hospital for gallbladder surgery. It turned out he was really on the run, because we talked to his lawyer, who called from Texas."

The man on the lam needed to decide whether he should come clean about his identity. Carey was more than happy to intervene. "So a woman and I decided to place this in a message to him in a book, which we went way up into the mountains to post." The man didn't see the message, which was inscribed on the book's flyleaf, and his bust later became front-page news.

"A lot of that sixties paranoia turned out to be pretty

well founded," Carey says. The government was indeed spying on radicals, and the outback was full of people trying to get away from whatever it was they once were.

Carey has written of this period before, in *Bliss*, and he revisits it now in a less comic vein and from the point of view of a child. Satire, he felt, was not really an option. "A lot of radicals in this period came from quite privileged backgrounds. And they ended up going all the way. A lot of my Maoist friends used to say, 'After the revolution, you will be shot.' They weren't entirely kidding."

But the people living in this "collaborative community were ahead of their time: They were worried about carbon footprints, about whether or not we could sustain this way of life we have going now, which we now know is unsustainable."

In beginning *His Illegal Self*, Carey decided he would not simply bring this world back. "It cannot be the same place," he says. "That place existed thirty years ago. A mirror or shadow of it remains in my head. Working with this afterimage, I fashioned a new place whose topography and inhabitants exist only to serve my story."

As he has aged, Carey has become less interested in satire and more interested in sentences. "Since *The Kelly Gang* I aspired to make a poetry out of an unlettered voice," he says, "and ever since, I've been obsessed with bending, snapping, and reshaping sentences, trying to join things in ways that are not at first apparent."

Coady, not surprisingly, has become his first audience,

often at the end of the day when, over a glass of wine, Carey reads to her what he has written that morning. Carey says she hasn't changed what he writes but is a superb reader.

"She can echo things back to me that are tremendous. And she will tell me when things aren't working. The beginning of this book, for example, had some problems and I told her, 'Don't worry, I'll fix it.' "

This workshop isn't the only one Carey has been conducting. After four years as the director, he is now the executive director of Hunter College's master of fine arts writing program, arguably the cheapest way of obtaining a writing degree in Manhattan, and now one of the best.

"This is the first time I have taken something like this on," Carey says. "I took it on because I could make something and I didn't see why the university couldn't be the best MFA program in the city."

Joining a school such as this in an age when privileged schools have a great advantage is almost a statement of political solidarity with working-class students.

Hunter is a state-run institution where an MFA costs about $11,000 a year; at an Ivy League university such as Columbia, it costs four times as much. Nor is it a glamorous place like the New School in Greenwich Village. "Many of the students are older," Carey explains. "They are the first generation in their families to go to college, and they often have other jobs." Many of them are not white.

However, "we have taken this thing and turned it around in four years," Carey adds, leaning forward in a rocking motion, his verbal hydraulics pumped up by the innate gusto of a born turnaround man. He describes how he has lassoed writers out of prior teaching commitments, coaxed money from skeptical patrons, and convinced smart students they needn't take on $60,000 in debt to get a good education. "And today the students are amazing."

Carey has bent over backward to provide for them, bringing in some of the world's best writers, from Annie Proulx and Ian McEwan to Michael Ondaatje, setting up a mentoring program that pairs faculty (such as memoirist Kathryn Harrison and novelist Jennifer Egan) with students, so the students don't just get instruction but can experience firsthand how a writer works. He has helped several students get jobs elsewhere.

The results are paying off. In recent years a number of his students have received book deals.

Now that he has rejuvenated Hunter, Carey isn't going to rest. In fact, from 8:00 a.m. to 1:00 p.m. every day, he has been working on a new book, using one of the Hunter College fellows as a crack research assistant. "This guy is tremendous; he will print out floor plans of old castles, and find out exactly the distance from one place to another," he says.

Carey's next novel is set in eighteenth- and nineteenth-century France, Britain, America, and Australia, he says, adding, "Lots of people have done research for me, including a French architectural historian." He says he has already written more than two hundred pages of the book.

Just as *Illywhacker* preceded his Booker Prize winner *Oscar and Lucinda*, and *Jack Maggs* preceded his second Booker winner, *True History of the Kelly Gang*, it seems *His Illegal Self* might be the beginning of a new stage in Carey's career, marked by momentum and tidier, snappier sentences.

I ask Carey again if this palpable sense of creation has to do with happiness in his personal life and again he shrugs it off. "I was working on *The Tax Inspector* when I was relatively keen and yet the sense of this dark book almost seemed to invade my life. It's hard to know what qualities of your life enter your work." Whatever they are, Carey isn't going to think too hard about them. He's been around long enough to know that self-contemplation isn't just the end of work but the end of happiness, too.

January 2008

Mo Yan

Mo Yan is one of China's most celebrated and widely translated writers. Born in the Shandong Province in 1955 into a family of farmers, he enlisted in the People's Liberation Army at the age of twenty and began writing stories at the same time. Mo Yan is a pen name, which means, in Chinese, "don't speak," a reminder not to speak so frankly in mainland China. He was eleven when the Cultural Revolution began, and his pen name comes from a warning his parents gave him as a child, when a loose tongue could get you killed. He has written several novels and story collections, including Red Sorghum (1987), Big Breasts and Wide Hips (1996), Life and Death Are Wearing Me Out (2006), and, most recently, Frog (2009), all of which draw on the vernacular patterns of Shandong and the storytelling architecture of the magical realists. Mo Yan's work is not realistic. It is Rabelaisian, satirical, steeped in blood, and filled with references to food and eating, a not unpolitical thing in a country where many millions starved during the Great Leap Forward. In The Republic of Wine, an inspector who has been sent to the fictional province of Liquorland, where decadence has been reportedly occur-

ring on a grand scale, goes on a bender and cannot tell whether the roasted meat he eats at a drinking duel is pork or human. I spoke to Mo Yan through an interpreter at the London Book Fair 2012, when China was the guest of honor. He talked about writing strong women, retaining idioms and puns even in translation, and avoiding censorship. Later that year he won the Nobel Prize in Literature, a selection that prompted a great deal of controversy given Mo Yan's reluctance to speak politically about human rights in China, and his membership in the communist party. He dodged the maelstrom and a few months later published two new novels, Pow!, *which had never been released in China, and* Sandalwood Death, *a ribald and densely poetic novel set during the Boxer Rebellion.*

Many of your novels are located in a half-fictionalized place based on your Gaomi hometown, in a way similar to, say, Faulkner's American South. What is it that makes you return to this half-imagined community and does having a global readership alter the focus at all?

When I first started writing, the environment was there and very real and the story was my personal experience. But with an increasing volume of my work being published, my day-to-day experience is running out and so I need to add a little bit of imagination, sometimes, even some fantasy in there.

Some of your writing recalls the work of Günter Grass, William Faulkner, and Gabriel García Márquez. Were these writers available to you in China when you were growing up?

When I first started writing it was the year of 1981, so I didn't read any books by García Márquez or Faulkner. It was 1984 when I first read their works and undoubtedly those two writers have had a great influence on my creations. I found that my life experience is quite similar to theirs, but I only discovered this later on. If I had read their works sooner, I would have already accomplished a masterpiece like they did.

Early novels like Red Sorghum *seem to be more overtly historical or even considered by some as romance novels, whereas in recent times your novels have moved to more overtly contemporary settings and themes. Is that a conscious choice?*

When I wrote *Red Sorghum* I was less than thirty years old, so I was quite young. At that time my life was full of romantic factors when considering my ancestors. I was writing about their lives but didn't know much about them so I injected many imaginations into those characters. When I wrote *Life and Death Are Wearing Me Out* I was over forty years old so I have transformed from a young to a middle-aged man. My life is different. My life is more current, more contemporary, and the cutthroat cruelty of our contemporary times limits the romance that I once felt.

You often write in the language of the local Laobaixing, and specifically the Shandong dialect, which gives your prose a flinty edge. Does it frustrate you that some of the idioms and puns might not make it into an English translation or are you able to work around that with your translator, Howard Goldblatt?

Well, indeed, I use quite a substantial amount of local dialect, idioms, and puns in my earlier works because at that time I didn't even consider that my work would be translated into other languages. Later on I realized that this kind of language creates a lot of trouble for the translator. But to not use dialect, idioms, and puns doesn't work for me because idiomatic language is vivid, expressive, and it is also the quintessential part of the signature language of a particular writer. So on the one hand I can modify and adjust some of my usage of puns and idioms, but on the other I hope that our translators, during their work, can echo the puns I use in another language—that is the ideal situation.

Many of your novels have strong women at their core— Big Breasts and Wide Hips, Life and Death Are Wearing Me Out, *and* Frog—*do you consider yourself to be a feminist or are you simply drawn to write from a female perspective?*

First of all, I admire and respect women. I think they are very noble and their life experience and the hardship a woman can endure is always much greater than a man. When we encounter great disasters women are always more brave than men—I think because they have their dual capacity, they are also mothers. The strength that this brings is something we can't imagine. In my books I try to put myself in the shoes of women; I try to understand and interpret this world from the perspective of women. But the bottom line is I am not a woman: I'm a male writer. And the world I interpreted in my books as if I were a woman might not be well received by women themselves, but that is not something I can do anything about. I love and admire women, but nonetheless I am a man.

Is avoiding censorship a question of subtlety and to what extent do the avenues opened up by magical realism, as well as more traditional techniques of characterization, allow a writer to express their deepest concerns without resorting to polemic?

Yes, indeed. Many approaches to literature have political bearings, for example in our real life there might be some sharp or sensitive issues that they do not wish to touch upon. At such a juncture a writer can inject their own imagination to isolate them from the real world or maybe they can exaggerate the situation—making sure it is bold, vivid, and has the signature of our real world. So, actually, I believe these limitations or censorship is great for literature creation.

Your last book that was translated into English, a very short memoir, Democracy, *narrates the end of an era within China from your own experiences as a young boy and man. There is an element of melancholy to it, which, coming from the West, is to some degree a surprise: We*

*often believe Progress with a capital P always means bet-
terment, but your memoir suggests something has been
lost. Is that a fair characterization?*

Yes, the memoir you mention is full of my personal
experience and my daily life; however, it also presents
something imagined. The melancholy tone you talk
about too is indeed very accurate, because the story features a forty-year-old man thinking back on a youth that
is now gone. For example, when you were young you were
probably once smitten with a certain girl but for some
reason this girl has now become someone else's wife and
that memory is indeed rather sad. For the past thirty
years we have witnessed China undergoing dramatic
progress; whether it be in living standards or in intellectual or spiritual levels of our citizens, the progress is visible, but undoubtedly there are many things that we are
not satisfied with in our day-to-day life. Indeed, China
has progressed but progress itself brings up many issues,
for instance environmental issues and the decline in high
moral standards. So the melancholy that you talk about is
for two reasons—I realize that my youth has already gone,
and secondly I worry about the current status quo in
China, especially the things I'm not satisfied with.

April 2012

Donna Leon

 *Donna Leon is one of the world's most in-tuitive crime writers. She published her first novel,* Death at La Fenice *(1992), at age fifty, after having lived around the world—in Switzerland, Iran, Saudi Arabia, China, and eventually Venice, where from 1981 to 1990 she taught English on an American military base. She has published a novel a year since making her debut, most of them set in or around Venice, all of them involving Commissario Guido Brunetti, a principled Italian police officer who always makes it home for at least one meal a day. Her books have developed a cult following, leading to cookbooks based on Brunetti's meals and travel guides to Brunetti's Venice. Leon has used the proceeds of her book sales to support her second great passion after Venice: opera.*

It's one week after the latest Commissario Brunetti novel landed in bookstores across Britain and crime novelist Donna Leon seems more excited than usual. The tiny sixty-two-year-old American with steel-gray hair and lively eyes rides what appears to be a triple-shot-espresso buzz into the lobby of Durrants Hotel in London and keeps it galloping for more than an hour.

"The situation is odd," Leon says, pausing briefly in her whirlwind conversation, "because in interviews I talk a lot. But in Italy I don't. I never know when I am going to find something potentially glorious for me."

It's not books that have her feeling talkative today, or even crime writing in general—which she has been pursuing for many years—but a passion nearer and dearer to her heart: opera.

"I write a lot of liner notes for CDs," says Leon, on the edge of her seat again. "But on this one I am getting an attribution in the cast. At the bottom, it says, 'Sword: Donna Leon.'"

The opera company Leon set up with fellow American exile Alan Curtis was recording an opera—Handel's *La Maga Abbandonata*—in which a sword had to be dropped to the earth. "Hey, Donna," she recalls the sound technician saying, "you wanna drop the sword?"

She is published in twenty-four languages and has won crime writing's highest awards, but nothing could have made Donna Leon so happy.

This sword cameo was probably the closest Leon has come to doing in real life what she has been up to in fiction. Over the past thirteen years, the New Jersey–born opera buff and crime novelist has dispatched lives often and democratically. Fishermen, a transvestite, American soldiers, even a flamboyant Austrian composer, have all died in her wake.

The job of sorting out who did what and to whom always falls to Leon's retiringly suave hero, Commissario Brunetti. A Venetian policeman and father of two, Brunetti has investigated international corruption, sex trafficking, illegal immigration from North Africa, animal rights, even the Catholic Church, allowing Leon to map all the fissures and fractures of Italian society. At the same time, he always manages to squeeze in sumptuous sit-down meals with his wry political wife, Paola.

Blood from a Stone is Leon's fourteenth book in the series, and though it may not disturb Brunetti's eating patterns it does draw our hero into some of the murkiest waters yet. At the beginning of the novel, just before Christmas, a Senegalese man selling knockoff handbags on a street in Venice is shot and killed in broad daylight.

In spite of the witnesses, Brunetti has trouble finding a killer or even a motive, and is soon warned off the case by someone high up in the police force. Is this because the man killed was an illegal alien? Or is there something larger at stake?

Leon, who has lived in Venice for more than two decades, stumbled on the story recently and felt, like Brunetti, slightly embarrassed at how long it had been before she had noticed what was right in front of her.

"I had my Saint Paul moment," she says. "I was walking across the Campo Stefano going to someone's house for dinner three years ago and I stopped in my tracks because there were about twenty of these guys on either side of the street. And I just said to myself, these guys are here but they are invisible. I knew I had to write a book."

As she has done with the previous thirteen books, Leon didn't exactly research *Blood from a Stone*, but then again she didn't make it up either. Rather, her novels seem to come together through a confluence of conversation and listening—as if Leon is recording what the city is thinking.

By way of an example, Leon tells me about a neighbor who responded to her comment that her next book would be about trafficking in infant children.

"She said to me, 'Oh, yeah, like last month. I just happened to notice a pregnant girl in that apartment that gets rented by the week.' Oh, really? What follows from here sounds suspiciously like a woman having a baby and not wanting anyone to notice—and then leaving town."

Leon pauses at the story's conclusion and rewinds through the facts, much as Brunetti would. "So this woman obviously was brought here, had her baby—not in the hospital, not registered—and then the baby somehow got filtered into the baby market." She shakes her head. "So that's my next book."

By combining these glimpses into Venice's underbelly with scenes of its elegantly unhurried domestic life, the Brunetti series has become a worldwide bestseller.

However, like her sober and skeptical hero, Leon won't get too ruffled by it all. "I'm a carpenter, not a violin maker," she has said. She refuses to allow her books to be translated into Italian, and few of her friends in Venice read them.

Leon knows her life could have gone in another direction and seems eager not to take her newfangled existence too seriously. "I wrote my first book as a joke to see if I could," she says. "I've become successful, but never because I wanted to be—it just fell on my head."

This might sound a little disingenuous if a quick tour of Leon's past didn't reveal so many dead ends and one-year jobs. She bounced around Iran, China, and Switzerland for years and had a stint as an English teacher in Saudi Arabia. She eventually wound up in Venice in the early eighties. It was where friends lived, where she knew the language, "a place I could love people again and people could love me," Leon says now.

For a while, she taught on Venice's American military base for six hours a week. Then one night she was backstage at the opera with a friend, expressing a wicked glee at the recent death of a conductor. They thought it would be fun to write him into a crime novel and kill him again. Leon did. And the rest, as they say, is history.

April 2005

David Mitchell

David Mitchell is one of the most electric writers alive. To open a Mitchell book is to go on an adventure. To dream. His books span the globe, from Tokyo in the near present to Korea in the far future, to England in the recent past and Japan in the Napoleonic era. They are full of sea captains and cannibals, terrorists and midwives and composers and star-crossed lovers. Genetically modified food-service workers. They are about people who live to an idea, but who also get blown sideways through life.

Mitchell was born in Southport, England, and raised in Worcestershire, where he grew up reading J.R.R. Tolkien and Ray Bradbury. He attended the University of Kent, where he obtained a degree in English and American literature and an MA in comparative literature. He moved to Japan in the nineties and taught English, and at the end of the decade published his first novel, Ghostwritten, a Chaucerian fable of ten interlinked stories set in different parts of the globe, which meditate on randomness and won him the John Llewellyn Rhys Prize. Number9dream, a futuristic and gorgeous tale about a nineteen-year-old Japanese boy's search for his father in *strobe-lit Tokyo, followed in 2001 and was a finalist for the Booker Prize.*

In 2004, Mitchell published the book that has made him the most emulated writer of his generation in Britain: Cloud Atlas, *six interlinked novellas that span hundreds of years and grow out of (or nest within) one another like Russian dolls. Lana and Andy Wachowski and Tom Tykwer turned the book into a motion picture featuring Tom Hanks and Halle Berry. Mitchell's subsequent novels include* Black Swan Green *in 2006, and* The Thousand Autumns of Jacob de Zoet *in 2010. A former bookseller, Mitchell lives in Ireland with his wife and two children. I met him there when* Black Swan Green *came out.*

David Mitchell loves to play with stories. To turn them inside out—as if the laws of narrative physics don't apply. With his latest novel, the two-time Man Booker Prize finalist takes this approach and makes it personal. But the deck being shuffled this go-around is not just any tale. This time it's his own life. "In a way I'm writing my first novel fourth," says the thirty-seven-year-old author, referring to the convention that literary debuts are often highly autobiographical.

In a seaside restaurant in Clonakilty, the Irish town where he lives with his wife and two kids, Mitchell makes his point. Jason Taylor, the narrator of *Black Swan Green*, shares many similarities with his creator. Like Mitchell, he grows up in Worcestershire in the eighties and struggles with an agonizing stammer. He uses the same slang

Mitchell once did, and even suffers some of the same indignities of adolescence.

But their paths diverge. For Jason's stammer is only the beginning of his problems. As he skates toward adulthood, his parents' marriage dissolves. Then he loses a watch that is precious to his grandfather. Bullies threaten at every turn. But none of these things happened to Mitchell.

Mitchell is expertly mimicking yet another genre—this time the bildungsroman. But *Black Swan Green* does not traffic in the veiled autobiography and wish fulfillment that has come to mar that form in recent years. "I kind of evolved a distinction between a personal novel and an autobiographical one," says Mitchell. "A personal one is where the protagonist and the writer have many things in common. An autobiographical one is where events and everyone around the protagonist or the narrator come largely from life."

This is a book about a boy who doesn't know what he knows—who has the entire world inside him but cannot spit it out. Although Jason's stuttering is a metaphor for the blind spots one grows out of in adolescence, Mitchell understands the condition well. "It's one of those things that well-meaning people won't bring up," he says. "They don't want to make you ashamed or embarrassed. They don't want to make you stammer."

It seems a cruel irony that a man so preternaturally gifted with language should have grown up so tortured by it. Mitchell concludes it was probably this affliction that turned him inward—toward the written word.

"It certainly increased my vocabulary size," he says, referring to the method he still uses, of being aware of several different "exit strategies" with each sentence he utters. The result is he speaks in clear complete sentences—almost like someone reading from a book.

"You can think of it like a fuse that burns during a Tom and Jerry cartoon," he says, describing how it feels to live with a stammer.

"It burns down—this is the time you have to get this word out, this word that you are not ready to say. And the time runs out, until boom, the bomb explodes. And then you've had it. You're stuck."

The trick, he says, is "to be able to make that fuse infinite. To honestly not care if someone is going to see you stuttering or not."

Mitchell is eager to talk about talking—and hopes the book will help people who grew up like him.

"I didn't think there was much good fiction that takes you inside what it's like to have a stammer," he says. "I hope it does some small service to explaining it to people."

Mitchell decided not to try to follow his blockbuster *Cloud Atlas*, first published in the United States in 2004, with another ambitious, globe-trotting novel.

"Oh," he says, discussing the intricacies of *Black Swan Green*, "it feels so good not to be talking about *Cloud Atlas*."

Mitchell thinks of writing as "controlled personality disorder." "It's controlled because in order to make it work you have to concentrate on the voices in your head *and* get them talking to each other."

Since *Cloud Atlas* was published, he has spent quite a

bit of time talking about that one book and its cast of characters. It was a finalist for the Man Booker Prize, the Arthur C. Clarke Award, and the National Book Critics Circle Award. The book's unlikely bestsellerdom has been a great boon for Mitchell, but it also makes him antsy. Already he is well into a new novel set in a Dutch colony on an island off Japan. The research will involve moving to Holland and then, probably, back to Japan, where his wife is from.

Not only does Mitchell like characters, he likes projects. And better yet, projects with very clearly defined parameters.

"I feel comfortable operating within stringent restrictions in all the books," he says—"a list of things I can and cannot do."

He picks up *Black Swan Green*, which is told entirely in Jason's voice.

"So, if you write a book in the first person, you can't give any information to the reader that the protagonist doesn't know—unless you smuggle it either through the narrator's stupidity or, in the case of Jason, of this device of him not knowing what he knows. Once you decide the rule, you can see how what happens is dictated. So you don't have to work out what happens, you just have to work out the rule."

Mitchell is just as methodical at peopling his book. Several characters in *Black Swan Green* emerge out of previous books—some younger, others much older.

"It's enormous fun," says Mitchell, about sculpting these cameo roles. "It is also creatively economic. If there's a vacancy for a role, and I can fill that vacancy—like a personnel manager—with someone I've already written, then they arrive as a preconceived character. They already exist."

Listening to Mitchell describe how he works, how he researches his way into a novel—often by reading classified ads because they tell him "what people were after"— his novels begin to sound like exquisite computer programs, to which they have been compared by some critics.

But there is something even Mitchell's own thorough descriptions of this method leave out, something he himself cannot entirely explain. It involves using the occult power of creativity to inhabit other worlds.

"What distinguishes someone," says Mitchell, is "by and large what they believe. And if they believe in something I don't know about, science or philosophy, then I need to know about it."

The trick to *Black Swan Green* is that Mitchell has, in one book, erased all the erudition he absorbed to write his dazzling books—and become thirteen years old again.

It is the opposite of what he has done before, and much as he enjoyed the challenge, he has come away with exactly what most of us feel driving by a middle school: "I wouldn't want to live through it again."

April 2006

John Updike

 *John Updike was a poet, short-story writer, novelist, and critic who for more than sixty years dominated the cultural life of the United States. Born in Reading, Pennsylvania, he grew up on a family farm in the small town of Shillington. The moods, memories, and textures of this place formed the basis of much of his early work, such as the tremendous story collections* The Same Door *(1959),* Pigeon Feathers *(1962), and* Olinger Stories *(1964), as well as his second novel,* Rabbit, Run *(1960), which began an enormous, sprawling tale of an ex-high-school basketball star and his rocky feelings about marriage, home life, and the potent mysteries of the tangible world. Updike followed Rabbit Angstrom through the tumult of the sixties and their aftermath in the seventies, the upheavals of the Reagan era's mania for wealth, and the uneasy peace of America in the nineties.*

*Updike's primary register was lyrical and melancholic, but he also wrote a thriller (*Terrorist, *2006), a romance (*Marry Me, *1976), comedic novels (including* Couples, *1968), and hundreds upon hundreds of essays and reviews about books, art, American presidents, travel, and the*

*value of a penny. Upon his death in 2009, he was revising
a final collection of poems, which walks a reader up until
his last breath. This interview, which I referred to in the
introduction, was conducted six years before he died,
upon the publication of his twentieth novel,* Seek My
Face.

Long before he began writing novels, John Updike
wanted to be a cartoonist. "Mickey Mouse and I are the
same age," says the twinkle-eyed novelist on an afternoon
visit to the New York offices of his publisher, Alfred A.
Knopf. "Disney used to make movies about working in
his studio. So I had a fairly clear image of what [a cartoonist's life] looked like, but I didn't quite know how to
get from Shillington, Pennsylvania, to Burbank."

Instead, Updike, now seventy-one, landed in suburban Massachusetts, where he launched a barrage of novels, stories, poems, criticism, plays, and children's books
unparalleled in modern American literature. With his
twentieth novel, *Seek My Face*, the author draws upon his
unrequited love affair with the art world to create Hope
Chafetz, a seventy-nine-year-old painter, who, as Updike describes it, witnessed the "go-go days of Abstract
Expressionism" and lived to tell the tale.

Seek My Face takes place in one day during an interview
that Hope grants to Kathryn D'Angelo, a twentysome-
thing art historian from New York. Their conversation
snags on Hope's early years, when she was married to
Zack McCoy, a volcanically talented artist based on Jackson Pollock.

While he lived in New York during the time that Pollock was gaining fame, Updike never crossed paths with the great painter, never hoisted a glass with him at the Cedar Tavern. That was not his scene.

"Art, however," he says, "was in the air." In the late fifties, Updike had just returned from the Ruskin School of Drawing and Fine Art in Oxford and was in the process of discovering he would not be a painter. "I used to paint these still lifes," he says with a chuckle.

For all his self-deprecation, Updike has nurtured a serious interest in art ever since, writing essays on exhibitions for *Artforum*, *The New Yorker*, and other publications. They were eventually brought together in the collection *Just Looking* (1989). He is also almost continuously involved in the production of his books, sometimes even bringing in jacket sketches and ideas for how he'd like them to look.

And yet *Seek My Face* is less an exorcism of Updike's failed career as an artist as it is an exploration of another man's tremendous success, and how that moment undid him. Not surprisingly, Pollock casts a long shadow over the novel, something that has earned Updike some harsh criticisms in America.

In a scathing review, Michiko Kakutani complained that "Zack's life is such a carbon copy of Jackson Pollock's that the novel reads like a graceless rewriting of recent art history."

When asked about this criticism, Updike, who speaks in low, measured tones, squints, then smiles and says, "Why not hang fairly close to the facts, which are so nicely set forward in a number of books, but especially the book that I credit, the big biography? I sort of saw the facts as the flowerpot out of which something surprising would grow."

Indeed, while Hope does resemble Pollock's wife, Lee Krasner, many of the details of her early and later life are invented, as is her interior world. The novel eventually moves on to Hope's marriages to husbands two and three, a pop artist and a financier respectively, neither of whom match up for Hope.

Like Updike himself, who fled New York in the late fifties for the peace and quiet of New England, Hope moves to Vermont, where she settles into a long, slow life of eating organic food and growing into her own gift for painting.

The big story of *Seek My Face*, then, is not its insight into postwar American art but the unlikely bond between Hope and Kathryn that develops during their conversation about it. "The intimacy is set by Hope," Updike explains, "who comes out pretty confessional, pretty breezy, pretty aware that on one side you have her exciting bohemian life. Yet she is old and arthritic. And here is this young woman, with not a very exciting life herself, but all of the assets of a young woman. So they are jealous of each other, yet fascinated by each other, too."

The notion of Updike scripting such a scene between two women may cause some feminists to gasp. His novels about the solipsism of men—especially the infamous Rabbit Angstrom, who lurched through three decades from *Rabbit, Run* (1960) to *Rabbit at Rest* (1990)—have angered some readers for their perceived objectification of women. It's not a criticism used lightly. His 1968 scorcher, *Couples*, for example, even had riffs on the color of a woman's pubic hair. This in a time when D. H. Lawrence's novels were considered racy.

It would seem, then, that *Seek My Face* is an apology of sorts. Yet this is not Updike's first attempt at creating a novel based around women, as he points out to me. In the eighties, he wrote three novels about women, including *The Witches of Eastwick*, which told the tale of three New England witches under the spell of a new guy in town, and *S.*, a rewriting of Nathaniel Hawthorne's *The Scarlet Letter* from Hester Prynne's point of view.

That New England puritanism—and the delicious pleasures of violating it—are again at the center of this novel. During the interview, Kathryn asks Hope about her finances, her parenting, even her sex life, which sends Hope on internal reveries about the tempestuous bedroom activities of her life five decades ago. Some of these she shares with Kathryn; others she does not.

This withholding is something Updike, who has been asked some pretty direct questions in his lifetime, can relate to. "[Kathryn's] forward in the way a starstruck person can be," he says. "People forget that you're not just a research resource, like an encyclopedia or a website, but you're a person with feelings and privacy."

In recent years, Updike has had to sit for more and more interviews. "When I first set out on this trail, in the fifties, writers were not expected to promote their books, go on the road, or sign them, none of that. You were supposed to produce the books, and that was about the extent of your responsibilities. Now producing the book is almost the beginning of your real responsibilities, which are to get out and sell it."

Although he has "gotten better at this part of the game" and has come to view such conversations as a necessary evil of sorts, Updike worries about their effect on art. "If an artist had a set of opinions to purvey he'd be a preacher or a politician. A work of art, a work of literary art . . . is an attempt to make a kind of an object, with the mystery that objects have. You can look at it in one way, find another light, and see another. All these breaches of [artists'] privacy are in danger of taking the art out of it."

Yet for a man who professes to dislike interviews, Updike remains unfalteringly cheery during an hour of conversation. Questions about his characters' motivations prompt the longest answers, launching him into minutes-long prose reveries, punctuated by the movement of his eyes, the waggle of his prominent eyebrows, and gestures of his hands, which are pink and somewhat gnarled, as if he has spent a lifetime vulcanizing words, rather than twisting them into shape on the page. When he strikes upon a particularly felicitous turn of phrase, his blue eyes flash with an immodest mischief.

Graciousness aside, in the end it is clear that Updike would rather be performing this wordplay on the page instead of into the microphone of a tape recorder. Criticism won't be stopping him anytime soon. "Thankfully," he jokes, "these things come out after the type has been set." Like Hope, Updike is excited every day by the prospect of making something new. "Although it looks increasingly foolish from the outside, it doesn't feel that way on the inside."

He is also motivated by fear. "There's the fear that somehow you neglected to say what was really yours to say," Updike says, for once his voice rising. "It's not likely: I've written a lot. I must have somewhere touched on almost every aspect of my life and experience. Nevertheless, there's this haunting fear that the thing you left out isn't going to be finally captured."

As if to underscore this, the day before our interview, Updike's editor received in the mail a large package bearing—what else?—the manuscript for his next book.

April 2003

Joyce Carol Oates

Joyce Carol Oates has created a body of work that is Victorian in scope and profoundly American in its preoccupations. Piety and the body, violence and its aftermath: These are but a few of her obsessions, which Oates has explored across novels, short stories, essays, poetry, and memoirs. Raised in Millersport, New York, a small, working-class town in the north part of the state, she attended a one-room schoolhouse and was the first in her family to graduate from high school. She won a scholarship to attend Syracuse University, and later earned a master's from the University of Wisconsin–Madison, where she met her husband of more than four decades, Raymond Smith, with whom she edited the Ontario Review until he died in 2008. Her most laureled novels, which make up the Wonderland Quartet, include the National Book Award–winning them, a brutal depiction of the decline of working-class America in the sixties. She has also written gothic romance, novels about celebrity (including Blonde, 2000), mysteries under two different pen names, horror fiction, drama, and more than ten works of criticism. She lives in Princeton, New Jersey, where she has taught for

more than three decades. I went to see her there on the
publication of The Gravedigger's Daughter *(2007).*

Joyce Carol Oates's rate of production has been staggering: more than one thousand short stories, some fifty novels, and a dozen-plus books of essays, plays, and poetry
since 1963. The year we meet she publishes three books.

Clearly, making things up has never been a problem.
But with her latest work, things have changed. Now it's
personal. A decade ago, she began cribbing from the life of
someone real and dear to her heart: her grandmother.

I go to see Oates at her airy modernist home, wrapped
around a leafy courtyard. But before she explains the gen-
esis of her latest novel, we have to agree what part of
her massive creative output we are to discuss. "Which
book are you here to talk about?" she asks, cloudy with
puzzlement.

That cleared up, we are on to *The Gravedigger's Daughter*. "My grandmother had experiences with her father
very similar to Rebecca's," she says, referring to the heroine of the novel, which tells of a woman who escapes
when her father kills the rest of their family.

"In actual life my great-grandfather was a gravedigger. Though he didn't kill his wife," she says, deadpan.
"He injured her and she was hospitalized. But he did
threaten his daughter, and he did commit suicide with a
shotgun. That's all true." In the book, Rebecca winds up
in the arms of an alcoholic husband. She flees when he
becomes abusive, turning herself into Hazel Jones.

Oates saw the novel through numerous revisions.

"The opening chapter alone was revised fifteen times," she says. "When I come to the end of the novel, I rewrite the ending and the beginning together. To me, that is what writing is."

The novel was finished several years ago, but it was bumped several times off the schedule by books that her publisher believed were more "controversial," Oates says, using his word, books such as *Missing Mom*, the tale of a woman who goes missing. In the meantime, *The Gravedigger's Daughter* cooled in a closet where Oates keeps a stack of fireproof drawers, incubating fiction already written and protecting documents. "Supposedly, if the whole house burns down, our wills won't," she says with a wry look.

She has written many tales of transformation, notably in her 2001 Pulitzer Prize finalist, *Blonde*, an imagining of the life of Marilyn Monroe.

"Norma Jean Baker sort of makes herself into Marilyn Monroe," she says, her voice high and quiet, not unlike that of the former sex symbol, "sort of like Rebecca, who becomes Hazel Jones. And many women become Hazel Jones to some extent—they don't always stay Hazel Jones. But it's kind of an American ideal."

Oates was fascinated that her grandmother had done a similar thing long before the era of extreme makeovers. And since her transformation was also long before psychotherapy had entered the mainstream, her grandmother didn't talk about it.

"The image I have of her is unfailing," Oates continues. "I mean, she never was the girl whose father had almost killed her and blew his head off with a shotgun. She was never that girl. She was never the woman whose husband had abused her and then left her. She never would have wanted to play those cards."

Oates's grandmother didn't play the victim, a role Oates believes Americans overplay today to their detriment. Writing about her grandmother's time, she grew to appreciate the hardships and starkness her ancestors, men and women, would have felt.

"If people came to America in 1890 and settled in the countryside, they were like pioneers," she says. "They were living in very primitive circumstances—of course, there was no plumbing and no electricity—so you can imagine what they were living in, a stone cottage in a cemetery."

Like Rebecca's father and mother, Oates's great-grandparents came to the United States—in the 1890s, not 1936, as in the book—and changed their name (from Morgenstern to Morningstar).

"I guess it was pretty common," she says. "They put aside their Jewish background completely, out of what trauma or devastation or terror or experiences in Europe I can only imagine. We never knew anything about this, and I didn't know my grandmother and her parents had been Jewish. That was never talked about."

As we sit in her living room, surrounded by the work of her Princeton colleagues Edmund White and Toni Morrison, as well as Melville and Hawthorne, this recently excavated history hangs in a loaded near silence. She speaks slowly, pausing at length, then starting again saying that her grandmother met a man named Oates. "He left her with a small child who was my father."

There is something deeply odd in hearing her discuss these matters, not because of the personal revelations but because her most famous novels—such as *them* and *Because It Is Bitter, and Because It Is My Heart*, as well as her trenchant essays—have become cultural shorthand for feminine consciousness. In other words, she has helped to create a world that would be totally unrecognizable to her own grandmother, let alone the heroine based on her.

"There's a good deal in the novel about playing with cards," Oates says. "Playing with the cards that you are dealt; you have a limited number of cards, which you have to deal very carefully, and people who choose to present themselves as victims, I think, are probably making a mistake."

She gives an example from *The Gravedigger's Daughter*, where Rebecca meets an appealing new man. "Does she feel for him what she feels for Niles [her first husband]? No, she's never going to be able to feel that again. But he's such a wonderful man, should she tell him what her background is?"

August 2007

Amy Tan

 Amy Tan was born in Oakland, California, in 1952 to a Baptist minister and a woman who had abandoned a past, and three daughters, in China. Her family was part of a social group called the Joy Luck Club, which got together and played the stock market. Tan's father and brother died when she was young, and Tan was sent away to Switzerland, where she attended high school and became a rebel. She returned to the United States and attended college in Oregon, where she met her future husband, and studied linguistics in a doctoral program at San Jose State University. When her roommate was murdered, she left the program and worked in the field of disabilities and, later, in business writing, before she turned to creative writing in her mid-thirties. At a writing conference in 1985, she tried out a short story that ultimately unraveled into The Joy Luck Club, a bestseller and worldwide phenomenon—as well as a finalist for the National Book Award, the National Book Critics Circle Award, and the Los Angeles Times Book Prize. In 1993, it became a film directed by Wayne Wang.

Tan's work since then takes many of the facts of her

life and refracts them through a robust storytelling aes-
thetic. Her novels are full of abandoned daughters
*(*The Kitchen God's Wife, *1991), sisters born between*
*China and America and the gap between them (*The
Hundred Secret Senses, *1995), and the friction between*
American-born Chinese daughters and their Chinese-
*born mothers (*The Bonesetter's Daughter, *2001). Her*
latest novel is The Valley of Amazement *(2013), the*
tale of a painting that is passed between three genera-
tions of women. Her 2003 memoir, The Opposite of
Fate, *laid out some of the true-life sources for these*
books. Tan's ability to channel different voices and
draw from these elements deep family portraits has made
her one of the most widely read novelists of her gener-
ation. Among literary writers in America, perhaps only
Toni Morrison and Cormac McCarthy have sold as
many books. I met Tan in 2005, when she was publish-
ing her fifth work of fiction, Saving Fish from Drowning, *which chronicles twelve Americans on a trip to*
China and Burma.

Amy Tan's fifth novel, *Saving Fish from Drowning*, begins with a rather cruel hoax on the reader. It introduces
Bibi Chen, a woman Tan professes to be real, only to later
present her as the narrator—from beyond the grave.

Sitting in her SoHo loft, surrounded by two feisty
Yorkshire terriers named Lilli and Bubba, Tan remains
unapologetic about having it both ways.

"Why would anyone believe me?" asks the fifty-three-
year-old novelist. "I'm a fiction writer! I make things up."

Indeed she does. Since debuting in 1989 with *The Joy Luck Club*, Tan has published three other novels, two children's books, and a collection of essays, and she was an adviser on a hit children's cartoon, *Sagwa*, based on her Chinese Siamese cat.

But recently Tan has begun to think about how faithfully people trust what is presented as true.

"I was starting to question where we get the truth," she says. "And I was interested in what happened when you looked at something that had the appearance of authority. Like a note to the reader—you automatically assume it's the truth."

In this sense, reading *Saving Fish from Drowning* is like looking in a funhouse mirror where everything is upside down and backward. Where what's true is false, and what's false is true. Or maybe not.

Unfolding in Bibi's cranky, if amused, voice, the book describes the misbegotten holiday taken by twelve wealthy, art-loving San Franciscan friends to the country of Burma, or Myanmar, as the military dictatorship that took over in 1990 calls it. Readers won't have to look hard to find a nod to Geoffrey Chaucer.

"I started outlining the story an hour after I finished writing *The Bonesetter's Daughter*," says Tan, "and imagined a '*Canterbury Tales* goes to Burma.'"

But Chaucer's travelers did not find themselves as lost in translation as do Tan's. Mostly rich, mostly white, and entirely unfamiliar with the culture into which they have dunked themselves, they make a number of errors. The whopper involves a celebrity dog trainer urinating on a sacred shrine.

Bibi Chen looks down on this debacle with lashing humor. She critiques the decor of their hotel and ridicules her friends for having a Christmas lunch in a Buddhist country.

"She is definitely the voice of my mother," says Tan, whose mother died in 1999 from Alzheimer's, after figuring prominently in Tan's previous novels, such as *The Hundred Secret Senses* and *The Bonesetter's Daughter*. It was the beginning of a very hard time for Tan. That same year she contracted Lyme disease, which attacked her body and then her brain, causing hallucinations and trances. It made it hard for her to write, too, which was a big setback for an author who came to writing almost as therapy. Tan had been working ninety hours a week as a technical writer for IBM in the eighties when an agent encouraged her to turn one story into a book—*The Joy Luck Club*.

That novel spent nine months on the bestseller list, sold more than four million copies, inspired a critically acclaimed movie, and put Tan's days of working as a technical writer behind her.

Saving Fish from Drowning was begun in the aftermath of recovering from Lyme, when Tan was "just happy to be able to write at all," she says. "I knew from the beginning it would be a comedy."

Humor and the topic of Burma do not often go together, but Tan felt an obligation to slip readers in the back door.

"The wonderful thing about fiction is it's subversive: You can get people into a very repugnant situation through fiction—and comedy is one way to get people to let their defenses down.

"The sad thing about Burma is that some of the most absurd things are the real stuff. You have a military regime which is called SLORC. Doesn't that sound James Bondian? It's State Law and Order Restoration Council.

"I think someone finally said, 'You know, it's not a very good name.' So they hired a Washington-based PR firm, and revamped their image, renamed them. It was ludicrous."

Tan captures some of this absurdity by having her merry travelers get kidnapped by a group of Burmese tribesmen, who believe that one of the tourists—a teenager who reads Stephen King and performs card tricks—is the Young White Brother, a man fabled to save them.

Harry, the aforementioned urinating dog trainer, is left behind and helps ignite a media frenzy to rescue the kidnapped Americans. Little does he know he is actually helping the military regime spread propaganda via a global news network called the GNN.

"I wanted to play with the idea that the news makes it happen," says Tan, explaining why she felt compelled to have the experience of her innocents abroad evolve into a media circus.

As a Chinese American with an enormous audience, Tan is frequently asked to use her platform in the media as a way to call attention to injustices in Asia.

"During the time after Tiananmen Square, people thought I should go to China, stand on the square, and denounce the Chinese government," she says. "And I just wasn't sure that would be effective. That would be me asserting my American rights to say anything, but does it really help people who are suffering? So my bottom line now is: How would it help people if I do something, and how would it hurt them?"

Tan became acquainted with this equation when she went to China several years ago after the BBC aired a documentary called *The Dying Room*, which showed secret footage of babies dying in orphanages. In response, the Chinese government shut the orphanages to Western observers, stopped doing cleft-palate surgeries, and refused money given to them.

"And I thought to myself," says Tan now, "did that save any lives?"

In her novel, the kidnapped travelers, who Tan depicts as bumbling but basically good people, experience this dilemma firsthand when they witness repression by the Myanmar government. They become convinced they must speak out. Doing so, however, means risking tipping off the government to the exact location of the tribesmen.

Tan believes these catch-22 moments are part of everyday life. For instance, the title refers to how Buddhists allow themselves to catch and kill fish.

"They scoop up the fish and bring them to shore," explains a man in the novel to one of the tourists. "They say they are saving the fish from drowning. Unfortunately . . . [the fish] do not recover."

Tan hopes readers will begin to see Burma on their radar again.

"This is a country that has been largely forgotten by people since the name was changed, and it would be nice for people to remember it. Burma has some of the worst cases of human rights abuse. It has the world capital of growing heroin."

Tan plans to keep writing and entertaining and to finish an opera libretto she is working on. And to support worthy charities. For instance, she recently helped Dave Eggers by lending her name to an event at his writing lab in San Francisco. In return for canceling her other plans, Eggers sent her a list of what he might do in return, from cutting her grass to fetching her coffee. Tan simply asked for his firstborn.

"I said, if it's a boy, I don't care. If it's a girl, I want her to be Amy Tan Vida Eggers."

Tan cackles for a bit. And only then does it become clear she's joking.

October 2005

Don DeLillo

Don DeLillo spent his childhood in an Italian American part of the Bronx, where he developed a lifelong affection for baseball, the varied and poetic sound of the American idiom, and New York City. He attended high school and university in the Bronx, and went to work on Madison Avenue for advertising firms when he couldn't get a job in publishing. His first short story appeared in 1960, and he began to work on his first novel after he left advertising. His debut, Americana, appeared in 1971, and told the story of an advertising executive turned filmmaker who is observing the corrosive effect of film and corporate life on Americans' sense of reality.

DeLillo published five other novels in the seventies, books that range in focus from football to rock musicians and their self-mythology and to Wall Street and the rise of terrorism and its effect on the imagination. In the eighties he published three of his most important novels: The Names (1982), which revolves around the use and abuse of language; White Noise (1985), which won the National Book Award; and Libra (1988). Aside from Underworld (1997), his kaleidoscopic epic of America from

1950 to the nineties, DeLillo's novels since this period have been short and elliptical, surreal in their imagery, and damning in their examination of characters lost in a world slowly being emptied of meaning. In form they are almost closer to the plays he has been writing since the eighties, the latest of which formed the occasion for this interview.

Don DeLillo is not an easy author to spot on the streets of New York. It's not that his author photo is decades old but rather that it doesn't capture how small he is, how slight. Perhaps this is why, on a recent afternoon, the author of *Underworld*, *White Noise*, and other contemporary classics was temporarily barred entry from the offices of his New York publisher. Apparently DeLillo didn't produce proper identification, or wasn't assertive enough about his right to be there. After much huffing and rolling of her eyes, the security guard waved the sixty-nine-year-old novelist through the gate toward the elevator bank. As DeLillo passed, she looked over his shoulder at me, with eyebrows raised, as if to say, "See the grief I get from these idiots?"

As it turns out, DeLillo prefers things this way. While some writers cozy up to the medal stand, he would rather lurk on society's margins, noticing without being noticed. This doesn't make for easy interviewing. Moments after passing the security gauntlet, DeLillo is ensconced in an empty office, in a chair pressed up against the wall. The position ensures that he remains partially obscured by a computer, his voice a disembodied whisper. "What do

you really see? What do you really hear?" DeLillo rumi-
nates, when I ask how he stays tuned in to the dream
waves of American life. "That's what in theory differenti-
ates a writer from everyone else. You see and hear more
clearly."

DeLillo has had his ear to the ground of late. The result is his fourth play, *Love-Lies-Bleeding*. It's a three-act
drama about a dying man and his family's struggle to
decide whether to keep him on life support. At the center
of the action is Alex Macklin, a landscape painter brought
low by a second stroke. Alex's ex-wife, Toinette, has not
seen him for some time and thinks he should be put out
of his misery. Alex's son, Sean, is not so sure, but his illu-
sions have long since run out. "He's not aware of you or
me or anything else," he tells Lia, Alex's current lover and
caregiver. "He can't think. He doesn't know what you're
saying to him. You are not Lia. He is not Alex."

Once again, DeLillo has scooped American newspapers. On the day of our conversation, the U.S. Supreme
Court upheld Oregon's assisted suicide law, the only such
rule in the country. When DeLillo finished the play, Terri
Schiavo dominated the news, as if summoned by his
imagination. Many Republicans argued that terminating
her life support would be premature. Schiavo's husband,
Michael, insisted it was the right thing to do. He won the
public battle and Schiavo died thirteen days after her feeding tube was removed. "I didn't have her in mind particularly," says DeLillo, skirting the debate, very aware of
how it became a political football. "But I did learn some
things from that event."

DeLillo would prefer politics be left out of this discussion. That's how he wrote the play. "They are in a state of stark isolation," he says of his characters, "outside of the influence of lawyers, doctors, and clergymen. I wanted them to be dealing simply with their own feelings, emotions, and predilections." Throughout the play, Alex sits on the stage like a silent witness to his own trial.

There is almost no medical equipment. America's most outspoken critic of technology has steered clear of it here. "I wanted a minimum of systems," DeLillo says. "There are feeding tubes, but I didn't want a hospital or a hospital bed. I wanted him sitting in a chair."

The starkness of this situation gives *Love-Lies-Bleeding* an eerie astringent feeling reminiscent of DeLillo's great 1985 novel, *White Noise*. That book told the story of a Hitler studies professor on a Midwestern campus terrorized by an airborne toxic event. Here the penumbra is personal, and the more the characters talk, the more it seems to loom. In the play's crescendo, a flashback, the emotions that lay buried rise up out of Alex's foretelling of his death. "You're the one blessing I know," he tells Lia, one year before the final stroke comes. "The last of the body."

Plays are becoming an increasingly large part of the only body DeLillo cares to share with us: his work. Though DeLillo is probably best known as the author of novels, his work for the stage has earned him comparisons to Beckett and Pinter. I ask him about these influences and he is flattered but confused. "I've seen some reviews that mention Beckett and Pinter, but I don't know what to say about that. I don't feel it myself."

In writing *Love-Lies-Bleeding*, DeLillo says he borrowed lines and structural elements from his first play, *The Engineer of Moonlight* (1979), published but never produced. "I wrote it experimentally," says DeLillo now. "I understood it was not producible, particularly in act two, which is very, very, very abstract."

DeLillo's later plays were only nominally less abstract. *The Day Room* (1986) is a curious two-act drama in which characters in a hospital room conduct a conversation that, in act two, is revealed to be a play itself. *Valparaiso* (1999) concerns a man who steps onto a plane going to a city in Indiana but winds up in Chile. At the end of the play the man is murdered onstage.

Death overshadows both of these plays, but it is more the idea of it—in *Love-Lies-Bleeding* it is real. "I suppose this is a play about the modern meaning of life's end," DeLillo says. "When does it end? How does it end, how should it end? What is the value of life? How do we measure it?" His talk skitters along these questions for a while then slides down a shale hill of silence into a full-blown reverie.

"Just yesterday," DeLillo says, "I remembered that in one of my earlier novels, I think it's in *Great Jones Street* if I didn't edit it out, there's a reference to patients in British hospitals being assigned to beds that are marked NTBR: not to be resuscitated. When I learned this, in the early seventies, I thought it sounded like the bleakest landscape out of some futuristic novel. Now it is widespread, the idea of people not being resuscitated."

DeLillo has never had to make such a decision. "If I did, I would probably speak of it only privately." As he says this, his gaze cannons out from behind the computer with intensity. Through large, slightly out-of-date glasses his eyes are huge, fierce without being spiteful. Just when I think I have blown it, the lines around his eyes break and soften, and he looks away. He is happy to go on to the next question.

It's odd to imagine this man sitting in the front row, listening to his words being read by actors, but that will happen soon. The Steppenwolf Theatre in Chicago has a production of *Love-Lies-Bleeding* scheduled. Without any false modesty, DeLillo admits he is already indebted to the stage and its actors. "The deceptive element is that, well, it's only dialogue after all. And much of the work will be done by others. A playwright realizes after he finishes the script this is only the beginning. What will happen when it moves into three dimensions: This is the test and surprise."

DeLillo greets this spring with another surprise. A screenplay he wrote fifteen years ago has finally given birth to a film, *Game 6*. It stars Michael Keaton as a playwright on a journey across town to confront a critic he worries will ravage his new play on opening night. "So here I am with a play coming out, and a movie about this situation," says DeLillo, the first real smile spreading across his face. As soon as the talk shifts to baseball, he grows more comfortable. "My baseball memory goes back a long way," DeLillo says. A longtime New York Yankees fan, he has grown disillusioned with the club's massive player payroll. As serious as he is about baseball, he will not make exceptions for it these days. He attends one game a year, and he does not watch it continuously on television.

And so DeLillo slowly backs out of the conversation, unrevealing himself piece by piece, until I'm not sure what, exactly, we are talking about. Or how we got there. When his publicist comes to retrieve him, DeLillo has become an almost avuncular presence, joking with her that we didn't really do an interview but simply played cards. So persuasively has he disappeared that, when I get home, I expect my tape to be blank.

April 2006

William T. Vollmann

*William T. Vollmann is an American re-
porter and novelist whose life and work
marry the crusading spirit of John Stein-
beck and the decadence of Henry Miller.
Born in Los Angeles, California, he grew
up partly in Indiana, where he acquired a
Midwestern accent and a set of old-fashioned manners.
When he was nine years old, Vollmann's younger sister
drowned while he was watching her, an incident that
haunts his fiction and partially explains his desire to help
and rescue people. Like Thomas Pynchon, whose sprung
diction his sentences recall, Vollmann graduated from
Cornell University. In 1982, he traveled to Afghanistan to
fight with the mujahideen who were resisting the Russian
invasion. Vollmann's account of this trip,* An Afghan Picture Show *(1992), hilariously details the burden he put on
his hosts as an unseasoned traveler and naïve pacifist.
Vollmann returned to America and wrote his first novel,*
You Bright and Risen Angels *(1987), an allegory of war in
which insects go to battle with the forces of civilization,
while working as a computer programmer, sleeping under his desk at work and living off vending-machine
food.*

Over the next twenty-five years Vollmann began a massive project that weaves between documentary reportage about violence and poverty—Rising Up and Rising Down *(2003), a 3,300-page study of violence, and* Imperial *(2009), a 1,300-page study of California's Imperial Valley—and historical fiction of the highest order. In 1990, he published* The Ice-Shirt, *the first in a proposed seven-volume fictional retelling of the conquering of the North American continent, the research for which took him to the Arctic Circle, where he wanted to see what it felt like to freeze to death. Vollmann is drawn to the margins of society, and to people who must make desperate bargains and moral decisions under the duress of history or grim circumstances. He has written three books about prostitutes, the best of which is the slim* Whores for Gloria *(1991), and one novel modeled off the work of Danilo Kiš,* Europe Central *(2005), which reanimates many of the players of World War II and shows them caught in the millstone of war. It won him the National Book Award. For many years he has made his base semi-anonymously in Sacramento, California, where he returns from long trips to write his long books. I spoke to him in 2000, as he was about to release* The Royal Family, *a soaring, visceral epic about prostitutes and a pair of brother detectives set in San Francisco's Tenderloin.*

The man some hail as the most vital and enduring link to gonzo journalism lives in a big white house with decorative pillars tucked away in a quiet neighborhood of Sacramento, California.

Sitting on a couch, sipping a whiskey, and describing how he read and reported his way out of a comfortable upbringing in this sunniest of America's states, William T. Vollmann seems earnest and abashed all at the same time—even when he is handing me a homemade bullet.

"When I was in my twenties," says the forty-one-year-old reporter and novelist, "I thought, gosh, what a shame I wasn't alive a hundred years ago, when there were all these parts of the world that weren't explored. And then I realized there are places still out there."

For the past two decades, Vollmann has made it his life's work to embrace this opportunity, even if it means going where American civilians often do not. His 1992 memoir, *The Afghanistan Picture Show*, described how at twenty-two he humped into the war-torn country with Islamic commandos, armed with a comparative literature degree from Cornell University. As it turns out, he wound up being a burden to those he wanted to help.

Since then, Vollmann has earned a reputation as a fearless, if sometimes pathologically risky, reporter, interviewing opium kings in Burma, smuggling an underage prostitute out of Thailand, and surviving a sniper attack in Kosovo that claimed the lives of two colleagues.

"It really was just chance that they were killed and I wasn't," he says, sounding rather far away. "One guy got hit in the face, and it took him a long time to die. He made these sort of groaning, vomiting sounds." The dying man had been a friend of twenty years.

These details informed *Rising Up and Rising Down*, his 3,300-page "essay" on violence, which was also published in abridged form—as well as *Europe Central*, Vollmann's slighter (at a mere 811 pages) collection of linked short stories about Nazis and Red Army officers at moments of moral decisions during wartime.

Part of what makes Vollmann distinctive as a novelist is the elasticity and stubbornness of his sense of moral responsibility. Accepting the National Book Award, Vollmann said, "When I was in elementary school, they showed me a film loop of burned corpses being pulled out of ovens. Later on, I understood I was partly German. I thought, am I somehow guilty for this? So I read and read and read my way into this awful history, and now it's over, and I'm happy I never have to be there again."

Like Tom Wolfe, Vollmann prepares with an intense amount of traveling and reading. For *The Ice-Shirt*, the first in his ongoing series of historical novels about the conquering of the North American continent by whites, Vollmann spent two weeks at an abandoned weather station at the magnetic North Pole to better appreciate what the explorers of that region went through.

Often Vollmann finds extreme stories in his own backyard, though. His most pressing preoccupation until recent years was with prostitutes, who he believes are "very close to the essence of life, everything is concentrated—violence, fear, experience, gambling." One of his earlier

books, with Ken Miller, is a series of photographs of
hookers he discovered living near his Sacramento home.

This fascination brings all sorts of hazards, not the
least being the threat of exposure to HIV and drugs.
While prepping for his 1991 novel, *Whores for Gloria*, he
interviewed hundreds of street women, pushers, and
pimps in San Francisco. To prove he wasn't a cop, Vollmann smoked crack with them. He says he lit up around
a hundred and fifty times.

Did he get addicted?

"You know, they say that stuff is addictive," Vollmann
says in a voice so flat, it at first seems phony. "But when I
wake up in the mornings, sometimes I can't help thinking
how nice it's going to be at eight when I get my coffee. I
never felt that way about crack."

On this sunny, quiet Saturday afternoon, it is hard
to imagine Vollmann in such a squalid environment. Tall
and beefy, with a slowness to his voice that seems Southern, he is an affable and sincerely polite host.

At the drop of a hat, he stomps heavily upstairs to
fetch his amateur photographs and the deluxe limited
editions of his poems that he crafts for CoTangent Press,
including one that features a bookmark made out of
"whore's hair."

Talking at his home and on a drive to San Francisco,
he comes across as an impassioned cynic, a libertarian
who has come by his cynicism by witnessing the awful
things people do to one another.

"It seems to me that America is entering a period of
decline, which is starting to become apparent. America

has never been so rich, and it also has never been so empty," he says.

But driving through some of the depressed towns of California's central valley, Vollmann suddenly lights up and says, "I bet if you and I spent some time there," pointing toward dismal Vacaville, "we would find some sort of fascinating secret."

July 2000

Louise Erdrich

 Louise Erdrich is a poet, bookseller, and bestselling novelist. In her childhood years Erdrich's family lived in Wahpeton, North Dakota. She attended Dartmouth College, where she met her husband, the writer Michael Dorris, who at the time was the director of the university's Native American studies program. Erdrich raised six children with Dorris, three of them adopted. Dorris committed suicide in 1997.

Erdrich began publishing poems and stories in 1978, and in 1984 released two books, Jacklight, a collection of verse, and Love Medicine, a novel in stories, each told by a different character. The novel made her the youngest ever winner of the National Book Critics Circle Award for Fiction. In her 1986 novel, The Beet Queen, she widened her fictional universe to include Argus, North Dakota, which she has revisited on and off for three decades in books, including three of her best: The Last Report on the Miracles at Little No Horse (2001), The Master Butchers Singing Club (2003), and The Plague of Doves (2008).

Erdrich's fiction blends Native American storytelling traditions and the narrative ingenuity of Eudora Welty's stories to create a mesmerizing, complete world. All these *elements come together in* The Plague of Doves, *her twelfth novel, released at the time of this interview. In 2012, she revealed it would be part of a trilogy.* The Round House *(2012), the second book in the sequence, won the National Book Award.*

Of all the fictional hamlets American writers have planted, from William Faulkner's Yoknapatawpha County to Garrison Keillor's Lake Wobegon, the most complex, luminous place might be a little town called Argus, North Dakota. Since 1984, when she first introduced the town in *Love Medicine*, Louise Erdrich has returned to it continually, conjuring the reservation it abuts, the love affairs that bolt down through the generations, the tensions that simmer between French Canadians, Catholics, and the native Ojibwe Indians, and their competing notions of God. It is amazing someone hasn't accidentally drawn up a Rough Guide.

So perhaps it is just a palpable sense of relief radiating off her at New York City's Penn Station on a rainy morning in May. Erdrich has swung through town to talk about *The Plague of Doves*, her first book in a while to spin out of Argus into new characters and territory. The enormous timeline Erdrich keeps in tandem with Trent Duffy, her copy editor, did not have to be consulted. Nor did she have to worry about veering off course from a main character's biography. She simply had to tell the story—or, as she likes to put it, wait for it to come.

"I knew this particular incident was going to be part of it," she says. "I just didn't know how I was going to approach it." The incident Erdrich refers to was a brutal one. On November 13, 1897, a mob of forty men broke into a North Dakota jail and lynched three American Indians—two young boys and a grown man—who were among a group being tried for the murders of six members of a white family. *The Plague of Doves* reimagines this event, bringing to life an entire fictional North Dakota community and tracing the crime as it filtered down through subsequent generations.

At the heart of the novel is Mooshum, an Ojibwe grandfather who was to be hanged but survived in part due to his mixed heritage. Mooshum tells his version of the events to his granddaughter, Evelina Harp, when she becomes infatuated with a teacher who is, as it turns out, descended from one of the men responsible for the killing. Later in the book she discovers that the genealogy of this killing extends all the way to the man she loves. "I could not look at anyone in quite the same way anymore," Evelina concludes.

As in all of Erdrich's books, revenge is a theme—but a complicated one, as families involved in the hanging intermarry. Memory is a battleground. The tribal members keep the story alive through folklore; the whites try to pretend it never happened. "In the beginning, the whites had all the power," Erdrich says, "but, as one reviewer put it, 'The Indians have the history.'" Her deft handling of this tension has earned her high praise across the United States. "Her most deeply affecting work yet," wrote Michiko Kakutani in *The New York Times*, while Philip Roth hailed it a "dazzling masterpiece."

Shuttling between these various modes of storytelling,

of remembering, has been Erdrich's lifework—on and off the page. Her father, Ralph, who according to family lore was born during a tornado, is German American; her mother, Rita, is French and Ojibwe. Erdrich was born Karen Louise in Little Falls, Minnesota, and grew up with six siblings in Wahpeton, North Dakota, a town of around nine thousand, where her parents taught at the Bureau of Indian Affairs School. One of the only books in the house was *A Narrative of the Captivity and Adventures of John Tanner*, the tale of a man who lived with the Ojibwe in the late eighteenth century.

The Erdrichs—regarded as the town eccentrics—were rigorous teachers. Ralph encouraged his children to memorize the poems of Frost, Tennyson, Robert Service, and Longfellow, paying them a nickel for every poem they could recite. Not surprisingly, two other Erdrichs are writers—Lise, a children's author, and Heid, the author of three poetry collections. Louise Erdrich has also published three collections of verse and four children's books. "I lived a very sheltered childhood, a very sweet childhood," she says. "We used to go for walks outdoors. I spent a lot of time around animals. I grew up without television."

She also spent a lot of time around storytellers. Throughout her work, including in *The Plague of Doves*, elder figures form the bedrock of stories. They are the long memory against which current action often plays out. "I was lucky to have grandparents around," Erdrich says—she listened to their stories and asked questions, something she continues to do when she drives to North Dakota, stopping off beside the road to write down ideas. There is a comically literal character in *The Plague of Doves* who constantly badgers Mooshum and his siblings for "the real story," to get the timeline of events straight. I ask Erdrich if she ever feels like this woman and she shoots back, "All the time," though this doesn't seem to bother her. "I still feel like I listen more than I tell."

This engagement with the past and her Ojibwe roots permeates every aspect of Erdrich's life. She left the plains in the seventies for Dartmouth College, the Ivy League school founded in the 1760s for the education of Native Americans in the New England area. It was there that she met her future husband, Michael Dorris, a fiction writer and anthropologist. Erdrich had returned as a writer in residence after graduating with a master's in creative writing. Dorris heard her read her poetry and was intrigued. They communicated by letter while he did fieldwork in New Zealand and she began to publish. She supported herself working at Kentucky Fried Chicken and as a construction flag signaler.

The two married in 1981 and began a working relationship that lasted more than a decade. Dorris encouraged her to work on fiction and even posed as her agent when they began submitting *Love Medicine* to publishers. The book was knocked back by numerous publishers before going on to sell four hundred thousand hardcover copies. She became a minor sensation and was named one of *People* magazine's Most Beautiful People in 1990. But there would be no flameout. *Love Medicine* was the start of a tetralogy that also included *The Beet Queen* (1986), *Tracks* (1988), and *The Bingo Palace* (1994). With

Dorris she published *Route Two* (1990) and *The Crown of Columbus* (1991). They had separated and were in divorce proceedings when Dorris committed suicide in the spring of 1997.

Erdrich has been guarded with the press ever since, but her books have not slowed down. She has unleashed a prodigious amount of work since then in fact—eight novels for adults, one of which, *The Last Report on the Miracles at Little No Horse* (2001), was a National Book Award finalist; five novels for children, one of which, *The Birchbark House* (1999), was also a finalist for the National Book Award; a collection of poems; a volume of collected stories; and a nonfiction work on books and islands in Ojibwe Country. She also founded Birchbark Books, a nonprofit bookstore in Minneapolis; raised her children; continued learning the Ojibwe language, which she feared was being erased; and taught workshops on Turtle Mountain with her sister Heid.

This level of activity would not suggest that Erdrich is willing to wait. But in person she is quiet and self-effacing. She called upon these qualities as she waited for *The Plague of Doves*, which has been with her since the early eighties as she worked on other books. The voices of the main characters—a college graduate, a judge, a grandfather, and a doctor—came over time, at odd moments, their story in shards. "I can't quite know I'm making a book," Erdrich says. "I really don't know where [the voices] come from. I just feel like I get to take down what they're telling me."

At times, Erdrich can sound closer to a medium than a fiction writer. But she is keen to correct that impression. "A voice that is going to take over a story is some-one you will have prepared for quite some time," she says. And in twenty-five years of publishing, these characters have taught her how cruel the world can be. "It's against my nature to believe how evil people can be," she says. "I didn't see cruelty a lot growing up. When it became apparent that the world was different from what I had known as a child, it took me a long time to understand it."

June 2008

Norman Mailer

 Norman Mailer was an American novel-
ist, screenwriter, biographer, journalist,
newspaper publisher, and mayoral candidate, among other things. Born in Long
Branch, New Jersey, in 1923, he grew up in
the same part of Brooklyn that Bernard
Malamud wrote about in his fabulist short fiction. Mailer
fought his way into Harvard University, where he studied
aeronautical engineering, and from there he enlisted in
the army in World War II, an experience that catalyzed
his writing career, even if he did not see much combat.
Mailer's energetic debut novel, The Naked and the Dead,
was published in 1948, just a few years after the war
ended, and went on to be a New York Times bestseller
for more than a year. Barbary Shore (1951), set in a Brooklyn rooming house during the heyday of the New Left,
and The Deer Park (1955), which fictionalized his time in
Hollywood, followed closely thereafter and established
Mailer's taboo-breaking voice. From the mid-fifties to the
mid-sixties, he reinvented his storytelling mode in genre-
bending nonfiction reports that invested the subjective
voice with all the flexion and energy of first-person fiction. He collected these reports in Advertisements for

Myself *(1959) and* The Presidential Papers *(1963), and finally returned to fiction with* An American Dream *(1965), which was serialized in* Esquire. *Mailer's most successful reinvention came in 1979, when he returned from a period of flabby, overambitious novels to write his greatest book,* The Executioner's Song, *a novel based on the real-life murderer Gary Gilmore.*

Mailer's career was full of spats, fistfights, breakups—he famously stabbed his second wife at a party—and promised returns to form. He was married six times and fathered nine children. At the time of this interview, conducted upon the publication of his last novel, The Castle in the Forest *(2007), he had mellowed and become a lion at rest in Provincetown, Massachusetts.*

There was a time when Norman Mailer used to talk about the Big Book. The subject, like a white whale, prowled at the periphery of the interviews he gave in the fifties, blasting into view and then diving into the darkness, where it would lurk until the next publication date.

With each decade, and each new book, from *An American Dream* to *The Executioner's Song*, it seemed as if Mailer might still drag his promised catch to shore.

Though Joan Didion argued in *The New York Review of Books* that Mailer finally got his big trophy—four times in fact—the lion remains unconvinced. And at eighty-four, America's most pugilistic novelist has done something unusual: He's beginning to say he may not get it.

"I may have made announcements fifty years ago of

the kind of book I was going to write," says Mailer at his home in Provincetown, the fishing village turned weekend retreat at the tip of Cape Cod. "But I'm not going to stick to those predictions."

What's unusual is that Mailer made this pronouncement on the eve of the publication of his thirty-sixth book, *The Castle in the Forest*, an audacious novel that tells the story of Hitler's first seventeen years through the eyes of D.T., an assistant to the devil himself.

Mailer has worked on the book long enough to lose track of when he started exactly. In the interim, his knees have given out, meaning he now walks with the aid of two canes. During the course of the interview he does not stand.

"There was one early review that was essentially favorable, but it irritated the hell out of me," he says, revealing a flash of his former feistiness, his smile turning wicked. "Let's say it irritated the shit out of me. Because the reviewer said in some long-winded way, of course, 'Mailer is just rewriting Freud.' Why? Because I paid attention to toilet training? Well, as a father of nine children I do know a little bit about toilet training."

The evidence of this assertion surrounds him. The end tables in the room are stacked four deep with photographs of Mailer offspring. Several paintings of Mailer line the walls—a large one hangs in the front office depicting himself and his sixth wife, Norris Church Mailer, and a friend in Havana. Large windows open onto the bay and the ocean beyond.

In this comfortable setting, it seems odd that Mailer should be so compelled to delve into "the reek of the urine, the shit, and the blood of Luther" so manifest throughout *The Castle in the Forest*.

But, as reviews have noted, that's exactly what he has done. This is an exceptionally dirty book that also happens to want to turn the clock of America's cosmology back some sixty years: Mailer believes the world is run by a threesome—God, man, and the devil—and that Hitler was the devil's response to Jesus Christ.

The most graphic scene of *The Castle in the Forest* involves Hitler's bawdy, raucous, incestuous conception—with the devil inserting himself into young Adolf's soul at the moment of his parents' climax. As provocative as this sounds Mailer says he is not being facetious. "We can understand Joseph Stalin in a way," he says. "One of the things about Stalin is that he was one of the very toughest men in Russia. Hitler was not that tough. It was as if odd gifts were given to him at extraordinary moments."

Mailer says such gifts can only have come from the devil, who he believes works all the time. "Maybe every year there are one thousand people invested by the devil, or a million people? Then they either come to fruition or they don't."

Hitler, in Mailer's view, was a high point of the devil's work, something he says his mother acknowledged early on. "My mother was very affected by Hitler," he says. "When I was nine years old, she knew already, long before the statesmen did, that Hitler was a disaster and a monster. That he was probably going to kill half the Jews, if not all of them."

Mailer has long thought he would write this book.

But first he had to get to *The Gospel According to the Son*, which told Christ's story in his own words. The idea for that book came to him in a Paris hotel room. Mailer couldn't sleep, so he picked up the Bible. "I thought, this is such a funny book. It's got sentences that are worthy of Shakespeare, but most of it was dreadful. Then I thought, there are one hundred writers in the world that could do a better job. And I'm one of them."

Mailer wrote the book and got slaughtered for it, and today, even he admits that "I felt I didn't quite bring it off. I felt like I was making a reach for the material," he says judiciously.

With Hitler, though, Mailer says he did not feel this barrier. For starters, spending time with a very bad man was not a problem, as he learned from writing about Lee Harvey Oswald in *Oswald's Tale*. "You know your characters don't need to be there to make you happy with how wonderful they are and how warmhearted they are and how human they are—you can write about a monster, and so far as you enjoy writing, enjoy the work."

Mailer used to put in marathon writing sessions but has become used to five, six hours at a stretch, sometimes without lunch if he becomes absorbed. Although the book contains an extensive bibliography, Mailer was pleased to be plowing the dark, too. "There is very little known about Hitler's childhood," he says. "He concealed much of it, to the best of his best ability." So Mailer ad-libbed. Long ago, he might have felt some apprehension with this project, knowing the kinds of reviews it would spark. Now he says he doesn't care. "One of the advantages of getting old is you really don't give a fuck anymore. What are they going to do, come and kill me? Fine, make a martyr of me! Make me immortal!"

As a Jewish writer, he says he has also long been ready to approach Hitler with a cool head. "I remember the first time I visited Germany, in the fifties, I was very much on edge." But not now. And with current events going the way they are, Mailer says there might be a lesson here for Americans. "My feeling now is all countries can potentially become monstrous nations—and I think the last few years here, it's not as if we became a monstrous nation, but for the first time in Americans' lives, the possibility is so."

In other words, the devil is not entirely responsible for Hitler's rise to power. Conditions made it possible, too. Vigilance is key. "Given the hideous conditions in Germany after the First World War, not only the shame and humiliation of losing that war in an extraordinary, thoroughgoing way," Mailer says, continuing to rattle off the social context of Hitler's rise, "given all that, all the conditions were there for a monster to take over the country." And yet, to say that that alone created Hitler, for Mailer, is not enough. "I'm not here to guarantee it. But I'm saying we won't understand this unless we go back to the notion that maybe God and the devil do exist!"

February 2007

James Wood

James Wood is a literary critic, a novelist, and a professor at Harvard University. The son of a professor of zoology in Durham, England, he attended Eton College and read English at Jesus College, Cambridge. Wood began his career as a reviewer at a very young age and by his late twenties was the chief book critic for The Guardian. *Wood's voice and fierce aesthetic approach to criticism made him stand out in a decade largely dedicated to fighting over identity politics. In the nineties he launched a series of devastating attacks on the work of Don DeLillo, Toni Morrison, and Philip Roth. He joined* The New Yorker *in 2007, at which point his scathing reviews gave way, to some degree, to an exploratory spirit. He has published three collections of reviews and essays; a novel,* The Book Against God *(2003); and one book-length exploration,* How Fiction Works *(2008), which was the occasion for this interview. Wood lives in Cambridge, Massachusetts, with his wife, the novelist Claire Messud.*

For the past fifteen years, the most talked about literary critic in the English-speaking world has been a tall, thin, agreeable Englishman from Durham with a crop-top pate and an apologetic air about him.

"I agree with Randall Jarrell that a critic who can't praise is not a critic," James Wood, forty-two, says as he sits in an empty café near Harvard University, where he teaches.

But this doesn't sound much like the Wood that readers are familiar with. That Wood has been the man lying belly down in the jungle, while big-game novelists lumber by, their award-fattened flanks exposed to his shots. Toni Morrison, Wood wrote, "loves her own language more than she loves her own characters," Don DeLillo has spawned a culture in which everyone with a laptop and a bit of paranoia is a genius, and John Updike forgot when to stop. "It seems to be easier for John Updike to stifle a yawn than to refrain from writing a book," Wood wrote about his short-story collection *Licks of Love*.

On a cold, windy day in Cambridge, Massachusetts, Wood doesn't disavow these statements. But he admits that he has exhausted the polemic. And if publishers want to send flowers to anyone for bringing about this change, they should start with his students.

"I became aware of a curious dual track," Wood says, looking slightly sheepish. "I would be polemicizing in pieces about things I didn't like, but almost never doing that in class. You can't do that with students; it's not fair to prejudice them."

Wood's concise, readable new book, *How Fiction*

Works, grew out of this engagement with students. It is an attempt to show what he does like and explain the novel as he sees it.

Constructed in 123 short sections, *How Fiction Works* covers narration, style, detail, and other basic elements in Wood's typically crisp prose, but there is one big difference: The primary mode is praise.

Here are Wood's maestros, demonstrating how it's done: Henry James using what Wood calls free indirect style in *What Maisie Knew*, George Orwell's mastery of detail in *The Hanging*, and Ian McEwan's shrewd manipulation of the reader's sympathy in *Atonement*.

For Wood, the modern novel began with Flaubert, when we started to see "that highly selective editing and shaping, by cutting out the chatty narrator that you get in Balzac or Walter Scott."

Through free indirect style, by which he basically means third-person narration that cleaves to one character or another, Wood says the novel has shown us more about consciousness than any other art form.

In recent years, however, he believes that the novel has become bloated with unnecessary facts and language, especially American novels. Buried inside *The Corrections*, for example, was a very good novel if only Jonathan Franzen could have stopped telling us how much he knew.

"The result—in America at least—is novels of immense self-consciousness with no selves in them at all," Wood wrote in a piece about the American social novel that Franzen and others were writing, "curiously arrested and very 'brilliant' books that know a thousand things but do not know a single human being."

Once Wood may have reiterated this point in journalism, but now he feels that he can have a greater impact by sharing his opinion with students. "I really felt a connection," he says of his Columbia University master of fine arts students in particular, "because these were people very interested in technique, and were willing to take what they learned and go away and apply it. This was my chance to say, 'Look, you all do this thing called free indirect style, it's instinctive; you have your own words for it. Here's a history of it: You can go all the way back to Jane Austen, or even the Bible, and see it's endemic to narrative. Let me give you some terminology, and let me give you a brief history of it.' "

In many ways, Wood is perfectly suited to this terrain. While other boys his age were playing rugby, he spent his time reading criticism by F. R. Leavis, Irving Howe, and Ford Madox Ford.

"It sounds very trainspotter-ish," he says, laughing, "but I used to sit in bed and read this stuff."

He was also obsessed with America. "I went through a phase where I loved everything having to do with America," he remembers. "Then someone gave me Richard Ford's *The Sportswriter* when I was twenty-one. That book just blew me away. No one begins a book like that in England: 'My name is Frank Bascombe. I am a sportswriter.' "

At Cambridge, Wood met the Canadian American writer Claire Messud, with whom he now has two children, Livia and Lucian. As Messud began her literary career, Wood spent the next decade making a name for himself as a critic in London.

But he eventually found himself stifled by the environment. "I got to the point where I knew who was in and who was out, and followed all the newspaper sections and watched who was doing what—and I hated myself for that involvement."

In 1995, Wood met the editor Leon Wieseltier in London and recognized a kindred spirit. Wieseltier invited him to write for *The New Republic*, the literary section of which he edited, and Wood leaped at the chance to go to America.

"I always felt in America there was more room to move around," Wood says. "There's just so much space that people will, by and large, leave you alone to do your work."

He was an immediate sensation. Coming from the outside, Wood cut a swathe through some of America's most hallowed names—a role that Dale Peck tried to take on, without much grace, because a good polemicist is not just a destroyer but someone who leads you to a new way of thinking. Still, Wood quickly found out how small the country can be.

In 1996, he attended the dinner for the PEN/Faulkner Award. Messud's novel *When the World Was Steady* was a finalist, alongside Richard Ford's *Independence Day*, to which Wood had given a mixed review.

"About halfway through the dinner I feel this shadow standing over me, and it's Richard Ford, who puts a hand on my shoulder and says in that voice of his, 'We need to talk.' I immediately said to Claire, 'We've got to get out of here!'" Wood successfully ducked his date with Ford.

In 1999, Wood published some of his pieces as a book,

The Broken Estate. That book—with its follow-up, *The Irresponsible Self: On Laughter and the Novel*—became secret handshakes for aspiring critics. A novel, *The Book Against God*, followed in 2003 and met surprisingly little payback. "People on the whole were very kind," Wood says. "But I know if I were to publish that novel again there are some things I would change and like to do better."

In the meantime, he now has a chance to reach a larger audience with his criticism. In the autumn of 2007 he moved from *The New Republic* to *The New Yorker*, where he joined Updike as one of the magazine's primary literary critics. If there is any awkwardness in sharing that post, he doesn't mention it.

In fact, it seems that Wood is getting just as much out of listening to younger critics. "I think that we're in a golden age for criticism," he suggests. That generation begins with his own children, to whom he has been reading Beatrix Potter and J. M. Barrie's *Peter Pan*, among other writers, remembering how good some literature is, and how little time a writer has to win over readers.

"You get such a ruthless interrogator of tale," Wood says with a glint of pride at his children's discernment. "And they're right: Sometimes I'm bored myself."

January 2008

Margaret Atwood

 Margaret Atwood is a Canadian novelist, short-story writer, anthologist, poet, and environmental activist. Her stories and novels are important texts of the feminist movement and have won her nearly every major literary prize, from the Booker to Canada's Governor General's Award (twice). Born in Ottawa in 1939, she spent large parts of her childhood exploring the woods of northern Quebec. Her debut work, The Edible Woman (1969), dives into and scrambles gender stereotypes through the story of a woman who is beginning to feel as if her body and mind have separated. Surfacing (1972) and Lady Oracle (1976) expanded Atwood's tonal register and deepened the mythical power of her grappling with the role of women in society. Atwood's definitive work, The Handmaid's Tale (1985), prefigures the apocalyptic work of Cormac McCarthy, imagining North America has been taken over by a chauvinist theocracy and renamed the Republic of Gilead, in which women (and undesirables) are stripped of their rights.

Love and romance, and the shifting boundaries between truth and falsehood in storytelling, form the core

of her bestselling novels The Robber Bride *(1993),* Alias
Grace *(1996), and* The Blind Assassin *(2000), which won
her the Booker Prize. Since then, she has begun to focus
more on science fiction, from the trilogy of novels that
began with* Oryx and Crake *(2003) and concluded with*
MaddAddam *(2013). Atwood's meditations on nature
and banking and science fiction have spawned much of
her most potent nonfiction. Her short fiction often treads
a line between poetry and prose. It was during the publication of* Moral Disorder, *one of three books she published in 2006, that this interview took place.*

Most authors are shelved in just one section of the bookstore. Not Margaret Atwood.

Since she made her debut in the sixties, the Canadian
writer and author of *The Handmaid's Tale* has published
in more forms than seems possible—poetry, short stories,
children's literature, thrillers, romance, criticism, and science fiction.

"I've never written a Western," says the sixty-seven-
year-old writer, sitting in a large hotel suite in New York.

"I think I'm this way because I never went to creative
writing school and nobody told me not to. Nobody said,
'You have to specialize,' or 'For heaven's sake, control
yourself.'"

And so she hasn't. But now Atwood is about to tackle
her most unlikely role yet, one that is just as perilous as
creating on the page: inventor.

Atwood is the force behind the LongPen, a robotic
device that allows writers to sign books remotely. So an

author in Miami could sign for a bookstore customer in Mombasa, or a lawyer in Minneapolis can sign documents in Manitoba, for that matter.

"It's like a very long pen," Atwood says. "I just say the ink is in another city."

Connected by an Internet feed, the author's end features videoconferencing, an electronic writing tablet, and a magnetic pen. On the receiver's end are a video screen and the document being signed. The pen had mixed results in early demonstrations, but Atwood says it's ready for its coming-out party.

"You can write anything with it," she says, an inventor's gleam in her eye. "You can draw little pictures. It reproduces every stroke that you have made, with exactly the same pressure."

Atwood demonstrated the product in Toronto with Alice Munro, Atwood's literary sister and another of Canada's most revered authors, who signed books at a Toronto bookstore from her location in southern Ontario. Atwood also interviewed her via the system.

Munro's appearance wasn't just good publicity; it also established why it's so appropriate that a Canadian author is the driving force behind this invention, which Atwood developed through Unotchit, a Toronto-based company she founded.

"Canada is a really big place," Atwood says, "so, sure, there is Amazon.ca, and there are more bookstores, but there are still a lot of people who would have a really hard time meeting an author."

Atwood understands this because at the beginning of

her career she was on the road when being an author on tour wasn't any great shakes.

"Back in the sixties and seventies, some places I'd go to didn't even have bookstores," she says. "So you would take your books to the reading at the school gym. You'd sell the books, make change, you'd put it in an envelope and take it back to a publisher."

Now she is published in thirty-five countries. Her publishers fly her around the globe to read in superstores. She works as she travels, clearly. In the nineteen months prior to our meeting, Atwood had published a collection of essays, two volumes of stories, and a book based on the life of Odysseus's wife, Penelope.

The last work was launched on the stage in London, with Atwood herself playing Penelope.

Atwood admits that this emergence as a literary superstar is a strain on her time, but it is also a triumph. In the eighties and nineties, Atwood's work—with its recurring examinations of female identity, violence, and the Canadian wilderness—was raked over the coals of deconstructionist theory, which posited that there is no author, just a "text."

But the tide shifted, says Atwood, with a Cheshire-cat grin. The importance of postmodern theory has waned and "the authors are alive again, I'm happy to tell you." In other words, even if she is signing her books by a remote pen, she is definitely their author.

It's a fitting resurgence. After all, Atwood's novels and stories, like the recent interlocking collection *Moral Disorder*, often concern a woman's struggle to wrest free from her identity or the identity others project onto her.

"You are your story to a great extent," Atwood explains. "But other people's versions of you are going to differ from one another, and they're all going to be different from your version of yourself."

Atwood found this out as a young woman, and then she found out the hard way as a literary figure by examining something one of two biographers wrote about her.

"It had a story about me at Harvard: that I kept a clam on my desk, and when asked why I liked it, I had remarked, 'It was very loyal.'"

Atwood gives a weary sigh. "First of all, you can't keep a clam in a jar on your desk for more than about twenty-four hours or it will die. Second, I never had a clam in a jar on my desk. Third, the story was some permutation of a real story about my sister-in-law, not me. She had a pet hermit crab, of which she had remarked, 'It is very loyal.' But it came to a sad end, because they put it in an aquarium on top of a TV set and it got too hot."

Now, thanks to her invention, readers far from Toronto will know what Atwood really has on her desk. It's a small, oddly shaped pen. As for what she's writing with her real pen, that will remain a mystery. Is she tempted to write a Western? "I never talk about my temptations," she says.

December 2006

Mohsin Hamid

 *Mohsin Hamid's life has given him a rare stereoscopic view of the perils of globalized culture. Born in 1971 in Pakistan, he was raised there and in America, where his father, an economist, taught at universities. Hamid studied at Princeton University under Toni Morrison and Joyce Carol Oates, but continued to Harvard Law School and then the consulting firm McKinsey and Company, where he worked to pay off his law-school debt. For three months of the year he was allowed to write, time he used to pen his first novel,* Moth Smoke *(2000), a sort of* Bright Lights, Big City *set against the backdrop of Pakistan's nuclear race with India. His second novel,* The Reluctant Fundamentalist *(2007), took seven years to write, during which time he moved to London and began working for a branding agency. It was upon its publication that I spoke to him. Two years later he moved back to Lahore, Pakistan, where he began to raise a family and finished his third novel,* How to Get Filthy Rich in Rising Asia *(2013).*

In the years since the attacks of September 11, 2001, the Western world went through a crash course on terrorism and radical Islam at its bookstores. And it wasn't just journalists or historians doing the teaching. A growing number of novels addressed the fallout of terrorism, from John Updike's *Terrorist* to Jonathan Safran Foer's *Extremely Loud and Incredibly Close*.

But with *The Reluctant Fundamentalist*, there was a literary first: a novel about post-9/11 America by a Muslim writer. And he is singing a slightly different tune.

"As horrible and wrong as they were," Mohsin Hamid says, "the attacks of 9/11 were a voice in a conversation. Something terrible was speaking to America, and immediately it was taken in at political levels which responded, 'We don't want to hear that.'"

When Susan Sontag made similar comments in *The New Yorker* two weeks after the attacks, she was widely criticized as unpatriotic and inappropriate.

Sitting at a hotel bar in lower Manhattan, Hamid believes now is the time for that conversation to be picked up again. He hopes his second novel, *The Reluctant Fundamentalist*, short-listed for the Man Booker Prize, will help.

The novel unfolds in the voice of Changez, a Pakistani man in a Lahore café, telling his life story to an offstage American, who may—or may not—be a CIA agent who has come to kill him. Over a series of short, monologue-like chapters, Changez describes how he traveled to America on a scholarship, performed well enough at Princeton to earn a coveted consulting job, and then quickly climbed the corporate ladder.

But Changez became so obsessed with fitting in that he lost himself—a fact mirrored by the desperate lengths to which he went to secure the affection of a white American woman.

"It's not the story of someone who begins hating something," says Hamid, eager to make it known this is not an America-bashing book. "It's somebody who loves something so much that they are willing to do things which, upon reflection, when their love is rejected, feel demeaning."

Hamid knows how Changez feels. He moved to the United States to attend Princeton University and Harvard Law School, later working as a management consultant for some years at McKinsey and Company in Manhattan—a famously competitive firm.

Hamid says burnout—and a feeling of having sold out—were endemic. As a Pakistani man, though, Hamid's malaise had a sharper, more intimate angle. He witnessed how the United States used its power to leverage Pakistan in its nuclear race with India. Like his character, he was mistaken for being Arab. Watching post-9/11 America cheer on the invasion of Muslim countries was painful.

It was doubly painful because Hamid had lived in California as a boy. His family returned to Pakistan, but then he came back to the United States for college. To this day, he says, "I cannot separate my Americanness out of me."

Hamid believes what's true about himself goes for the world at large, even the parts that look on America with disgust. There are even American echoes in the tenets of radical Islam, especially, he believes, in the martyrs who cast themselves as heroes.

"Much of the world thinks of itself in filmic, narrative, and cultural ways that are heavily influenced by America," he says. The bombers think of themselves as "the knights errant of the modern day. Instead of slaying dragons, they kill three thousand innocent people. The failure to grasp the Americanness of all this means the U.S. doesn't get what's going on."

He stresses that the suicide bombers are not "robots from another cultural world . . . they are from the same world as us—with some differences."

Hamid, who works part time at a brand-management agency in London, knows that what he is trying to capture in this novel is a rather large shift in American thinking, and he knows there are hurdles: for instance, what he perceives to be the U.S. media's one-note portrayal of Arabs and Pakistanis.

"Our number one television talk-show host in Pakistan is a transvestite," Hamid says. "We have a huge indie-rock band scene; we've got fashion models wearing next to nothing on catwalks; we've got huge Ecstasy-fueled raves." But you don't see these things on American TV, he points out. We get "the guys in the caves instead."

And for all the personal or imaginative narratives about Islam to emerge since September 11, all too often, Hamid feels, they come from a certain perspective. "The ones [Americans] read are now almost solely from people who have chosen, often through the result of very unfortunate circumstances, to utterly reject that aspect of themselves. Ayaan Hirsi Ali stories—it's the we-hate-Islam Muslims."

Or John Updike's *Terrorist*, a book Hamid read with

frustration. "What's interesting about *Terrorist* is how deeply such a talented and gifted novelist can fail at a project," Hamid argues. "He fails for the same reason that America as a project fails: That leap of empathy is just one step too far."

The Reluctant Fundamentalist is Hamid's attempt to make the leap a little shorter, to be a bridge across a chasm that has been filled, already, with rhetoric. At less than two hundred pages, it may look small, but it is profoundly important.

October 2007

Richard Powers

Richard Powers is one of the world's most intelligent novelists. A close study of his books will reveal a restless mind at work, with interests that range from choral singing to computer programming. He was born in Evanston, Illinois, in 1957, and moved to Thailand with his family at age eleven. He returned to America for high school having fostered a love of music and the ability to play the guitar, cello, and clarinet. Upon completing graduate school, in 1980, Powers moved to Boston to become a computer programmer. It was a short-lived career: He quit after seeing the photograph Young Farmers *by August Sander so that he could begin his first novel,* Three Farmers on Their Way to the Dance *(1985). Powers's next seven novels meditated, in some way, on the world he had left behind: science and technology's ability to quantify, the human heart's inability to live within borders. He broke through his reputation as a brainy novelist in 2006 with his moving and elegant ninth novel,* The Echo Maker, *the trigger for this interview, which took place an hour before he won the National Book Award.*

Arriving at the National Book Award ceremony in New York, Richard Powers makes a nerve-racking discovery. He has left his finalist's medal at the hotel. "I really should go back and get this thing," said Powers, looking around nervously as he enters the grand ballroom of the Marriott Marquis hotel. Seeing the throng of editors and writers, he sprints back to his room.

As it turns out, Powers's hunch was right. His ninth novel, *The Echo Maker*, beat out Mark Danielewski's *Only Revolutions* and three other books to take home the prize—the same award, incidentally, that anointed Jonathan Franzen's *The Corrections* and Thomas Pynchon's *Gravity's Rainbow*. It amounts to a powerful boost in prestige and sales, and one could have forgiven Powers for being skeptical about his chances. After all, in America, as Powers's reputation has grown, he has remained the perennial also-ran in the awards sweepstakes. He has been a finalist for the National Book Award once before and has traveled to the National Book Critics Circle Awards four times and each time come home empty-handed.

"I have been luckier than any novelist," Powers demurs in his suite at the Algonquin Hotel, an hour before the awards. The room is quite small, and Powers is very tall. In black tie, with his attentive eyes and large, full head of hair, he appears like a well-dressed Gulliver who would rather be out chopping wood. He has certainly worked hard at helping his readers keep up with the times. Over the past two decades, he has stuffed his novels with an enormous amount of information, about DNA (*The*

Gold Bug Variations), virtual reality (*Plowing the Dark*), medicine (*Operation Wandering Soul*), the rise of capitalism (*Gain*), computers (*Galatea 2.2*), and singing (*The Time of Our Singing*), among other things. "He gets 'brainy,' and earns it," wrote the novelist Colson Whitehead in a *New York Times* book review, for writing about "the intricacies of Watson and Crick, virtual reality, artificial intelligence and the ins and outs of making a good bar of soap. 'Chilly' comes from people who think he can be remote at times."

Neither of these charges has been leveled at *The Echo Maker*, however, which critics have described as Powers's most mysterious, warm, and heart-pounding novel yet. The story begins with a car crash in the middle of the night on a Nebraska road. Twenty-seven-year-old Mark Schluter awakens from a coma suffering from a rare, real-life syndrome called Capgras. He can recognize his loved ones but doesn't believe that they are who they claim to be. Complicating matters is a note left by his bedside that reads: "GOD led me to you so You could Live and bring back someone else." As Mark tries to reenter his life and divine the provenance of this message, his anguished sister, Karin, attempts to convince him that she is indeed his sister. Meanwhile, a neuroscientist author named Gerald Weber tries to focus on his case but is derailed by the spectacle of the nearly half a million cranes that settle on the Nebraska plain near the site of Mark's accident.

Powers's nephew was once in a car wreck and received a similarly mysterious note. But the moment the novel became a possibility arrived when Powers was driving across the Midwest on his way to visit his mother in

Tucson. "It was getting on towards sunset. I was in the middle of Nebraska. And I looked out off the interstate and I saw this large, three-foot-high biped, then another. Then, as far as I could see, it was this continuous carpet of birds." Powers speaks in the rough and clipped tones of a Chicago accent, and there is something unusual about hearing him go into an extended digression on the beauty of the birds, which Native Americans call echo makers. "I almost drove off the road, it was such a hypnotic and fascinating sight," he continues. "I pulled off and the next town was Kearney, Nebraska. I got a hotel room for the night and started asking around, and they just laughed at me. I was the first person to stumble on this by accident. People come from all over the country to see it."

The image of this huge flock of cranes coming back every year to the same spot was in the back of Powers's mind as he began to read about Capgras syndrome. "It's the most eerie, unintuitive, impossible syndrome imaginable," says Powers, who watched many tapes of people suffering from it being interviewed. To him, it highlights a false division that has risen in how we talk about emotion. "All the different ways we know the world all come from the brain," Powers says, "and they all depend on each other to make sense."

When Powers gets excited, it's easy to see the enormously intelligent, slightly nerdy youth he must have been.

Born in Illinois in 1957, he grew up one of five children in a house animated by music. His father, a headmaster, would have guests over for accompanied sing-alongs. Powers's instrument was the cello. But he was also fascinated by the sciences. He adored Darwin's

The Voyage of the Beagle as a youngster, and later enrolled at the University of Illinois at Urbana-Champaign as a physics major, with an interest in technology. In his off-hours, he taught himself how to program computers—a skill that led him to his first and last day job: writing code in Boston. He had never considered writing fiction until he saw a photograph of three farmers in a retrospective of August Sander's work. Two days later he quit his job to write their story.

As a young novelist, Powers's most important influences were James Joyce and Thomas Hardy, but it was coding that gave him an education in how to put a book together. "I think that discipline gave me many ways of thinking about form and structure as a fiction writer," he says. It is useful to remember that William Vollmann, who won the National Book Award the year before Powers, also began his career writing computer code. Their back-to-back wins are seen by many in New York circles as a kind of changing of the literary guard. Powers, however, believes that their rise in popularity reflects a shift in readers' acceptance of a new way of telling stories. "This idea that a book can either be about character and feeling, or about politics and idea, is just a false binary. Ideas are an expression of the feelings and the intense emotions we hold about the world. One of the things that Capgras really reveals is how dependent upon feeling [an] idea is in order to be reliable at all."

One of the most convincing aspects of *The Echo Maker* is its portrait of the mechanics and feel of hospital life—the tensions of getting better, and then not, of how research creates hope for treatment and then runs into the hard wall of organic unknowability. Powers's brother is a surgeon, and the novelist spent quite a bit of time with him while writing his earlier book, *Operation Wandering Soul*, a fable-like tale set in a children's hospital in the near future. "The stories that we tell ourselves—we the healthy when someone near us is in danger, undergoing treatment—can be profoundly moving," he says.

Powers also believes that technology is a primary conduit for how we tell our stories. He wrote his novel *The Time of Our Singing* on a wireless keyboard, sending his words across space and onto the screen. *The Echo Maker* was composed using voice recognition software. Powers dictated the words onto the screen like a twenty-first-century Henry James, with software as his amanuensis. "We build our technologies as a way of addressing all our anxieties and desires," Powers says. "They are our passions congealed into these prosthetic extensions of ourselves. And they do it in a way that reflects what we dream ourselves capable of doing."

Ranging far and wide across several disciplines, Powers has dedicated himself to knowing and exploring all those dreams. "Novel-writing is the only place where someone who would have liked to do anything can still do that vicariously," he says. "So the books have been explorations, through characters, of these different ways of knowing the world: history and biology, digital computer technology." If only he could get a computer to tell him when he leaves his medals behind.

December 2006

Ian McEwan

Ian McEwan has in the past decade become England's most popular and critically acclaimed novelist. Born in 1948 in Hampshire, the son of an army officer, he had an itinerant childhood across Singapore, Germany, and Libya. He studied at Sussex University and at the University of East Anglia under Malcolm Bradbury. McEwan's early fiction, such as First Love, Last Rites (1975) and The Comfort of Strangers (1981), is dexterous, densely poetic, and frankly sexual. Like Kazuo Ishiguro, he began writing for film in the eighties and continues to do so to this day. In the nineties he published four of his most significant books, The Innocent (1990) and Black Dogs (1992), both of which revolve around betrayal and history, and Enduring Love (1997) and Amsterdam (1998), which both explore relationships so intense they warp into abnormal attachments. Amsterdam was a single-sitting entertainment but it won McEwan the Booker Prize, and Atonement (2001) won a National Book Critics Circle Award. It was with the latter of these two books that McEwan became a worldwide bestseller, a position he has maintained ever *since. This interview took place during the publication of* Saturday *(2005).*

There are two kinds of men in an operating room: those who get spooked, and those who do not. Ian McEwan discovered he belongs firmly in the latter camp. A year ago, the fifty-six-year-old prizewinning novelist began a new book and, as part of his research, accompanied a neurologist during brain surgery.

"I didn't know what my level of squeamishness was," says McEwan in an interview in his large London home. "But as it turned out, I just had total fascination. From the very first use of the skin knife to part the scalp, it was just amazing. I couldn't wait until [the doctor] cut through the dura and got to the brain itself."

Although McEwan claims this lack of disgust came as a surprise to him, readers familiar with his earlier nickname—Ian Macabre—might find this hard to believe. After all, this is the writer who wrote "Solid Geometry," a story about a man who keeps a pickled penis on his desk. *The Cement Garden*, McEwan's 1978 novel, tells a tale of children who entomb their parents.

Over the past three decades, though, McEwan has come a long way from those ghoulish early works, graduating to robust meditations on family (*The Child in Time* and *Black Dogs*) and the moral bargains of the writing life (*Atonement*).

Nowhere is it more apparent quite how far McEwan has come from his early roots than in his gripping novel

Saturday, which follows a day in the life of a British neurologist named Henry Perowne.

With deceptive boldness, the novel writes itself "right into the present tense," as McEwan says, referring to how the book references the war in Iraq. In the process, it chronicles a man's thoughts more closely than McEwan has done before.

That doesn't mean *Saturday* is a novel devoid of menace. For starters, Perowne has a bit too much going for him. He drives a Mercedes 500 SL and lives in a home that sounds like a design magazine fantasy. He has a good wife and a happy family, terrific health, and fantastic taste in food.

But from the moment Perowne wakes on this Saturday in February 2003, something is off. In the middle of the night, he climbs from his bed, pads to the window, and sees a plane making what appears to be a crash landing at Heathrow.

This terrifying spectacle casts a pall over the coming day, during which Perowne expects visits from his out-of-town daughter and his eminent father-in-law.

As Perowne sails forth into the morning, making breakfast and climbing into his Mercedes to go to play squash, he carries that alarming moment with him like a Doppler wave of anxiety. An enormous antiwar demonstration rages nearby, blocking traffic and steering him into a minor car accident that threatens to turn violent when the other driver, a mentally unstable man, confronts him.

"I wanted to sort of do pleasure," says McEwan. "But I also wanted to describe in detail the mental processes by which our pleasure is interwoven with our anxiety. As we sit here worried about the state of the world," he says during the interview shortly after the tsunami disaster in South Asia, "we're certainly not about to do anything about it."

For many people in the Western world, anxiety runs "like a fugue with our pleasures," says McEwan, neither one upsetting or overwhelming its counterpart. Although we might donate to tsunami relief funds, we are not about to get on a plane to Phuket, or to Baghdad, for that matter.

Saturday twists the knife by pitching Perowne into two situations that give him a similar sense of futility that an international disaster might. One is his run-in with the unstable driver, a violent man whom the doctor can diagnose but not control. The other is a visit to his mother, who, as McEwan's mother once did, suffers from vascular dementia, a condition that has robbed her of her memory.

"I wanted to capture what it's like to sit with your mother and have her not recognize you," McEwan says. "You can have all the descriptions of disintegrated neural nets, deficiencies, but that doesn't relieve you of the tragedy of her mind closing down."

Saturday may be one of the first in a wave of literary novels that address, among other things, the sense of apprehension that came in the wake of 9/11, one that lingers and interacts with our day-to-day concerns.

McEwan was not expecting to go in this direction. In 2001, he was set to write a comic novel, but the terrorist attacks happened.

"I didn't think about writing at all," he says. "I

watched news programs, read newspapers, read books about Islam. Like everyone else, I suppose." He also wrote two strong pieces for *The Guardian*. When he emerged from this period, McEwan decided he had to engage with the present.

"I was thinking then, well, now that there was clearly going to be an invasion of Iraq, I'll let history lead the course of the novel. Then I thought that would be too complex. I needed structure, so I based it around a single day."

Although *Saturday* is more contemporary, more cinematic than anything McEwan has published to date, it does have a significant relationship with what came before it, specifically *Atonement*, his sprawling 2001 novel about a small girl's fib that destroys a man's life and makes her a writer in the process.

In an interview on Radio National when *Atonement* was published, McEwan described how he became aware of his own consciousness at the same age as Briony, the narrator of the novel.

"It was the Mediterranean spring, and I had the day to myself . . . and I had one of those little epiphanies of 'I'm me,' and at the same time thinking, well, everyone must feel this. Everyone must think, 'I'm me.' It's a terrifying idea . . . yet that sense that other people exist is the basis of our morality. You cannot be cruel to someone, I think, if you are fully aware of what it's like to be them. In other words, you could see cruelty as a failure of the imagination, as a failure of empathy. And to come back to the novel as a form, I think that's where it is supreme in giving us that sense of other minds."

Saturday is the adult counterpoint to *Atonement*, providing a wintrier look at consciousness and writing. Throughout the day, Perowne recalls the books his daughter, Daisy, a budding poet, instructs him to read: *Madame Bovary*, a life of Darwin. Neither moves him. To Perowne, literature is a work of accretion, not genius, and it certainly doesn't give him entree to the heads of other people. For that he has the knife.

With *Saturday*, McEwan has set out to explain a man's empathic response to the world based not on religion or art but on matter.

"I've always thought that there was a sort of kidnapping," says McEwan with a wry grin, "that the major world religions have tried to persuade us that they're God's gift to morality, and that forgiveness can only come from religion. I wanted to show that Perowne could arrive at a similar kind of forgiveness from entirely different means. That to believe that consciousness proceeds from matter can give you an infinitely rich hold on life, a quite celebratory one."

In the past five years, McEwan has emerged from a tumultuous divorce to remarry, publish his bestseller to date, win both the National Book Critics Circle Award and the Los Angeles Times Book Prize, see his work on the screen again (with the chilling and beautiful adaptation of *Enduring Love*), and move into a beautiful old town house just off a central London square where V. S. Pritchett once lived (although at a time when the address wasn't so grand).

All this good fortune has not made McEwan paranoid or boastful. Rather, he projects a profound and appealing sense of ease. Over several hours, his conversation ranges from the writers he calls "the senators" (the trinity of authors that is Roth, Bellow, and Updike) to the war in Iraq, from cooking to the prime minister, to the sadness of watching his mother die. He is a curious man.

"I remember my naïve surprise when I went for a total health checkup," he says, "which involved running on a machine for thirty minutes while my heart was monitored. Then, afterwards, the consultant showed me a scan. And there was my heart, as we were talking, pulsing and writhing away. And I was so astonished."

And that is McEwan's breakthrough: *Saturday* is not just a book about a man watching himself think; it is the story of a man watching himself feel, too. Impossibly, patiently, the novel allows for the possibility that they are the same thing.

March 2005

Michael Ondaatje

 Michael Ondaatje is a poet and novelist who has developed a fragmentary, sensual style that feels magnetized by the compass turns of his life. Born in Sri Lanka in 1943, he moved to England in the fifties and continued his university education in Quebec and finally Toronto, where he has lived—with trips to California to write in a small cabin—since 1970. The American West and its rangy, searching literature inspired some of his earliest work, such as The Collected Works of Billy the Kid (1970), a novel which channels the myths and legends of the American outlaw, and Coming Through Slaughter (1976), a novel about the New Orleans jazz pioneer Buddy Bolden.

Genres bleed between books in Ondaatje's work. His novels can feel like memoirs, and his memoir, Running in the Family (1982), has the sonic uplift of fiction and the sudden beauty of poetry. Ondaatje's best work—such as In the Skin of a Lion (1987), which fictionalizes the lives of immigrants who helped to build Toronto—often deals with people who are uprooted from their lives, by choice or by reason. His best-known work is The English Patient (1992), the Booker Prize–winning novel about a

Canadian World War II nurse and her mysterious, badly burned patient. It was made into a film by Anthony Minghella, which won nine Oscars, including Best Picture. Ondaatje has maintained an interest in film, working on scripts and taking part in dialogues, such as The Conversations: Walter Murch and the Art of Editing Film *(2002), a series of interviews with the great editor and sound engineer. It is one of the most useful books about creative work published in the last two decades. I spoke to Ondaatje in 2007 as his novel* Divisadero *was being published.*

If you see a man or woman holding a Michael Ondaatje novel, chances are they can be romanced with language. "I've gotten letters to this effect," the bearish, gentle-eyed writer says, sitting in the office of his New York publisher.

Ondaatje will no doubt set off another whole generation of backpacker romances with his new novel, *Divisadero*. It is his most ambitiously evocative novel yet. The book was short-listed for the Giller Prize, Canada's most prestigious literary award.

"It's a novel about how art protects us all, and in some cases hides us all," Ondaatje says. The tale begins in the seventies in the California Sierras, skips ahead a few years, then flows backward through time, winding up in France, where it concludes in the form of a novella about a long-dead writer, whose life and work has resonance with what comes before.

"One book I remember loving was Willa Cather's *The Professor's House*," says Ondaatje, referring to his book-within-a-book structure. "It's this great story, and then right in the middle there is this other completely different story. I just love that form. What is this doing here, you want to ask. But it does everything. It deepens everything which is around."

In Cather's novel, the rupture is caused by a house. At the start of Ondaatje's narrative in *Divisadero* lies a much more explosive event. A widowed American farmer discovers that his daughter Anna has been having an affair with Coop, a young man he has adopted and given work as a laborer. In a fit of rage, he nearly murders the twenty-year-old man, and Anna runs off forever, ultimately for France. Claire, the other daughter, winds up in the San Francisco public defender's office, helping people in court cases that create formal divisions the likes of which descend upon her family. Here is the division alluded to in the book's title.

Ondaatje began the book during a year he spent teaching at Stanford University. "I was living at a farm in Petaluma," he says. "It was stunning country, really beautiful. And I started to write the book pretty much as soon as I came there. For the next three years, even when I wasn't teaching, I came back and rented a place there." With each visit, Ondaatje imagined an odd nuclear family living on such a farm. "I began writing that world, the world of horses," he says, "the pace outside the normal pace of North America." He began steeping himself in archives and learning about the San Fernando valley, towns like Bakersfield and Fresno.

Such research projects have always threatened to become a vortex for Ondaatje. "All the things in the book are things I'm interested in," he says. "It's a curiosity that becomes an obsession at times." This is something that has been part of his working method since he began publishing. "When I was doing *In the Skin of a Lion*, there was the whole thing about Macedonians, and apparently they distinguish themselves among each other by having a certain kind of purple plant on their front lawn. I finished the book, and went through it three times thinking, 'Where can I work this detail in naturally?'"

In *Divisadero*, Ondaatje says, he tried hard to allow such information to seep into his characters rather than live on the page. Coop winds up in Lake Tahoe as a cardsharp, and while his sections are told with an almost card-dealer-like flick of words, Anna's progress is in a smoother, slower register, saturated in memory. It's clear she is more haunted by the past than Coop, and she has sublimated this instinct through scholarship. But while she is on assignment to research the life of the French novelist Lucien Segura, Anna begins "filling a notebook with fragments and even drawings . . . If there was the sound of a bird through the open door by her table she would try to articulate it phonetically on the page." Accidentally, she becomes a writer herself.

Ondaatje admits that his books contain an unusual number of storytellers and readers. Books appear in the hands or at the bedsides of almost every character in *Divisadero*, like talismans, like clues. So do songs, including some by Tom Waits. "I love Tom Waits," Ondaatje says. "I love reggae. I think we are all the children of songs. I can probably recite two or three poems by heart, but I know the lyrics to thousands of songs." You won't find him trying to write his own, though, anymore. "I did write a couple of songs in Canada, and I just didn't have it—my friend said, 'You don't have to rhyme every line, you know? Okay?' And mine were always about animals."

The one thing Ondaatje will keep doing, however, is writing poetry. When *Anil's Ghost* was published in 2000, he had chased that book into the world with *Handwriting*, a book of poems that became almost like a guide to the novel. *Divisadero* doesn't have anything similar, in part because Ondaatje feels the poetry is in the book.

"I edited the death out of it," he says. "When I am editing, it's like going into this dark room for four or five years, I have to give it a more professional shape, so I am moving things around."

Ondaatje spends a lot of time at readings and interviews trying to account for the echoes even he doesn't quite understand, or really want to. Ask him if he is aware of the mysticism in his books and he thinks for a bit. "I'm not conscious of that, either," but "I do see I am taking off the ground a little bit," he says, moving his hand across the desk like a plane taking off.

"There's a great poem by Raymond Carver," he says by way of example, "which is like a shopping list— onions, eggs, milk, New Zealand, Australia?" Ondaatje gives a little giggle as if to say, of course this doesn't make sense. This isn't the way the world works. But our minds do go sideways and up sometimes, and when Ondaatje is charting its movements, chances are there will be liftoff.

October 2007

Salman Rushdie

Few writers have had their work and life politicized to the same extent as Salman Rushdie. Born in Bombay in 1947 to a teacher and a businessman, he left home early for boarding school and later studied history at King's College, Cambridge. After university he worked as a copywriter for Ogilvy & Mather and Ayer Barker. His first novel, Grimus, *the science-fiction tale of an Indian woman who is given the gift of immortality, was published in 1975, but it is his second,* Midnight's Children, *that launched him into the stratosphere of world storytelling. The sprawling, magical book tells the story of India's partition and transition to independence. It won the Booker Prize in 1981. In 1988, the publication of his fourth novel,* The Satanic Verses, *gained international attention when Ayatollah Khomeini, then the spiritual leader of Iran, proclaimed a fatwa demanding the execution of Rushdie for the insults he perceived the book leveled at Islam. With a bounty on his head, Rushdie was forced into hiding. The book inspired riots in which several people died, and Rushdie's Japanese translator was killed and his Italian translator beaten and stabbed. Rushdie eventually moved to New*

York City, where, as Thomas Pynchon has proven, it's possible to hide in plain view. Throughout the fatwa period and after, Rushdie has published prolifically—short stories (East, West, 1994), essays (including Imaginary Homelands, *1991), several novels (including* Shalimar the Clown, *2005), and his memoir of the fatwa period (Joseph Anton, 2012). He has also been an outspoken critic of the dangers of militant religion. In 2004, he became the president of PEN American Center, the writing organization dedicated to free speech. It was during this period that I spoke to him.*

Two months ago, in an amber-lit auditorium tucked away in New York's Greenwich Village, a group of world-renowned writers gathered to discuss how literature might determine the shape of Europe after communism. Perennial Nobel candidate Cees Nooteboom had arrived from Holland by way of Spain, while Russian-born novelist Andreï Makine represented his adopted homeland of France. The audience of readers was made up of New Yorkers—they could have been from anywhere.

It shows how the world has changed that the most luminous literary figure in the room—the one most intimately connected with the perils and pleasures of a global society—could slip into the back row and watch undetected. His name is Salman Rushdie.

No longer wearing the longish, almost prophetic, signature beard, suddenly there is a lot of Rushdie's face to see. Gone too are the other accoutrements of anonymity:

the dark glasses and baseball caps. As a result, in person, he seems smaller and somewhat diminished.

Though he still travels in a wake of whispers, it has been several years now since the Bombay-born novelist lived under the fatwa put upon him by Ayatollah Khomeini. In 1989, Khomeini, then the head of Iran's fundamentalist Islamic republic, condemned Rushdie to death. Khomeini accused Rushdie of committing blasphemy against Islam in his novel *The Satanic Verses*. The work can almost define itself as *a* novel now, rather than being referred to as *that* novel. And Rushdie can once again enter and leave restaurants through the front door.

Still, Rushdie is a powerful icon—a kind of enduring symbol of freedom—a form of capital he drew upon as president of the PEN American Center to corral hundreds of writers and critics from around the world into the New York Festival of International Literature, a weeklong series of readings and discussions showcasing literature and ideas from around the globe. The event concludes with a party hosted by fashion icon Diane von Furstenberg.

"I'm really proud of how it went," says Rushdie, on the eve of a lecture trip to New Haven, where he will give a talk about, among other things, secularism and nationalism, the importance of free speech, and the writing life. "It's something I very much wanted to do: to stress the international aspect of literature, and to allow people in New York to see the world's very best writers."

As Rushdie noted in a recent *New York Times Book Review* article, the percentage of literature entering the United States from other countries is woefully, historically low. The last PEN festival was held in New York twenty years ago. Convened by Norman Mailer, that festival brought together authors from around the world during Reagan's presidency at the height of the Cold War. Among the participants were the Palestinian poet Mahmoud Darwish; the Nicaraguan author Omar Cabezas, who was a Sandinista; and American writers from Kurt Vonnegut to Susan Sontag.

This year's PEN festival also brought writers from all parts of the globe, including some authors whose work had yet to be translated into English. The event was a huge hit, playing host to sellout crowds—even when the authors were as obscure as the German writer Patrick Roth, whose work is not available in the States even though he lives in Los Angeles.

In Rushdie's mind, the alacrity of this reception shows how eager Americans are to read outside their backyard, something from which he draws great comfort.

"The lack of translation means Americans don't have an opportunity to find out about the best stuff, but when you do bring it to them they are very, very receptive," he says.

As the PEN festival also revealed, now that Rushdie has his freedom, he is gingerly stepping out again, not least with the help of his fourth wife, Padma Lakshmi, a model and ambassador for the United Nations Development Fund for Women who also has a cooking show on television. The couple married last year and have quickly become a fixture on New York's social scene.

Lakshmi recently added fuel to the New York City gossip cauldron when she revealed that she often likens her shoes to her husband's books, and explained, "When he says, 'Why do you need more shoes?' I say, 'Why do you need more books? My shoes are the same as your books; they are part of who you are.'"

For the past year, however, Rushdie's professional attentions have been focused on his role as president of the PEN American Center, which involves not just putting on gala fund-raisers but filing legal action. Mention the U.S. government's attempt to ban literature being imported into the States and Rushdie immediately turns serious.

"PEN has been fighting that particular regulation for a long time," he says and then explains some of its details. "The U.S. government is just now beginning to plane back on it. The question is whether the damage is already done."

It seems somewhat ironic that Rushdie should survive a period of life-threatening danger, living in thirty houses in nine years, and wind up in "the land of the free" only to discover that he must start campaigning for freedom all over again.

If there is resentment, though, he doesn't show it. Rushdie has lived part time in New York for more than five years, and he's not about to stop. He can at least now play table tennis with Jonathan Safran Foer without first greeting photographers outside. Were it not for the occasional diaries published by his wife, which refer to him as S and describe movie dates with Lou Reed, his whereabouts might be entirely unknown.

About his own fame, he says, "The only thing it's good for now is getting tables in restaurants."

There is a friendliness and humor to his manner. It

takes a while before you twig to the fact that you have heard this before, only in his novels. In them, as he does in person, Rushdie speaks with enthralling speed and ease.

With his hectic schedule of social appearances, it's hard to imagine Rushdie sitting still at his desk long enough to produce new work. But in five years, he has published a novel (*Fury*), a collection of essays (*Step Across This Line*), a theatrical adaptation of *Midnight's Children*, and dozens of articles, mainly for the New York press. His desk has not become his mistress? "No, no, not a mistress at all," Rushdie says, giggling, "but a wife. And a shrewish one at that."

In fact, he was spending quite a lot of time at his desk until the PEN event, which will be apparent when *Shalimar the Clown*, his latest novel, is published. Weighing in at four hundred pages, it arrives with a whiff of triumphant return.

Beginning in Los Angeles in 1991, the book opens with the fatal stabbing of a former ambassador to India by his Kashmiri chauffeur. As it turns out, the man, who calls himself Shalimar the Clown, is not a meek and silent servant but a former war hero, who has plotted this event with chilling patience. As we go deeper into his history, we discover that the murder is not just political but deeply personal.

Like *Satanic Verses* and *Midnight's Children* before it, *Shalimar the Clown* evolves into a huge rollicking narrative that tells not just the stories of its four principal characters but also the tale of the age in which they live: an age of hyperbole and bloodshed, assassination and fundamentalism. Rushdie draws on Indian mythology, Los Angeles fakery, Hindu culture, and the limits of the English language to capture it all.

Rushdie has never felt trapped or hemmed in—in part because his frame of reference as a novelist is so broad. "One of my good fortunes as a writer is to have access to a lot of traditions—and not just inside Western culture, high culture or low culture. Remember, I am a child of the sixties generation—I was twenty-one in 1968—I am also somebody who is passionately in love with the language of cinema, so all this stuff, music, movies, it's just readily available, not something I have to bone up on."

In this sense, Rushdie sounds not unlike the American novelists of yore, from John Dos Passos to Hart Crane, who had an almost journalistic urge to squeeze all the sights and sounds of America into their novels. I ask him whether he thinks this way while walking New York streets. Rushdie ponders that and refuses to get too personal.

"If a novelist is smart, he or she will realize the novel is not an ivory-tower form. It's a form which requires what people are getting up to, what's really going on in their heads, how they think and feel—if you don't know that you can't write about it. The bolder you make your range of experience, the richer your work will be. One of the things I really like about New York is that there's just so much going on."

And he will continue to love it, but there is a choice coming up. Now that Rushdie and Lakshmi are married, he will have the option to obtain dual citizenship. Chances are Rushdie will not leap at the opportunity. "My British passport gets me around the world just fine," he says. "If you're like me, and you grew up with an Indian one, where it made getting to some places difficult or impossible, you can appreciate what you have."

Besides, he's also just beginning the research for a new novel and he's starting to feel that tidal tug toward deeper waters. "I am trying to develop an idea for a novel which I've had for quite some time," he says in a burst of candor. "It would be a historical novel in which I imagine a connection between the millennial empire of India and Rome. I'd be creating an imaginary ambassador who would bring India and Machiavellian Florence into collision with each other."

It's a fanciful connection, a perfect skeleton on which to hang the arabesques of plot and intrigue Rushdie loves to play with, even though he remains a "literary" novelist. "One of the things that happened in the wake of modernism is that you wound up with popular fiction which told great page-turning stories but had no other qualities," says Rushdie. "And you had the so-called literary novel, which had all those other virtues but didn't tell a story."

Ultimately, the story has always been this author's driving passion in life, whether in his magical literary tales or in his essays in defense of free speech; his chief concern has always been to create voices and make them heard.

Even with his new sense of freedom, Salman Rushdie has lost none of his fight.

Marilynne Robinson

Marilynne Robinson was born in 1943 in Sandpoint, Idaho, a small town on the shore of the state's largest lake, surrounded by three mountain ranges. The texture of this world is beautifully conjured in Robinson's 1980 debut, Housekeeping, *which elevates moments of domestic fracture to a sublime and stilling art. Raised a Presbyterian, and with a PhD from the University of Washington, Robinson is able to draw on traditions of faith and storytelling in equal measure, and remains one of America's rare and compelling advocates for the importance of spiritual life in serious literature. As an American from the West, awe comes naturally to her. Robinson's Pulitzer Prize–winning second novel,* Gilead *(2004), told the story of a Congregationalist preacher, and her Orange Prize–winning third book,* Home *(2008), followed his offspring into adulthood. Robinson has been publishing nonfiction essays since the early eighties, and this interview was conducted at her home in Iowa City upon the release of her fourth book of essays,* When I Was a Child I Read Books *(2012), a series of arguments about faith, democracy, and empathy.*

Marilynne Robinson's teaching and writing, including the novels—*Housekeeping*, *Gilead*, and *Home*—have been crucial to a generation of writers. Now she has a few corrections that she would like to make to the record.

"One of the things that focuses questions for me is simply coming across something and thinking, that can't be right," says the sixty-eight-year-old novelist.

Sitting on a couch, dressed entirely in black, before a table heaped with books, papers, and two laptops, Robinson looks like an intellectual detective who has been on the case.

She has been in this mode before. In her seminal 1998 essay collection, *The Death of Adam*, Robinson dismantled misunderstandings that had shrouded the teachings of John Calvin.

But the idea Robinson worries is now being misinterpreted is not a text or a notion but America itself. By America, Robinson means democracy, and by democracy, she refers to faith and respect in the power of community.

Our "culture is more abusive in certain ways than it has been in a long, long time," she says. "Prisons that are run for profit and so on—you have to go back to the eighteenth century to find that."

Robinson ought to know. For four decades, alongside her life as a fiction writer, she has been an Americanist, rooting around in the old documents to hear the story the nation tells itself: who is included, who is left out.

When I Was a Child I Read Books is the result of some of her more recent errands in this vein. Its essays ruminate on the global financial crisis, the role Moses has played in American political thought, her own Idaho childhood, and the idea that generosity is essential to a community.

For a writer known for the twenty-four-year gap between her first and second novels, Robinson has been prolific of late. This is her second book of essays in three years. In this mode, Robinson is rigorous, starchy, a throwback to the era when Ralph Waldo Emerson, William Cullen Bryant, and others lectured to packed halls.

Like Emerson and, more recently, Barry Lopez, she claims the soul as an essential part of intellectual life. "The way I use the word *soul*, I suppose I am describing what I'm taking to be an individual's deepest experience of himself," she says.

Rather than divide citizens, Robinson believes this experience of individuality—meditative, spiritual—can nurture empathy among people.

"Who could ever dispute that we are part and parcel of the universe? We didn't come from anywhere else," she says, practically quoting Walt Whitman. Robinson credits her rural childhood in the forties with fostering the habit of solitude. And through solitude she learned to pay attention.

She attended Pembroke College, the former women's college of Brown University, when, as she writes in these essays, a woman became educated so as to better reflect upon her husband.

The climate of academia has changed over fifty years, but Robinson still believes women need to speak up: "Over my life as a teacher, women have been too quiet. I'm quiet myself. I don't think I said three words the whole of graduate school."

This did not stop her from becoming a teacher, a task she calls "a very ancient, beautiful engagement between people."

She has been at the Iowa Writers' Workshop for more than twenty-five years. Her ex-students are a veritable who's who of young writers: from Nathan Englander to Paul Harding to Chinelo Okparanta.

Her work with them has been rigorous and time-consuming, but she would never trade it for another novel with her name on it.

"I've learned a lot about writing from listening to my students talk," she says. "It's sensitizing. It can remind you of really important things. I've probably written less but I've probably written better than I would've otherwise."

Gilead won the 2005 Pulitzer Prize. *Home*, which continues the stories of the characters in *Gilead*, won the 2009 Orange Prize for Fiction. If these novels are driven from a private sense of purpose and curiosity, Robinson's teaching—and ongoing commitment to her local United Church of Christ—have fed her larger sense of civic purpose.

A few months after we speak, she plans to take this act on the road, lecturing first at Oxford University and then in Greece. "After I give this lecture in Athens, they want me to talk to students in Athens—what a great idea. I'll feel like Plato."

May 2012

Edmundo Paz Soldán

The novelist and short-story writer Edmundo Paz Soldán is for the novel of Latin America what David Mitchell has been in Britain: a weaver of traditions, a crossroads between cultures, and a leader of a new wave of writers who see past the boundaries of genre. Mario Vargas Llosa has called him "one of the most important Latin American writers of the new generation." Paz Soldán was born in Bolivia, began writing in earnest in his adolescence, moved to America, where he completed a PhD in Hispanic languages and literature at the University of California, Berkeley, and has more or less remained in the United States while continuing to write in Spanish. His first book, Las máscaras de la nada, a collection of short stories, appeared in 1990, and has been followed by nearly a dozen other collections, novels, and anthologies of Latin American writing. I met him at Cornell University, where he teaches. When I spoke with him in 2006, his latest novel, Turing's Delirium, had just been released in English.

Five years ago Edmundo Paz Soldán harbored very little skepticism about globalization. Indeed, the collapsing of international markets, especially in the realm of intellectual capital, had worked out for him. Paz Soldán moved to America from Cochabamba, Bolivia, in 1988 on a scholarship, and within five years he had earned a master's degree in Hispanic literature. Within ten years, the stocky Bolivian was a professor at Cornell University, the same Ivy League institution where Vladimir Nabokov lived in the late forties and early fifties.

But that's when things began to slow down. Paz Soldán soon found himself in another, less comfortable position similar to the Russian-born novelist. "People used to ask me," recalls Paz Soldán, sitting at a Vietnamese restaurant in Ithaca, New York, " 'When will I get to read your novels? Are you really a novelist?' " After almost two decades of publishing, none of his fiction had been translated into English. Privately, he made excuses for his life apart. After all, he was published in Spain by the prestigious Alfaguara house, and is in constant demand as a columnist and journalist in Bolivia and Chile.

He went home to Bolivia in May 2000. "A transnational water company called Bechtel had bought up the water rights," says Paz Soldán. "There were these riots that left ten or twelve people dead." As a result of the chaos, Bechtel was forced from the country—a victory, some say the first, in the antiglobalization movement, but it was a mixed victory. "Now Cochabamba still struggles with the water," Paz Soldán says. "The poorest neighborhoods do not have good water."

At the time, Paz Soldán was working on a short abstract novel about a battle between a code maker and a code breaker. It was Borgesian, Nabokovian, even. "When I got home, though, it hit me that that's what I needed," he says, "that setting: globalization, this resistance to transnational companies." The combination proved explosive, and the novel it became, *Turing's Delirium*, won Paz Soldán the Premio Nacional de Novela in Bolivia, and catapulted him, at last, into an English translation.

Set in Rio Fugitivo, the fictional Bolivian town at the heart of Paz Soldán's previous fictions, the novel imagines that a group of antiglobalization activists set upon the government and GlobaLux, a multinational that has taken over the town's power grid. Their weapon: a computer virus.

The hero, of sorts, is Miguel Sáenz, a cryptanalyst for a government spy agency called Black Chamber. In the past, Sáenz's code breaking has saved the country from radicals and coups d'état, earning him the nickname Turing, after the famous code breaker Alan Turing. Sáenz knows this new rash of cybercrimes presents an opportunity for him to reclaim his former glory, to prove that computers have not made him obsolete.

Technology has always played a large role in Paz Soldán's fiction. A decade ago, he became involved with the McOndo Literary Movement, named after the fictional town in which Gabriel García Márquez's novels are set.

Composed of writers from Chile, Argentina, and Peru, the group rejected magical realism and rural essentialism in favor of a more contemporary approach to storytelling. "In the eighties, Latin America became less rural and more urban," Paz Soldán once told *The Boston Globe*. "Four of the largest cities in the world—Mexico City, São Paulo, Rio de Janeiro, and Buenos Aires—are in Latin America."

Initially, Paz Soldán received heavy criticism for reflecting this shift in his short stories and novels. "As recently as fifteen years ago there was very little urban fiction," he says. "The majority of Bolivian novelists felt this obligation to show the state of Bolivia, rural Bolivia. When I started publishing in the early eighties I can remember the critics saying, 'These are stories but where is Bolivia? Where are the Mayans?' "

Since he lived in the United States, Paz Soldán's critics could also claim he was out of touch. "I got this kind of guilt trip, like I am not a good Bolivian." So he created his fictional town of Rio Fugitivo. "It was very liberating," says Paz Soldán. "But I remember a friend of mine telling me, it's still very close to Cochabamba. He said, 'You need to have a square with a statue of Bob Dylan.' So in *The Matter of Desire*, there is a statue of Bob Dylan. Now nobody can say anything to me about accuracy."

But the real world has not been left behind entirely, especially in *Turing's Delirium*. GlobaLux bears obvious similarities to Bechtel, and the characters of the novel whiz about using their Motorola and Ericsson mobile phones. "All these brand names have lots of connotations in a country like Bolivia," Paz Soldán says. "It's a very poor country, but you have these islands of modernity. My friends, they have satellites, they have iPods, they have Nokias. They are so afraid of being backwards that they overcompensate."

From Ithaca, Paz Soldán will continue to think about these issues—but will not put answers in his fiction. "This is a novel about politics but it's not a political novel," he says. "I think there is a difference."

August 2006

Susanna Clarke

Susanna Clarke is one more reminder that there is no such thing as an overnight sensation. In 2004, her eight-hundred-page fantasy novel, Jonathan Strange & Mr. Norrell, *seemed to appear out of nowhere, but in fact she had been working on the book for a decade. The idea first came to her while she was teaching English in Spain in 1993. She returned to a coastal town in England and began to write, amassing some material, which she brought to a science-fiction writing workshop taught by her future partner, Colin Greenland, and the writer Geoff Ryman. Their response was so overwhelming she continued, writing short stories along the way that, like* Jonathan Strange & Mr. Norrell, *blur the world of magic and the nineteenth-century tone and authorial access to characters' inner lives from the works of Jane Austen and Charles Dickens. Those tales were published in 2006 under the title* The Ladies of Grace Adieu and Other Stories. *I spoke to her in Darbyshire, England, two years prior, just before* Jonathan Strange & Mr. Norrell *hit the bookshops, and the magnitude of what was about to happen made Clarke cagey, excited, and protective. We sat outside*

during the interview with a view of the countryside,
Clarke's partner at her side the whole time.

In a pub many miles north of London, Susanna Clarke
sits down and declares she needs a glass of Absolution.
Given that she is poised on the brink of one of the noisiest
literary debuts in memory, it would be easy to mistake her
beer order with the confession of some Faustian bargain.

After all, even Clarke expresses bafflement about how
the buzz over her eight-hundred-page first novel about
two early nineteenth-century magicians, *Jonathan Strange*
& Mr. Norrell, is primed to eclipse the hype generated by
upcoming books from Philip Roth, Tom Wolfe, and six
Nobel laureates.

"I think most people involved have been somewhat
taken aback by the response so far," says the silver-haired
writer, sipping her ironically named Sheffield microbrew.
"I certainly have."

Not bad for a former cookbook editor who ten years
ago took a class on how to write fantasy fiction.

Spend five minutes with *Jonathan Strange & Mr. Nor-*
rell and you'll realize that at forty-four, Clarke is an
apprentice no more.

Narrated in the wry voice of an offstage observer and
studded with faux-scholarly footnotes, the novel conjures
the gaslit world of Regency England, where performing
magic tricks makes one the life of society parties.

At the center of this community is a curmudgeonly
scholar and book hoarder named Gilbert Norrell. He
sets mouths flapping when, in an effort to restore respect

for the lost art of true magic, he casts a spell causing a church's gargoyles to call out and dance.

The plot takes off when Norrell's comfortable existence is disturbed by a handsome and charming young upstart named Jonathan Strange, who works the crowds like a classier, 1800s David Blaine.

"They have completely opposite personalities," Clarke says. "One sociable, adventurous, careless; the other fearful, solitary, pedantic. Yet each recognizes in the other his intellectual and magical equal. They have no other colleagues and so in an odd way they belong together.

"They are linked in the public mind—and the more they are so linked (or shackled), the more infuriated they become at each other."

During the Napoleonic Wars, Strange misleads French troops by creating roads that lead nowhere and assists the Duke of Wellington, commander of the Allied forces, by sending spoken messages via enchanted songbirds. Strange's confidence turns dangerous when he becomes fascinated with the villainous Raven King, a powerful magician raised by "faeries," who was once the King of England.

To Clarke, the current popularity of magic in fiction— from Harry Potter to Philip Pullman's His Dark Materials trilogy—is only natural.

"It's a very important function of novels to take you out of your everyday life and into somewhere else for a while," she says, citing C. S. Lewis and Roald Dahl as her childhood favorites.

"Magical novels achieve that very well because they take place in a world very clearly not our own," she says.

By combining fantasy elements with witty social commentary, Clarke strikes an unlikely blend of her twin influences of J.R.R. Tolkien and Jane Austen. The book also gives Potterites who have outgrown Hogwarts a place to go for more-sophisticated storytelling.

"I think the novel is viewed as something new," Clarke says, "blending together a few genres—such as fantasy and adventure and pastiche historical—plus there's the whole thing about slightly knowing footnotes commenting on the story."

In person, Clarke is reserved but not shy: more Norrell than Strange. After an hour of conversation, though, her inner geek and outward literary panache come into perfect alignment. The discussion zigzags from her collection of comic books and her favorite TV shows (*The Simpsons*, *Buffy the Vampire Slayer*) to Austen and back again to Buffy.

"I've never been to a convention of fans," she says, "but I can obsess over detail with the best of them."

Clarke may well end up as a featured guest at some future fantasy books convention. *Jonathan Strange & Mr. Norrell* is being published almost simultaneously in the United States, England, and twenty other countries, followed by a twenty-city promotional tour for Clarke. Weeks before the novel's release, an early push from independent booksellers has sold out the reported 200,000-copy first printing.

Clarke responds to the pressure by leaning on her partner, sci-fi author and critic Colin Greenland, whom she met in that fateful writing class. He was the instructor; she, his student.

"Everything I know about publishing has come from editing nonfiction," Clarke says, "so it's nice to have Colin's career as a guide," even if the scope of her work takes her into unchartered territory.

As we finish our beers, Clarke has the slightly tense expression of someone who'd prefer a cloak of invisibility to a career guide. But if given the power to cast spells, she would do something small, "like turn my mobile phone into a hedgehog" she jokes.

"My first thought was world peace, but I saw the episode of *The X Files* where Mulder tried for that—and everybody disappeared."

August 2004

Orhan Pamuk

Orhan Pamuk is a novelist, memoirist, and writing professor whose work melds a child's eye view of his home city of Istanbul with profoundly sophisticated reimaginings of Turkish history, the Ottoman myths, and detective fiction. Pamuk grew up a bookish child in the household of a merchant family of declining wealth, a period described in his novel The Black Book. Pamuk attended school to become an architect, after giving up on a dream of becoming a painter, but abandoned that too to start writing. He graduated from the Institute of Journalism at the University of Istanbul in 1976 and won a prize for a first novel in 1979. Cevdet Bey and His Sons, which remains untranslated, is like a Turkish Magic Mountain, telling the tale of three generations of a moneyed family in Istanbul. Pamuk's novels grow more complex with time. Silent House, which was first published in 1983 but not translated into English until 2012, has the frothed pace of a Turkish soap opera. With The White Castle, through a framing story about a historian who first appeared in Silent House, he began to peer into Turkish history. And with My Name

Is Red *(2001), he exploded it, using a footnote about min-iaturists within the Ottoman Empire to create a cascad-ing narrative about the tension between East and West, and the secular and religious desire for transcendence that exists within humankind.*

I spoke to Pamuk at Columbia University in 2010 shortly after he published The Museum of Innocence, *a long novel about a wealthy man in love with a poorer woman who must satisfy his desire for her by collecting objects related to her. In 2012, Pamuk opened a museum in Istanbul based on the one described in the book.*

As I was walking here I passed a wedding party, which felt like a fitting prelude to our chat since the novel you are just publishing, The Museum of Innocence, *is a big love story stretching across three decades, a love story be-tween a man and a woman but also between a man and a place: Istanbul. I wondered if you could talk just a little bit about Istanbul in the seventies, which is where the book opens and where we start on this long and wonder-ful journey.*

I don't, on the one hand, want to be deliberately self-conscious about representing Istanbul. I always underline the fact that I am in the end a writer who's more focused on human beings. But I came across humanity in Istan-bul, so indirectly I am, yes, a writer that also heavily writes about Istanbul.

I also argued in my previous autobiographical book on Istanbul, called *Istanbul*, which is also my autobiography to the age of twenty-four, that if you live in a city for quite a long time that city turns out to be a sort of an index for the emotions we live in the city: say, a fountain or a square or a building reminds us of happy times, manic times, hopeless times or times we are in love, arguing that for the insiders a city gains its depth and meaning through memories, while for outsiders it's something more exotic, something to watch from a distance.

But here, obviously, my characters are in love and the love is troubled, has a melancholy aspect, and I also think that the art of the novel works best if—*if!*—the writer finds a sort of an objective correlative to the sentiments of his or her characters. In the end the sadness of the melancholy love, the sadness of the love of my characters is represented by the city's landscape. But this is no accident, because I had this sense of melancholy, especially in my childhood in Istanbul. So, in ways, what I wrote about Istanbul in my autobiographical book now I elaborate it more and pin it more accurately in a grander scale in this novel, *The Museum of Innocence*.

Kemal, your main character, is caught between two women: a much younger cousin, Füsun, and a woman more of his society, named Sibel. What is preventing him making the choice that his heart wants to make?

Fear of tradition. Your question is so relevant and so to the heart of this novel; this novel, on a deeper level, is about belonging to a society, embracing its rituals, no

matter how stupid, how shallow, how pointless and (gar-
bled) these rituals are. My character Kemal is, I think, and
I argue, a typical Istanbul, upper class, bourgeois, in the
sense that he just follows the rituals of society to belong
rather than think in a logical way that they are necessary.

There is that desire to belong, or in fact, not to pick
any fights with the community—which the majority of
the people have in oppressed societies. One's first instinct
is not to be rational or to follow one's own humor or anger but to just follow what everyone else does. No one
breaks an engagement in 1975 in Turkey just because
they fall in love with someone else. And that has been not
only the Turkish tradition; it is the tradition of belonging
to a community in the whole of human history, I would
say. Modernity is trusting your own individuality and
judging the whole world through that premodern attitude,
whether you're posing as an upper-class Westernized bourgeois or just a simple person who's not educated. Premo-
dernity is in fact following the dictum that just because
you belong to a community everything will sort out itself.

And *The Museum of Innocence* is, in the end, deeply
about belonging to a community or not; following your
love, or as I did in my life, following your desire to be a
writer, or following your artistic methods, or just joining
the others. In the end, love is a little instrument or excuse
to polarize these two attitudes in the novel. I think that
your question highlights that for me the fact that yes, in
the end, this is a novel about love, trying to understand
its various aspects, arguing that more or less we feel the
same, the way we work out our heart's emotions, desires,

is heavily embedded in history, culture. I would say, unfortunately.

Your life has changed quite dramatically in the last five years: You've won the Nobel Prize; you were prosecuted under Rule 301 of the Turkish code; and you have described in other interviews that your method of working is, in some ways, to meander around cities—in this case Istanbul—and take the inspiration when it comes to you. And I imagine that that method of working has been somewhat disrupted by your life in the last four or five years. How have you found a kind of way to keep working through all of this?

In fact I've survived these five years easily—or easier, perhaps—because I was writing this novel. If every day I wake up and it's seven o'clock at my desk and I'm writing five hours and adding one page, or two and a half pages, to the novel, the rest of the day will be easy for me. The idea that one has to have a peaceful life to enjoy writing a novel may be as true for me as it is for many novelists. But on the other hand, I have a habit of being able to write in bad times. In fact writing helps me overcome the hardships of life, whether it's a political pressure, whether it's a personal problem, whether it's an economical problem— whatever. Writing and being away from the daily journalistic imagery always makes me keep going. In fact that's why I became a novelist: a person who, although pointing out reality, is partly living in fantasy. I think the desire to write novels is also heavily parallel for being away from the present, although the novel may point out contending elements of the present.

The novel Snow *in particular is set much more in the present world. It doesn't have the sort of fantastical sidebars and diversions of* The Black Book *or* My Name Is Red *and some of your earlier work. And I wonder did anything change in your thinking as an artist in the first decade of this new century, because these novels do feel very different from what has come before.*

Good question. I can only answer this: When I was writing my early novels, *White Castle*, even earlier ones, during the years when I announced to my family and friends that I'm not going to pursue architectural studies and painting, that I'd be a novelist, everyone said "Well! You're twenty-five; you can't write novels at this stage— what do you know about life?" And at that time I would get very angry to these people—saying, "Novels are not about life, they're about literature!" And arguing that I love my Borges, I love my Calvino, I love my Kafka. And these people don't know *any*thing about literature, that's why they're saying this, I would say to myself. Now, thirty-five or forty years later, I, tongue in cheek to myself and to the same people, those who are alive, say, "Well, perhaps you were right when you said that, when I was twenty-five. Novels are about *life* of course, and now I have seen enough of life."

Museum of Innocence, in that sense, is about the things I have seen in Istanbul between 1975—at that time,

as I also point out in the book, I was twenty-three—
and the oncoming decades. This book is full of images,
experience, little details, social rituals, conventions, lives,
weddings, clubs, bars, movie houses, newspapers—

—*and soft drinks.*

Yes, or even soft drinks . . . of Istanbul that I have
seen, and it was such a joy to write and put them in a
shape.

January 2010

Ayu Utami

 Officially, no one has sex in Indonesia. At least, some MPs would like it to be so. Since 2004, a minority group in the government of this Muslim country has tried to pass an antipornography bill that would fine couples $29,000 for kissing in public. A housewife who wears a skirt that is too short could wind up with a whopping $111,000 fine.

"The bill had almost nothing to do with pornography," says Indonesian novelist Ayu Utami on a recent trip to New York. "It was just a way to try to control people's behavior." In this context, Utami has, once again, become a political novelist.

In 1998, Utami published her first novel, Saman, and single-handedly launched chick lit in Indonesia. There, the genre is called sastra wangi (fragrant literature) because its other practitioners, Djenar Maesa Ayu and Dewi Lestari, are also young and attractive. Of this pack, Utami is the most literary.

Saman is told through multiple perspectives and follows various plot lines. Imagine As I Lay Dying set in and around Indonesia and twice as lush in its prose. The book's shadowy protagonist is a priest who is imprisoned *after allegations are made that he is a communist. Upon his release he becomes a human rights activist and the lover of a sexually adventurous woman.*

Through her characters, Utami presents a kaleidoscopic view of contemporary Indonesian life, from the plight of migrant workers on oil derricks to the tension between Christians and Muslims, and the presence of sensuality and sexuality in the lives of everyday citizens.

After her final event at the 2006 PEN festival in New York, the petite thirty-seven-year-old sat down for a beer at a Chelsea café. She talked freely about why her political conscience prevents her from getting into her next book.

You used to be involved in something called Indonesia's Alliance of Independent Journalists.

I started it with some friends to protest the closing of some newspapers. It was in the nineties, when I was still a journalist and the government was trying to crack down on free media. We did many things they didn't like. We had sort of retired it, but then this antipornography bill came back. Now, instead of working on my next book, I find myself distracted again.

I recently interviewed a Chinese chick-lit writer named Wei Hui, and she said that Henry Miller was a huge influence on her. What about you, were you influenced by him?

I liked some American writing, but I didn't get to it

until I was older—when you just like something or don't, but aren't shaped by it. I guess I wasn't soft, or I was too old to be soft.

Saman has sold a hundred thousand copies in Jakarta, which makes you the literary Dan Brown in that country.

It was published the year that Suharto was ousted, so I think there was an atmosphere of hope for a breakthrough. His fall brought an end to some terrible things. But I don't regard the book as controversial. Most of the text referred to in it is biblical. I was too afraid to address some Muslim topics directly.

But there is sex in the book.

Well, barely. I'm not very interested in writing sex scenes. But I am interested in sexuality and how that plays out in the lives of a country of people—what it means. It's not that I am against sex in books, but the urgency was not to arouse people but to make them think, to make them celebrate the idea of sexuality. I don't want to be exotic about this, but I don't want to write erotica, either.

Where does this curiosity come from?

I don't know. I come from a very conservative family— my mother is a devout Catholic and my father also became of faith. But my parents were very open in the sense that they can accept that if I do something the consequences are my responsibility, and they still love me unconditionally.

Were they shocked at all when they read Saman? *There is one riff on masturbation that I imagine would make a parent wince.*

Not really. You have to remember, people in Indonesia can talk about sex openly, just as long as it's not through a formal medium. As long as it's not printed. If you walk through Jakarta you will feel the difference between what is public and what is private. Officially, nothing bad happens, but everyone knows people get divorced in droves, people go to love hotels, but they have to keep up the façade of righteousness.

What about you, are you married?

I'm not married; I don't have any kids. It's not that I hate marriage. I have no trauma about it. I just want to be able to respect the fact that you have a choice, that you don't have to get married. That's not an issue so much here in America, but it's still an issue in Indonesia. Still, it presents a problem about what to call my partner. I can't call him my boyfriend, because he's definitely not a boy.

I guess you could call him your lover?

That's too French.

I know, and it makes him sound like he should be lounging in a smoking jacket.

Well, I'm going to keep thinking. He'll remain my partner for now.

May 2006

Jonathan Franzen

Jonathan Franzen is the most popular literary novelist in America. Born in Illinois in 1959, he grew up in a suburb of St. Louis, the backdrop for his debut novel, The Twenty-Seventh City (1988). Franzen began writing the novel while studying at Swarthmore College in the eighties. His follow-up, Strong Motion (1992), set in Boston and braiding family seismology with actual earthquakes, follows strongly in the vein of Don DeLillo's novels about the systems—both cultural and capital—that govern American life. These novels were well-reviewed modest sellers. It is his third novel, however, The Corrections (2001), completed after a long stretch during which the author reconceived of the importance of the social novel, that put Franzen on America's cultural map to a degree not seen since John Updike topped bestseller lists in the sixties. A devastatingly funny glimpse into the dysfunctions of American family life, The Corrections was the one novel published just prior to the attacks of 9/11 that was not ultimately swamped or outdated by them. It was selected by Oprah Winfrey for her book club, a show segment that never aired due to a disagreement between the author and the *host, and went on to win the National Book Award. Franzen has also published several collections of essays, including* Farther Away *(2012) and* How to Be Alone *(2002), the latter of which includes "Perchance to Dream," an essay he wrote for* Harper's *in 1996. In that piece, like Babe Ruth pointing at the center-field fence and then hitting a home run, Franzen laid out all the things he believed socially engaged fiction could do in a society that had forsaken it.* The Corrections *put those ideas into a story. His 2010 novel,* Freedom, *completed after a long gap between works of fiction, was a huge commercial success as well and catapulted Franzen onto the cover of* Time *magazine, the first time a novelist had graced its cover since John Updike appeared there in 1982.*

Jonathan Franzen has love on his mind. It is among the recurring themes of his third essay collection, *Farther Away*, and on a cold afternoon in December, he comes back to the topic frequently over conversation in his Manhattan kitchen—in his own unique way.

"I used to be deathly afraid of throwing up," Franzen says.

"And when I first began to date the woman I'm living with, she flew out to New York to visit me. She came twice, and I knew she couldn't come a third time, so I offered to visit her in California."

Franzen took a plane out to the Bay Area, and she picked him up at the airport and drove him on the long ride to her house.

"The road was really winding and twisty, and sure

enough I began to feel really, really sick. We got to her house, which was this cabin up in the redwoods, and I immediately became violently sick.

"And for a whole day, I lay in bed up among these trees and was sick, and yet I didn't feel ashamed or anything. I just felt very safe. And I knew I was in love."

Sitting in his extremely tidy kitchen, wearing his trademark glasses and an expression of earnest bemusement and yes, lovesickness, Franzen shrugs at the strangeness of his equation—love equals being able to vomit and be unabashed.

"What can I say, I'm a seventies kind of guy. I mean, I'm a process kind of guy."

Franzen is referring, partially, to growing up in America at a time when the information-processing models of computers became the model for how we understood experience. We became the stories we told about ourselves.

But he is also demonstrating how he managed to make such a startling leap as a novelist: from a mid-list writer working in the shadow of Don DeLillo with his first two novels, *The Twenty-Seventh City* and *Strong Motion*, to America's reigning literary novelist.

He has done so by making a deal with readers. "I want to be honest with readers. That is my pact with them."

And so here we have, as he writes in *Farther Away*, "the dirt that love inevitably splatters on the mirror of our self-regard." And just as we love Larry David for letting us laugh at Jerry Seinfeld's neuroses, we love Franzen for letting us see them in him and, by extension, ourselves.

·

It has taken some time for Franzen's frankness to be seen simultaneously as a comedic and a literary device.

In the mid-nineties, when he called out American novelists in *Harper's* for abandoning social engagement, he was the lugubrious auslander. The buzzkiller. The nerd king: right in concept but perhaps too knowing of his rightness.

All that changed with *The Corrections*, which proved he was capable of more than just heckling from the nosebleed seats.

What made the book so powerful was its unvarnished view of sacred American pieties: the family, our consumer culture, and the way the two are melded by the notion that we can improve upon the mistakes of our upbringing by starting our own families. Family 2.0.

There are moments of humor in Franzen's first two novels, but they are satires and social critiques, mental laughs rather than belly laughs. "I always wanted to be a comic writer," Franzen says, "and that's still what I want to be."

Chip, the main character of *The Corrections*, is over-educated and underdeveloped emotionally. Living in Manhattan at the height of the tech boom, childless and unmarried, slipping down an academic ladder, his life has become one white lie after another, told for the purpose of maintaining superiority over his own Midwestern roots.

The book's long opening set piece, in which his parents, Enid and Alfred, fly in from fictional St. Jude to visit him, is one of the funniest stretches ever written in American fiction. Here are all the pressures of a consumer state—its status-frenzied call to do more, better—bearing down on someone who has internalized their message while at the same time hating them. In one of the apogees of this segment, hoping to impress his parents with his cosmopolitan adult skills, Chip steals a salmon steak at Gourmet Garage, pressing the fish to his groin where it feels like "a cool, loaded diaper."

Franzen tried to write the novel in the late nineties and failed, and the subject of that failure became some of his best essays. Ruminations on the failure of the American social novel, the society itself, and himself.

He once would have said he was too angry to write, but now, looking back, he thinks it was a blessing. "I was lucky to have had that anger because that kind of rage tends to engender comedy, and I was, you know, I was—I was transforming the anger into a kind of cruel comedy."

He honed his success through failure. In the long gap between novels two and three a sea change took place in American publishing. "I did, I believe, one reading from *The Twenty-Seventh City* when it came out—it was FSG's lead title, and I did one reading from it—one bookstore reading. For *Strong Motion* I did two."

In the late nineties, though, bookstore readings became hugely popular. And even though Franzen didn't have a new book, he was "in perennial need of funny stuff to read at these readings which would suddenly become de rigueur in the literary culture."

"Because the things were being written, chunks were being written for reading aloud," he adds, "I would get to hear them, and I would start cutting lines, ah, a lot of it for comic timing: 'Okay, that's too many sentences without a laugh—there's a problem here, going to have to cut, cut something.'

"In that sense, yes, I think maybe I did become more deliberately a comic writer."

Even just a few years ago, his mood still contentious, Franzen would have backtracked and immediately undone this statement. He became famous, in interviews, for being the person who interviewed the interviewers' questions.

As the light begins to fall in Manhattan, though, Franzen comes across as a much milder, warmer, and funnier man than he is often portrayed to be. When he is in California, where he lives half the year with the writer Kathy Chetkovich, he listens to the stand-up Mitch Hedberg while he drives.

"He died—heroin, I think. But he was—he was as funny as it got. He had the perfect voice."

Franzen adopts a super-flat voice register and imitates it.

"The reason I gave up tennis: I knew I was never going to be as good as a wall."

"I played a wall once . . . It was relentless."

He keeps going for a while until he can't speak for laughing. Once his laughter dies down, Franzen veers into talking about Kafka, whom he reads primarily as a comic writer.

"He read the entire manuscript of the *Metamorphosis*

aloud to his friends and they were just, you know, gasping for air because it was so funny. And it is. It's hilarious!"

Twenty-five years into his writing career, Franzen still writes for misfits. He writes for the people who will find a man who turned into a bug funny.

"Misfits come in all sizes, shapes, colors, and income brackets," he says, as if to remind me he is still one. "And one of the really heartening things for me is the amount of reader mail I get from people in their teens and twenties, and a number that I see at readings, you know: We're still somehow producing . . . misfits."

The publication of a Franzen novel now gives him a chance to meet all these people. *The Corrections* was a surprise blockbuster, but the release of *Freedom*, nine years later, proved it was no fluke.

The book was an instant number one *New York Times* bestseller. Oprah Winfrey made it a book club selection, and this time Franzen went on the show. Barack Obama was seen carrying it on holiday.

All of which is terrific, if you root for literary novels to be at the center of American culture, but it's also very strange since the novel has so many dark things to say about the country and the cult of family life.

The book, which tells the story of the Berglund family and their fraying in the face of complex relationships, takes aim at the hallowed notion of the word in its title. Namely, that our concept of unfettered freedom is deeply corrosive to the things that keep a family together, such as self-sacrifice and loyalty.

Even though the novel traces these fault lines, it is far kinder to its characters than *The Corrections* and everything that came before it. Franzen argues this absence of rage has nothing to do with where America has gone in the time he wrote it: "It has to do with becoming less angry and so for some reason all the things that so pissed me off about the country, piss me off less now."

It seems more likely, however, that Franzen has finally moved beyond a mean kind of humor into something closer to comedy, with grace. He has a little more than half a collection of short stories, all of them break-up stories, which he published in *The New Yorker*, but he doesn't think they will be his next book.

"I just don't have the heart to write any more," he says, "to be in that mean-funny kind of mode it requires to write them."

He is writing, however. Normally he is quiet about these things, but, like a person in love, he cannot keep it in. "I'm a ways in," he says, and before he says more and jinxes himself, he changes his tack to explain what it is like.

"Smells are more powerful, I get on the subway and ride somewhere and everywhere I go I am thinking of it . . . I see things more clearly, colors are more vivid. Everything which feels broken in life feels, in moments like this, more complete.

"I have been publishing for almost thirty years now, and the four years it took me to write my four novels have been," and here he pauses, silently bracketing the Californian with whom he shares his life, "among the happiest years of my life."

Jonathan Franzen happy? It is, for those who have read his books, as Kafkaesque a notion as a man waking up and finding he has turned into a bug.

December 2012

Jeffrey Eugenides

 *Jeffrey Eugenides was born in Detroit in 1960, the son of a Greek American mortgage broker and an Irish American mother from Appalachia, and grew up in Grosse Pointe, Michigan, one of the city's leafier, wealthy suburbs. This twinned identity—of being both outside and inside a culture as an immigrant, and being both inside and alien to a wealthy society as an outsider—filters through Eugenides's three novels, which are so distinct from one another that it might appear they were written by three different writers. In a sense, they were, given how far apart they have been spaced. The Virgin Suicides (1993) spins a swift, dark fable about a group of bewitching sisters who commit suicide. It took Eugenides nine years to finish his second novel, Middlesex (2002), a family saga as seen through the life of Cal Stephanides, a man who is raised female in circumstances much like Eugenides (minus the intersexual identity)—in Detroit, the child of second-generation Greek Americans. Where Eugenides's first book was taut and poetic, Middlesex is a bulging, old-fashioned, Great American Novel, earnest where its predecessor was cool. I spoke to Eugenides when his third novel,* The Marriage

Plot *(2011), an enormously likable tale about love and
storytelling, had just begun its life in paperback. We sat
before a fire while Eugenides's dog snuffled our feet.*

Jeffrey Eugenides has a funny idea about how to be a
rebel. On a recent knuckle-skin-splittingly cold Monday
in Princeton it involves playing me some jazz on a school
night. Dressed in slippers and a turtleneck sweater, the
hawk-eyed, fifty-two-year-old Pulitzer Prize–winning
novelist has tiptoed up- and downstairs to make sure
his daughter is getting ready for bed. Now he is flipping
through a stack of vinyl in search of something by Dex-
ter Gordon. He racks the record and the horn comes
out soft and warming, like the thick-cut glass tumbler of
bourbon Eugenides has just handed me.

Thirty years ago, when he was a college student at
Brown University, Eugenides's idea of rebellion was a bit
more ascetic. It was the early eighties, and while his fellow classmates were smoking cigarettes and learning how
to deconstruct books, or love—any kind of intimately
felt idea, really, except the belief that ideas were bogus—
Eugenides did something radical. He got religion. "I could
have been a punk and had a Mohawk and that would
have been normal. But to actually go to a Quaker meeting
or Catholic Mass to see what it's like, was a very strange
and rebellious thing to do."

If you were to characterize this experience along William James's spectrum of variety it was a lukewarm one,
but it was real. Reading lead to exploring, and eventually
Eugenides made a serious commitment. "I thought that

the fascination should not be merely intellectual," he recalls. "Can I go and devote myself to the sick and the poor in Calcutta or am I not that person? I don't know yet because I'm only twenty, so let me see if I can do that. I wanted to test myself."

Eugenides took a year off from college and, in January 1982, packed himself off to India. He arrived in Calcutta and very quickly, very colossally, failed his own test. He was not a saint, not even close. The suffering made him squeamish and he was not very good at self-denial. But the trip and its impetus stayed with him. For twenty years he tried to write about it, and finally, a few years ago, he found a place in his latest novel, *The Marriage Plot,* which is a tale about crisis of faith—not just in God but in ideas, in people, in narrative—disguised as a novel about love, under the guise of a novel about campus life.

The book begins with a love triangle. Madeleine Hanna, its heroine, is a well-bred New Jersey native who is unlucky in love and both drawn to and repelled by the craze for deconstructive theory. The two of these tendencies collide when she reads Roland Barthes's *A Lover's Discourse*, a book Eugenides remembers cutting a swath through his classmates' ideals. "You became very suspicious about love," Eugenides recalls of its effect, and then laughs, "and yet in the midst of [reading it] you often still fell in love!"

And so it goes for Madeleine. She falls in and out of love with Leonard Bankhead, a tall, mentally unstable genius whose experience of his mind's fragility tells him that there are no ideas, really, worth believing in. Mitchell Grammaticus watches on from the near distance, agonized that this woman he has fallen for has chosen such an arrogant, unreliable mate. Mitchell's solution to the problem is to leave the country and, like Eugenides, go to work for Mother Teresa in Calcutta.

Sitting on a sofa in his den, thirty years removed from his own trip, Eugenides is hard on his younger self, the burgeoning ascetic reading Thomas Merton. The young man who believed he could conquer desire by removing it from the equation. So it is for Mitchell in the book. "But there's a question that arises as to whether it is some kind of desire to not have desire," Eugenides says. "And that even saintliness is some kind of greed. Certainly we have a lot of difficulties because of all the things we want."

Even though America is a deeply religious country, Eugenides's investigation is, within literary worlds, rather unusual. You could almost say unhip. Atheists, by and large, reign, and, aside from Marilynne Robinson and a small number of Jewish literary writers, there are very few who talk about God. "I think it's odd that no one is allowed to," Eugenides says, with slight irritation. "Certainly a lot of people are still interested in these questions. And they haven't gone away entirely."

Eugenides was baptized in a Greek Orthodox church, but religion was not a big part of his childhood. His father was a second-generation Greek immigrant mortgage broker, whose success took them out of Detroit into Grosse Pointe. Eugenides's mother was an Irish American who grew up "extremely, extremely poor in Appalachia," Eugenides says. Her people, he adds, had come to Detroit from Kentucky to work in the auto industry. Eugenides's uncle was a tool and die worker. "He was always going to work at a factory and getting fired."

Detroit then as now was a city with haves and have-nots. In the seventies it began looking for ways to collapse the divisions between its classes. The city considered busing children from wealthier neighborhoods into the city schools, which is how Eugenides wound up going to University Liggett School, a rigorously academic prep school whose purpose was to instill the values of WASP America and prepare its scions for future education in the East, and in the Ivy League.

It turned out Eugenides was not alone in being a partial fit. Parents of all kinds of descents had the same fears—fears Eugenides admits are partially racist—of having their kids go to an inner-city school. "I fit in with this group that came, because we all did not belong there, and we were ethnically various: Italian kids, Greek kids, kids of Arab Americans. We dressed differently, and our families operated differently, and I got a real sense of class structure in America from going to that school, and it made me want to assimilate to a kind of WASP, upper-class behavior that has since almost disappeared in America."

The school gave him something else valuable, besides the insider-outsider-ness, which has allowed him to watch and participate at the same time: Catullus. It was a poem by Catullus, a love poem, that made Eugenides want to become a writer. Eugenides continued to write poetry for many years. At Brown University, Eugenides even won a prize for poetry. The novelist Meg Wolitzer came in second. But by then his interest had waned. "I never really considered becoming a poet after that point," Eugenides says. What he really wanted to be was a novelist.

It took Eugenides a long time to figure out how to do that. His aesthetic absolutism was stoked when he arrived at Stanford, where Gilbert Sorrentino taught. The writer wanted his students to reinvent how to tell a story. "He hated everything in *The New Yorker*," Eugenides remembers, "hated almost everything, was fatigued by it, and was fatigued by it not because he was stupid but because he was incredibly smart, and he could see exactly what the writers were doing."

Eugenides obliged, but in a pattern that has persisted for his whole life as a writer, he kept his own counsel. So he would write stories that thumbed their nose at realism but didn't entirely give up on plot or story. It was this approach he took to writing his first novel, *The Virgin Suicides*, which tells the story of five sisters in Grosse Pointe who commit suicide. The novel tells the story in a first-person plural voice, something that had not been done in American literature with any success.

Yet Eugenides was not going to throw away plot and suspense. "For a while I had them dying each chapter," Eugenides remembers now. "And it became incredibly predictable. It was just awful. And then I realized you just have one die, and then nobody dies, and then even though the reader knows what happened the reader starts to get to the end of the book and thinks, how are they all going to die?"

In literary terms, *The Virgin Suicides* was a success. It sold through its hardback run and began to backlist in paperback. In 1996, Eugenides was chosen for *Granta*'s Best of Young American Novelists issue. Among the writers on that list was another Midwestern writer living in New York, Jonathan Franzen. Like Eugenides, he was working on a novel and things were not going well.

Over tennis matches and meals at diners, the two became friends. "He was writing what became *The Corrections* at that time, and having a really difficult time, and I was writing *Middlesex* and I was having a very difficult time, and he was throwing away most of the book—he had to redo it. And I went through a similar thing."

Their disillusionment was born as much from what was not working in their novels, as it was with the novel as a form. "We had a lot of conversations about whether or not the novel is dead," and both of them came to an astounding discovery for two young novelists writing in the age when the so-called systems novelists, Thomas Pynchon, William Gaddis, and Don DeLillo, were universally assumed to be the smartest guys in the room: The nineteenth-century novel had something.

Eugenides wasn't, of course, totally ignorant of the form's history. He had read *Crime and Punishment* as a teenager and been mesmerized. But it took a long time for him to come back to the time period in a serious, volitional way. He was in his late twenties when he finally got to *Anna Karenina*, "and that's when the switch was thrown," he says. Talking to Franzen, working on *Middlesex*, he would figure out a way to import its deep absorbing qualities into the twenty-first century.

The germ of *The Marriage Plot* was born in this reversal. Madeleine is in "the exact same situation that novelists are in, in our period," Eugenides explains. Just as she is being told love is dead, it is a chemical reaction, "we are also being told that narrative is old hat, that stories have been told. And yet the allure of narrative seems to override some of these intellectual prohibitions against it."

In other words, storytelling and plot, and deep involvement with characters who feel real, will always be an important thing. It took Eugenides years to figure out how to write *Middlesex*, the book that grew out of this discovery. He took a fellowship in Germany and moved to Berlin with his new wife, the sculptor Karen Yamauchi, whom he had met on a writing retreat. When the fellowship ran out they stayed. "It was cheap and wonderful and the city felt like my city."

It was a startling thing for a kid from Detroit to live in a European city, not just because the apartment Eugenides and his wife lived in was reportedly in the same building where David Bowie had spent time in the eighties. The city's history was tangible, its trains worked. People didn't leave. "Europeans can't abandon their cities as we can because they don't have enough space," Eugenides observes now. "They can't just leave the Rust Belt and go to Arizona, like we do. They have to deal with it."

Some of this knowledge surely made its way into *Middlesex*, which tells the story of Cal, an intersex child who

grows up, like Eugenides, mixed up about where he belongs in Detroit in the sixties. But he's also mixed up about
what kind of sex he is. Sprawling from the tale of Cal's
parents and grandparents, and their trip from Asia Minor to America, to Cal's quest for an operation, the book
is a grand, nineteenth-century-size tale.

Franzen had his moment with *The Corrections*, which
was published in 2001 and won the National Book Award
and became a colossal bestseller when Oprah Winfrey selected it for her book club. Eugenides broke through with
Middlesex. Arriving twelve years after *The Virgin Suicides*, which had by then become something of a cult
book thanks in part to Sofia Coppola's extraordinary debut film adaptation of it, *Middlesex* was received with
excitement and sales and the Pulitzer Prize. Winfrey selected it for her book club in 2007. Since its publication
it has sold more than four million copies in America.
Jeffrey Eugenides was no longer a cult writer.

The wind has picked up outside and Eugenides would like
to take a pause to play me another record. After he loads
the turntable, he stokes the fire and goes to the wet bar to
offer me a beer. It's a nice spread here, and Eugenides is a
generous host. He doesn't fully settle until I am comfortable and insists that if the weather gets too bad I can stay.
He nuzzles the dog with a slippered foot. He plays some
more music. He gives the impression less of someone happy
for company than a man who knows how to enjoy pleasure.

If the commercial success of his books has made Eugenides's life financially a little easier, it hasn't changed

his writing life. His perfectionism has remained, grown even stronger. "There are just pages and pages. It's a bloodbath," he says, his mood dipping as he begins to talk about how hard it is to write well. "I throw away so much." Eugenides clearly doesn't like to be pegged as the slow guy, especially when there are others—Franzen, notably, but also Junot Díaz and Marilynne Robinson and Edward P. Jones—who take their time, sometimes even more. But he knows no other way to do it.

"I never can plan my novels. So I have to live the experience of the book with the characters while I'm writing it. And understand where the possibilities of the plot will go."

Not surprisingly, with this kind of life, one of the biggest obstacles to writing is being Jeffrey Eugenides. It's not just that writing is hard, but that his success has made it possible for him to imagine the book out there in the field. He can imagine how it will be marketed and sold, and when that happens, he says, work is dead in the water.

He is not going to complain, though. He knows it could have gone another way, his life and career. "It's a crapshoot," he says. "I think of all the people I was in graduate school with, who were really accomplished, and one doesn't hear much about a lot of them now, and I don't know what happened. It's a tough thing. Luck of the draw."

Now he and Franzen are at the top of America's heap of novelists. It's a position Eugenides doesn't guard, and he knows that eventually there will be a new wave. He can even in some ways see it coming. "Now and then there's a literary party and I see these guys looking at me, guys I used to be, and I'm sure that they are in that same ferment and state, and ambitious and talking, showing their work to their friends, and I'm sure it's still going on. The look in their eyes that I see is the same I expect my eyes looked like back in 1992."

February 2013

Edwidge Danticat

Edwidge Danticat is a writer who is drenched in memory. Her books—stories, novels, memoirs, essays, children's tales, and anthologies—vigorously re-create the Haiti she left behind in the early eighties and the changed world her characters (and their ancestors) arrive to in America. Lush yet precise, sexy but born of a culture that has a strong Catholicism, her fiction began appearing in magazines when Danticat was still a teenager and has developed a huge following since then. Her best works are fragmentary in structure, yet create a complete whole that is shattering in its effect. Krik? Krak! *(1995), the story collection that earned her the first of two National Book Award nominations, feels like modern folklore. Her memoir,* Brother, I'm Dying *(2007), tells the agonizing tale of Danticat's father and his brother, one of them struck down by pulmonary fibrosis, the other by heart failure while being unnecessarily and roughly detained by the Department of Homeland Security when, after many years of coming to America for visits, he arrived declaring political asylum. He was eighty-one.* Claire of the Sea Light *(2013) is a novel in sto-*

ries that unfolds in linked chapters when a girl disappears from a small seaside village in Haiti.

This interview was conducted in 2004, upon the release of Danticat's Story Prize–winning novel, The Dew Breaker. *Danticat is forty-four and lives in Miami with her mother, two daughters, and her husband, Fedo Boyer, who runs a Creole-translation agency.*

Since immigrating to Brooklyn from Haiti in 1981 at age twelve, Edwidge Danticat has always had a foot in two cultures, and writing has always been her way to connect the two.

"When I got here, I felt so lost, in a way," Danticat said recently by phone from Mount Holyoke College in South Hadley, Massachusetts, where she was giving a talk.

"Writing was a way to interpret my world," she says, "to incorporate the new things I was learning."

Danticat was a quick study indeed. Her first book, *Breath, Eyes, Memory*, was begun when she was still in high school and later was made a selection for Oprah's Book Club.

Krik? Krak!, a collection of interrelated stories, was named a National Book Award finalist in 1995, when Danticat was just twenty-five, and *The Farming of Bones* was an American Book Award winner in 1999.

She has made her name as a writer who can depict characters caught between the past and the future—a Haiti mired in the past and an America where remnants of that past are surreally out of place.

Danticat's third novel, *The Dew Breaker*, appeared with cruel timeliness as Haiti nearly tipped over into anarchy. The book revolves around a former "dew breaker," a transliteration from Creole of the name given to enforcers from the Duvalier regimes. These torturers would come for their victims in the hours before dawn, hence the name.

The book opens in 2000. Danticat's dew breaker has moved to Brooklyn to put his past behind him, but in the opening sequence, he must reckon with his crimes when his daughter crafts a sculpture of him.

"Ka," he says, addressing his daughter with a nickname that means "body double," "when I first saw your statue, I wanted to be buried with it."

A note in Danticat's acknowledgments makes clear that unlike *Breath, Eyes, Memory*, this novel is not a very autobiographical book.

"After the first piece [of *Dew Breaker*] was published in *The New Yorker*," she says laughing, "a friend of mine came up to me, and said, 'Aren't you worried people are going to think your pop is a torturer!' "

Danticat's father actually drove a cab, but she does know what it feels like to live in close proximity to people who may have done very bad things.

"At the time I came to Brooklyn, when I was about twelve, you had a huge wave of migration. In the early stages of a dictatorship, in the fifties and sixties, you had the brain drain. In the eighties, you had a lot of other people coming out, people from the countryside.

"Mixed in with the victims, you also had the perpetrators. There were always these whispers that so-and-so was here now and is now something else."

The Dew Breaker dramatizes this frisson of fear and dread by taking a round-robin approach to narration. The first story is narrated from the perspective of the dew breaker's daughter and then expands to include people in his East Flatbush neighborhood, including barbershop customers, Haitian Americans who barely escaped him, and his wife. Some chapters don't even touch on the man but evoke the brutal memory of living under the threat of violence.

"They'd break into your house before dawn, as the dew was settling on the leaves, and they'd take you away," remembers a retired dressmaker.

The book's interlocking story structure aptly mirrors the fabric of this community and how it must weave itself together through the stories it tells about itself.

"This is a book as much about creating art out of mystery, or out of pain, as much as it is about the man," Danticat says. "It's about piecing together fragments, pieces that are thrown to us and [we are] forced to make wholes out of disparate parts."

Part of Danticat will always be in Haiti. Not only does she have a past there but she has relatives, too—a worrisome thing now, given the political upheaval still raging there.

"Like everybody else, I check in with them regularly," she says. "Thankfully, they're not yet in the region that's having the most trouble. Like everybody else, they are praying for an outcome. My uncle, who raised me, who I was with before I came here, he's eighty-one years old; he's in the capital. They're not amongst the powerful people. They are just waiting for people to settle things."

Danticat recently moved to Florida to be with her husband, so she is now closer to Haiti, though not close enough. But she does not bemoan having to write her way to wholeness.

"Dealing with two places is a gift; a rich life is what every artist seeks," she says. "Having two cultures to draw from is great in terms of creativity, in finding nuance. That's not tragic—it's wonderful with possibilities; it adds layers to one as a person."

In *The Dew Breaker*, Danticat proves what wonderful layers it can add to fiction as well.

March 2004

Geoff Dyer

 *Geoff Dyer is a British essayist, novelist, and award-winning literary critic. Born in Cheltenham to working-class parents, Dyer was educated locally until he won a scholarship to Corpus Christi College, Oxford, where he studied English litera-ture. In the eighties, he lived on the dole in England, a period he memorialized in "On the Roof," a notable essay for* Granta *magazine. He made his literary debut in 1986 with* Ways of Telling, *a short study of the work of John Berger. Dyer took Berger's restlessness with form to heart, and in the next decade published two novels (*The Colour of Memory, *1989, and* The Search, *1993), a genre-bending book on jazz (*But Beautiful, *1991), a travelogue about memory and World War I (*The Missing of the Somme, *1994), and a book about not writing a book about D. H. Lawrence (*Out of Sheer Rage, *1997). In these works Dyer has created a persona of an engaged dilettante, a fla-neur, a slacking autodidact. His writing on photography in* The Ongoing Moment *(2005), and on everything and anything in* Otherwise Known as the Human Condition *(2011), has won him several awards. His novel* Jeff in Venice, Death in Varanasi *(2009), a hilarious update to*

Thomas Mann's novella, took home the Bollinger Every-man Wodehouse Prize for Best Comic Novel.

I spoke to him as yet another unclassifiable book was being published. Yoga for People Who Can't Be Bothered to Do It *(2003) might be singular in being published first in America as nonfiction and then in the United King-dom and beyond as fiction.*

Whenever Geoff Dyer finds himself in a rut, he packs up his belongings and heads to the airport. In this fashion, England's hippest middle-aged novelist and critic has cir-cled the globe several times, living everywhere from New York and New Orleans to Rome and Paris, and writing about his travels in heavily fictionalized nonfiction or heavily autobiographical fiction.

"It's that thing about the importance of elsewhere," Dyer, forty-four, says over the phone from his current home base in London. "Let's say you are feeling really pissed off. The classic advice is to get out of the house and go for a walk for an hour. I just enlarged the scale."

This strategy for keeping things fresh would be sensi-ble were it not for the fact that a new city often throws Dyer woefully, hilariously off track. When he moved to Paris in the early nineties to write a *Tender Is the Night* type of novel, he wound up churning out three books— all of them about a man flaking out and not writing a book. Now Dyer has bundled together tales of his other humorous false starts—in Bali, Cambodia, Rome, and elsewhere—and come up with *Yoga for People Who Can't Be Bothered to Do It*, a collection of essays on the lure of somewhere else and the pleasures of just being. If you're the kind of person who fantasizes about disappearing in the throng of some European city, here is your bible.

The book's first piece, "Horizontal Drift," starts off with Dyer and a girlfriend delivering a car from Los Angeles to New York. They are using the free automobile as a way to see the heartland, just as Dean Moriarty and Sal Paradise did four decades earlier in Kerouac's *On the Road*. Along the way, they pass through New Orleans, a town Dyer loves so much that he later returns to it and lives there for three months.

The stories that follow are like a game of intercontinental hopscotch, played with colorfully named paramours—one is called Dazed; another dubs herself Circle—and buddies who really enjoy their psychotropic drugs. One chapter revolves around a rain-sodden day spent high on mushrooms in Amsterdam; another takes place in Paris, where Dyer convinces a lady friend to smoke some skunk (a powerful kind of marijuana), getting her higher than either expected. The book's title piece details a trip Dyer took through Southeast Asia, where he encountered lots of other people doing the "self-journeying" thing. All of them were too busy baking their noodles to actually do anything as physical as yoga. As a joke, Dyer comes up with the idea of writing a self-help book for these dropouts from conventional life.

This series of vignettes could easily be mistaken for a slice of life in the tune-in and drop-out sixties. But, lest *Yoga* make Dyer the hero of bohemians around the world, the author points out that all events described in the book did not necessarily happen as they are written.

"Sure, it's only an inch away from what happened," explains Dyer, who is careful to keep the particulars of his fictionalization mysterious. "But all of the art is in that inch."

Dyer has condensed timelines, changed names, and simply invented things. "Somebody was asking me," Dyer recalls, "'Is it embarrassing to reveal this kind of stuff about yourself?' And, in some weird way, I feel more embarrassed talking about it over the phone, because when it is the 'I' in the book speaking, it sort of has nothing to do with me."

Besides providing Dyer with a scrim behind which he can hide—for the record, Dyer was married two and a half years ago, and the autumn of his drug use has long since become winter, he claims—breaking from the record allows him to shape a narrative out of his often shapeless travels. And so, over the course of two hundred and fifty pages, *Yoga* charts a journey from existential restlessness to arriving in "the Zone," which, Dyer explains, means "a place of absolute contentment—a place where the possibility of there being other places isn't a goad or torment."

Reaching this state of beatitude and making the pursuit of it into a good story are two different things. Happily, Dyer manages to do both. *Yoga* is full of elaborate, lyrical descriptions of doing nothing in Rome, of playing endless games of table tennis in Bali. There are even paeans to his shoes of choice—Tevas—that accompany him on all of his trips.

While another writer might have us yawning during such stretches, one actually slows down to savor Dyer's lively prose and turns of phrase. The attention to language is contagious: The reader begins to treat this book as Dyer would have us treat life—insolently, with nary an eye on the clock.

But the book also contains grueling riffs on the kind of self-loathing that is the flip side to so much idle time. "There is always the fear," Dyer admits, "[that] maybe I am just being lazy."

Since there is no name for the mixture of nonfiction and fiction that Dyer is perfecting, let alone a category under which to shelve it in a bookstore, self-doubt constantly plagues the writer.

"Let's say you are writing a novel," he says. "It's going well, it's going badly, whatever—at least you still know it's going to result in a novel. My anxiety is redoubled by the fact that I have no idea what [a project] is going to be."

Even though it might be easier to go back to writing in conventional genres, Dyer wonders if he'll ever write another novel (he has written three to date, the latest of which is *Paris Trance*, 1998). He imagines that as with *Out of Sheer Rage*, his book about failing to write a book about D. H. Lawrence, his future projects will arise out of an obsession of one sort or another. Currently, he is writing a book about photography, an avocation he touches on throughout *Yoga*. So far, he says, it's not going so well. "I just can't see where it's going to end," he says despairingly.

Not surprisingly, Dyer has set his sights on another city: San Francisco, where he stayed recently for a few months during his wife's sabbatical. Mention the place, and Dyer's voice dips into honeyed tones, proving that even after writing *Yoga*, the Zone, that place beyond torment and temptation, is as elusive as ever.

"It would be really sad if I didn't end up moving there," Dyer says, his voice trailing off. "Just unbelievably tragic. I feel, at some level, it's my destiny."

January 2003

A. S. Byatt

A. S. Byatt is an English novelist, short-story writer, and critic from Sheffield, England. With a father who was a Quaker judge and a mother who was a Browning scholar, Byatt became an academic herself in the sixties, when a woman's presence in academia was something that had to be fought for. Her debut novel, The Shadow of the Sun, was published in 1964 when she was not yet thirty. Byatt later fictionalized her early years in academia with an autobiographical quartet, starting with The Virgin in the Garden (1978) and ending with A Whistling Woman (2002). She became a major bestseller with the publication of her tremendous 1990 novel, Possession: A Romance, which marries a story of a poetic Victorian romance with the story of contemporary scholars in pursuit of that ancient love affair's literary crumbs. Byatt is also the author of numerous collections of short fiction, which tend to be as dark and mysterious as her novels are vaulting and sardonic. A generous supporter of younger writers, Byatt is one of the few vital connections between academia and the general public in Britain, and she continues the revival of storytelling brought on by Angela Carter and Salman Rushdie.

"If I weren't here I'd be with a group of people discussing 'Is science our new mythology?' " says A. S. Byatt in New York. Such is the life of a polymath. The sixty-eight-year-old author had been booked for a radio show in Britain, but has flown to the United States instead for a lecture and reading tour.

"My lecture is on something I think about a lot," says Byatt, her eyes big and attractive. "I think about how much thinner literary characters have got since the disappearance of Christianity."

This acknowledgment of Christianity's gift to the novel might seem an odd concession coming from a born Quaker, but Byatt has always been a remarkably ideology-free thinker. She studied English at Cambridge at a time when literature was a commentary on life, not the other way around, which left Byatt free to form her own interpretations about a book's meaning. Or, as she is fond of saying to people when they ask who her role model was as a girl growing up, "I was brought up to believe you should think things out for yourself."

This mixture of impatience with ideology and brisk self-reliance might explain why Byatt had so much fun needling the sacred assumptions of academia in her 1990 blockbuster Booker Prize winner, *Possession*, or lambasting Boswell's profession in *The Biographer's Tale*. Both of these novels won a grinning victory over the deadening effects of theory: No matter how much theoretical hardware one uses to pry them apart, Byatt's storytelling brio keeps them whole, artful, and mysterious.

Not surprisingly, Byatt has a theory about the wider triumph of storytelling in British fiction. "British literature suddenly began to flower in the seventies because the novelists realized they didn't give a damn about literary theory. Or literary critics," she says. "And they started telling stories. And the reviewers were still saying, you know, 'Stories are vulgar. Everything in the world is random, haphazard, this great miasma.' Meanwhile, the storytellers—people like Salman Rushdie and Angela Carter—continued telling stories."

Byatt managed to straddle this divide for more than a decade as a university professor, and continues to do so in her work (she has published five volumes of criticism to date). Her critical interests feed her fiction and vice versa: Reading and writing remain the same activity for her. So even though she doesn't teach anymore (not since 1984, "a good year to give something up," she says), she continues to take an interest in the work of younger writers: people such as Adam Thirlwell, David Mitchell (whom she met when he was still selling books at Waterstone's), and Lawrence Norfolk, who she thinks "has it in him to be a great novelist."

"The British novel is going through a wonderful phase right now," she says, warming to the topic, allowing that novels such as Monica Ali's *Brick Lane* and Zadie Smith's *White Teeth* have brought over a kind of American-style reportage. "As in America, the novel is becoming representative of society, not just about it."

To connect Monica Ali with John Dos Passos takes some critical engineering, but Byatt seems to enjoy such surveying work. Comments on her own work often boomerang into the literary ozone, landing in some unexpected places, such as Dame Edna Everage. "If I were a different kind of writer I'd write a story about how she scares Barry Humphries," she says wickedly.

I am about to encourage Byatt to go ahead and execute this idea, but I realize it would be filed into a long queue. "I have a notebook," says Byatt, "and I think I've got a list of eighteen more stories that I'm going to write right now. So, for example, when I decided on the title of *The Little Black Book of Stories*, I picked out the ideas that went in my little black book and wrote them."

Like the dark sorts of fairy tales Lewis Carroll might have written if his audience were entirely adult, *The Little Black Book of Stories* represents the flip side of Byatt's sunnier 1998 collection, *Elementals*. Before that volume came three others. "I have a story called 'Arachne,'" says Byatt, "which I really love and I am really tempted to write some stories to go with it so I can have a book of my own with it inside. Yet every time I say to my editor, 'Can't we do a book of stories?' she says, 'Yes, yes, I'm collecting them in a drawer.'"

For a moment, Byatt sounds not unlike the petulant child she surely once was, the asthmatic who spent her time in bed reading Austen, Dickens, and Scott, and inventing plotlines of her own. Back then, short stories did not inspire her—nor would they for some time. "If you'd asked me twenty years ago if I could write a short story, I would have said, 'No, I can't do it.'"

And yet after the death of her young son in 1972—the victim of a drunk-driving accident—something changed in Byatt. She had taken a teaching post at London's University College to pay his school fees, but he was killed the week she started the job. Somehow she felt she had willed the nightmare into being. "It didn't feel like an accident; it felt like something I had caused by thinking about it."

As a result of this loss and a decade and a half of thinking, she came to believe there had to be more to storytelling than just realism. The only problem was she had begun a quartet of novels about an academic turned novelist named Frederica Potter.

"I had already become a quite different writer, but I *owed* those books," Byatt says. "They needed to be written, so I made a lot of compromises and a lot of discoveries about how you could put things into English realism that weren't in English realism, like all the awful fairytale stories of *Babel Tower*."

Perhaps this is why Byatt's short fiction remains the most accessible bridge between her critical and creative impulses. Her big novels *Possession* and *Babel Tower* bait readers into discussions of intellectual issues, while her stories are pure seduction—they take the passions of Byatt's mind and put them into a kind of ominous action.

I am about to share this theory with Byatt, but she beats me to the punch, with yet another theory of her own. She's returned to her planned lecture and explains to me how the pornographic emptiness of Philip Roth's *The Dying Animal* isn't a failure but a statement. "I realized Roth is saying that without religion we've been reduced to sex and death." She lets that simmer for a while and then it's time to leave.

Almost as an afterthought she asks, "What should I read tonight?" I am about to answer her, but before I can open my mouth I realize this is a question as much to herself as to me. And so I pack up my tape recorder instead, and in the un-awkward silence of a conversation completed, I see, or think I see, her face settling into the look of someone who has already made up her mind.

March 2005

Michael Cunningham

 *Michael Cunningham is one of the most seductively pliant writers in America. From* A Home at the End of the World *(1990), which reads like the novel Christopher Isherwood would have written if he had moved to New York City in the eighties, to his Pulitzer Prize–winning triptych of tales inspired by the life of Virginia Woolf,* The Hours *(1998), Cunningham reinvents his craft with each book. His characters have richly evoked inner lives, through which Cunningham dramatizes questions of loyalty and love. All while the big city, usually New York, heaves in the distance.*

I spoke to him in 2005, in the middle of the Bush years, when Specimen Days, *his long-awaited follow-up to* The Hours, *was just hitting the stores.*

On a hot Manhattan summer evening in June, Michael Cunningham kicked off the publication of his much-awaited fifth novel with a reading at the Union Square Barnes & Noble, the five-story superstore where the grandest of grandes dames in world literature read when they visit New York City. Capacity crowd is several hundred, and the store was full.

At the conclusion of the reading, applause rolled across the bookstore for more than a minute. It had been seven years since Cunningham published *The Hours*, three years since Dave Hare's cinematic adaptation earned a mantel shelf of Oscar nominations. The crowd seemed grateful the wait was over. Tall and handsome, with the affable good looks of a daytime soap star, Cunningham twinkled in the glow.

Then the Q&A began. First there was a softball, and then came a more involved inquiry. Then finally, the question *Specimen Days*, a novel haunted (or inspired) by the poet Walt Whitman, seemed destined to provoke.

"Do you believe in angels?" asked a woman. Cunningham attempted to sidle out of the question, but she wasn't backing down. "It's a yes or no question: Do you believe in angels?"

Cunningham paused and then grew firm.

"Actually, I don't think I have to answer that question."

The woman tried to push again, and before things could get contentious, Cunningham did what he has become so good at doing: He improvised.

"Actually, I'm sorry: I'm not going to answer this question. You know why? It is exactly this kind of insistence on either/or in matters of faith that has got us in the situation that we're in now in America."

The applause roared up again and it didn't stop for another minute.

·

Two weeks later Cunningham was just as poised if slightly more relaxed. He was in Michigan on the eve of July Fourth, having smoked his book tour straight down to the filter. "I'm overlooking beautiful Ann Arbor," the fifty-two-year-old author said by telephone, with more than a hint of weariness. Happily, the angel incident in New York turned out to be an aberration on his tour of red and blue America.

"You know, it crossed my mind: I wondered, 'Is this going to attract every crazy person in each town?' But actually that's the only time that happened."

Read *Specimen Days* and it's hard not to see why Cunningham might have been a little worried. The novel explores how belief and the beyond seep into our everyday lives, topics that have remained on the frontal lobe of this nation in the wake of the 2004 presidential election.

But the spiritualism that Cunningham is writing about isn't born-again or churchy but mystical instead. For this we owe thanks to Walt Whitman, the Long Island–born poet who flits throughout the book like a guardian angel. The great bard's lines, "I sing the body electric" and "every atom that belongs to me belongs to you" actually burble up through one character's voice, like the outbursts of someone with lyrical Tourette's.

The book takes its title from one of Whitman's lesser-known books, *Specimen Days*, a hybrid work of essays and reportage which describes soldiers dead, dying, or maimed in the Civil War. It also includes journal entries of the most staggering beauty. The contrast is striking. The "procreative urge" that convulsed Whitman throughout his poetry was suddenly turned inside out by the Civil War and represented here in all its awful chaos.

Although Cunningham says he chose this title "because it sounded good," the echoes between Whitman's book and his own are profound. Just as *The Hours* did with *Mrs. Dalloway*, this novel looks to *Specimen Days* and expands upon its themes, most specifically tying the scenes of death and destruction Whitman witnessed 150 years ago to those Americans feasted on over the TV during 9/11.

Cunningham is aware of these resonances, and they are the reason he is glad to find that Gotham is once again at the heart of his book. "I love New York and I know it better than I know any other place. I think 9/11 demonstrated that New York is fragile, which is not an adjective that comes to mind when you walk the streets."

Unlike, say, Jonathan Safran Foer's 9/11 novel, *Extremely Loud and Incredibly Close*, which directly invokes the falling towers, Cunningham comes at this trauma from a side angle. The first narrative unfolds in the city during the Industrial Revolution, the second takes place during the present day, and the third far into the future. Each section tries on a different style and a different genre. All three of them feature a man, a boy, and a woman, in different combinations.

Although it is tempting to make a comparison to David Mitchell, whose Booker Prize–finalist *Cloud Atlas* pulled off a similar stylistic tap dance, cycling from science fiction to hard-boiled crime and back again, the better comparison here is to Cunningham's own work.

Ever since he left Pasadena, California, where he grew up the son of an advertising executive and a housewife, Cunningham has been learning how to improvise—as a writer and as a man. He didn't start out as a writer but as a visual artist, who matriculated at Stanford University in 1972 to study painting. "I wasn't bad at it," he said in an interview with the *Milwaukee Journal Sentinel*. "I just wasn't good enough."

He was, however, good enough at writing. So he took literature classes and graduated with a degree in English, which he quickly put to no practical use, falling in love with a woman and moving with her to Nebraska, where she had inherited a run-down farm. It didn't work out and soon he was bartending in queer-friendly cities like Laguna Beach and Provincetown.

Before he could wash his talent entirely down the drain, Cunningham enrolled in the Iowa Writers' Workshop, the alma mater of one of his strongest literary forebears, the short-story writer Flannery O'Connor.

The training and discipline paid off. His first short story was published in *The Atlantic Monthly* when he was twenty-nine. Other stories followed in *Redbook* and *The Paris Review* within the year. Cunningham was on his way. Desperate to publish a novel by age thirty, Cunningham cranked out *Golden States* (1984), a decision he now regrets. He will not allow the book to be republished now. "I don't think anybody has read it," Cunningham says with a let's-make-this-go-away chuckle. Copies of the book are rare enough that they now sell for as much as $400 online.

He could have used some of this money back then.

The following five years were tough ones for Cunningham. He worked a day job at the Carnegie Institute and became involved in ACT UP, the radical activist group determined to raise awareness over the spread of AIDS. It was during this period that Cunningham chained himself to the White House gate and also got arrested for interrupting a speech given by President George H. W. Bush.

Political frustrations dovetailed with artistic roadblocks. Things got so hard that in order to prove to his partner how difficult it was to get stories published, Cunningham fired off a submission to *The New Yorker*, expecting it to come right back.

Instead it wound up in the magazine and became the seed of *A Home at the End of the World*, Cunningham's highly regarded second novel. The story of a gay teenager who comes to New York to live with his childhood best friend, the novel describes the collision of middle America with gay America—and how many New Yorkers wind up in the city like refugees from their past. The novel was made into a movie last year starring Colin Farrell. Cunningham wrote the screenplay.

Each one of Cunningham's books since then has reinvented his form and style, just as they have expanded the boundaries of what constitutes an American family in this country's fiction. *Flesh and Blood* (1995) was a dark and sprawling epic about three generations of a Greek American family from the Great Depression to the present day.

"I certainly write each book differently in order to keep from ever feeling like an expert at it," says Cunningham, the audible hiss of a cigarette giving the phone a sibilant exhale. He had quit but the pressure of the tour has made him light up again. "I think a novel that's worth anything probably involves trying to do something you can't do—otherwise it's really just like making Chicken McNuggets."

And so when he began to write his fourth novel, Cunningham decided to take a risk. "It was to be my artistic book," Cunningham explained in 1999 to *The Guardian*. "The plan was to try and make it up with the next book which would be the best-seller."

That plan backfired because against all odds out came a book that made him both rich and famous. In *The Hours* (1998), Cunningham took a deep breath and blew one of the most arresting riffs about an artist's life and work ever captured between two covers: covering the life and work of Virginia Woolf as seen through the eyes of the novelist herself, a housewife in California in the fifties, and a woman named Mrs. Dalloway in New York City in the present day.

The book was published to tremendous reviews, winning not only the Pulitzer but the PEN/Faulkner Award, and bouncing on and off the bestseller list for two years. Cunningham, who was used to literary poverty, lapped it up for a while. "To tell you the truth," he told the crowd at Barnes & Noble back in June, "no one had ever asked me if I wanted to go halfway round the world to give a reading. So I was like, um, yes!"

Eventually the whirlwind stopped and Cunningham got back to writing and he found himself drawn to experimentation again. "The first and the third sections were both difficult for me to write but for different reasons—the first section it was really hard to get the voice right."

Of the three segments that make up *Specimen Days*, this one might be the most powerful, as it deals potently with the themes of loss and remembrance and family that have haunted Cunningham's work for two decades now. Lucas, the main character, becomes convinced that his brother's ghost is trapped in the machine that took his life. The belief leads him to a decision that seems, well, suicidal.

"It was hard to create a ghost story that didn't necessarily require the readers to be ghosts," says Cunningham, coming back, as he often does, to questions of craft. "My model was actually Henry James's *The Turn of the Screw*, which can be read either way. Are those ghosts the hysterical delusions of the governess, or are they really phantoms?"

The one ghost that seems to hover around all of Cunningham's work is New York City itself—and it takes many shapes, from the smoky urban apocalypse in *Specimen Days* to the funky bohemian hangout represented in *A Home at the End of the World*.

Cunningham has lived in the city on and off for more than two decades. Although he now spends summers in Provincetown (the small New England arts colony he wrote a short travel book about in 2002), much of his time is spent teaching at Columbia and writing in a rent-controlled studio downtown, where he works.

This neighborhood remains the kind of pivot point of

Cunningham's recent fiction. From James's old neighbor-hood of Washington Square down to Houston Street, between Mercer Street and Eighth Avenue: on a map it is called Greenwich Village. Capturing this section of the city on the page was one of the goals of *The Hours*.

"In *The Hours* I was working from Woolf's beautiful lyric celebration of London, on an ordinary day. I can't think of a better record for the people of the year 3000 than Woolf's description of London on that day in 1923. And I'm not the artist Woolf was. I hoped to set down what New York was like at that moment."

In the years since he has lived here, New York has changed from a bombed-out shell of a city wracked by drugs and impoverished with debt to a moneyed playland for the rich. Cunningham has seen the city through much of this time.

During the 2004 election he was active in an organiza-tion called Downtown for Democracy, which raised money to "un-elect" George W. Bush. He also frequently gives pro bono readings at Housing Works Bookstore in SoHo, a nonprofit that raises money to help homeless New Yorkers with HIV and AIDS get housing and job training.

He is also busy giving his time to other New York writers. When Jonathan Safran Foer gave his first public reading from *Extremely Loud and Incredibly Close*, it was Cunningham who introduced him—simply because he liked his book so much. Every now and then, he will ex-travagantly blurb a young writer's work. And it helps.

But his greatest gift to the city that has nurtured him might turn out to be *Specimen Days*. Like Whitman himself, who reached out his arms to the sooty and the poor, Cunningham presents a story about the city's past and present and future and allows all of its characters— from the freaks to the futuristic denizens—a place to live, and breathe, and sing, and die. We'll see what they think in the year 3000.

June 2005

Jennifer Egan

Jennifer Egan is an American short-story writer and novelist, whose work straddles as many genres as it does decades. Born in 1962 in Chicago, she grew up in the Bay Area and began publishing fiction in her late twenties. Her debut collection, Emerald City *(1996), jumps from continent to continent as it portrays women trying, and failing, to grow up in a world not designed to protect them. Aside from Don DeLillo, she is the American novelist with the deepest interest in image culture, and in her four novels follows its variations across the countercultural movement (*The Invisible Circus*, 1995), terrorism (*Look at Me*, 2001), and the music industry (*A Visit from the Goon Squad*, 2010), the last of which masterfully weaves between genres as it meditates on mortality. That book won her the Pulitzer Prize.*

I met her on a snowy Friday afternoon in Brooklyn, where she lives with her husband and two sons, after she had finally finished what amounted to a three-year world tour prompted by the book's sudden popularity.

Until she was thirty-five, Jennifer Egan used to fantasize about becoming a cop. "My husband is relieved that deadline has passed," jokes the fifty-year-old novelist, sitting in a Brooklyn bistro, referring to the NYPD's age cutoff for its exam. "But I loved all of it, the stories and the crimes and the uniform. Yes the uniform."

It's not hard to imagine her with a shield. Egan is a steely kind of woman, her long blond hair running slightly to gray. The warmth of her face comes with an aftershock of something hard.

Had the fantasy become a reality, Egan would have been following in a family tradition. One of her sisters is a lawyer married to a U.S. marshal. Egan's grandfather was a cop in Chicago who acted as Truman's bodyguard when he came through town, both before and after his presidency. Egan remembers, laughing, "one can only imagine what kinds of crazy things he witnessed."

Instead, two things drew Egan away from this possible destiny. Her parents divorced when she was six and her mother remarried Bill Kimpton, an investment banker, whose work took them to San Francisco, where Egan grew up in the seventies, during the countercultural movement's long back draft. Kimpton and her mother divorced when Egan was eighteen, and he later founded Kimpton Hotels, a boutique hotel chain. He died in 2001.

And Egan, of course, has spent her life writing, deploying the narrative jolt of crime, in direct or subtle ways, in all of her fiction. From *The Invisible Circus*, her 1995 debut novel, the tale of a woman's obsession with her sister's mysterious death, to *A Visit from the Goon Squad*, a series of linked stories set within the music world, her books are animated by a notion that the world is not as it seems.

Very often this break in reality in Egan's books is transmitted through what happens to women. Her novels possess nothing of the morgue-like feel of Joyce Carol Oates's work, but the women in them are frequently in danger, at risk, threatened. A world that at first seems safe and adoring is revealed to be anything but.

In "Black Box," a story that appeared in *The New Yorker*, a spy who infiltrates a criminal ring transmits intel back to her base through a chip embedded in her brain. Told in the second person, the story proceeds in brief imagistic bursts, like a tale told by telegram. It was serialized over *The New Yorker*'s Twitter feed across nine days.

The form is more than a gimmick. As the danger heightens there is a blurring between what the character needs to do as a spy and what a woman must do to be liked. "Your physical person is our Black Box," the story begins, taking its name from the recording device all airplanes have to keep a record of their flights. Later, after the spy has had to sleep with her prey to earn his trust, Egan writes: "Remind yourself that you are receiving no payment in currency or kind, for this or any act you have engaged in. These are forms of sacrifice."

Egan knows why, for most of her career, she has thought a lot in her books about image culture and how it impacts women. At the end of her high school years, and before college, she worked as a model. "It had a gigantic impact on me, to be judged so acutely by how I looked," she says now, partially because she was not successful at it. "People would say to me, 'Your look would have been perfect ten years ago.' I felt terrible at having failed."

The near miss with modeling affected her deeply because, at the time, it confirmed something she felt about herself. "I was very pretty as a little girl," she says. "I had white-blond hair, and I was aware of having this effect on people. But within just a few years I changed, we all get older, and in my head I became a kind of debased version of myself."

This was in San Francisco in the seventies, and looking back Egan says she sometimes wonders how she survived it. She was not as wild as some, but she shudders at the risks she took. "I started dropping acid at fourteen and walking around everywhere barefoot." If she was late for school she would occasionally hitchhike to class.

Much of this atmosphere makes its way into *The Invisible Circus*, which is about a woman growing up in San Francisco in the seventies, when the movement's radicalism curdled into something meaner. The party, if it can be called that, of the countercultural days is over.

"In the seventies in San Francisco, there was this funny lull there," Egan says of San Francisco. "I know now that there was an ugly aftermath, but I feel like I missed that then. I didn't realize I *was* the ugly aftermath."

After her brush with rebellion subsided, Egan became increasingly aware of what she calls her own crushing ignorance. She went east for college, to the University of Pennsylvania, in the heyday of critical theory. The mental gymnastics of it were appealing, but she still craved real experience.

"I thought, 'I can't go another minute without seeing Europe.'" So on and off through college and afterward, she traveled with a relentlessness of someone determined to map the world and its limits. She traveled in Africa and the Far East, a scattershot trajectory that ghosts through her first story collection, *Emerald City*.

Ultimately, she realized she was failing at this, too. "I wanted to see things, but there was always something else—a new limit I hadn't crossed." Egan went to China in the eighties, just before Tiananmen Square, only to learn that the really brave thing to do was to get into Tibet, which a friend of hers did in fact do by disguising herself as a monk. "I thought, 'Okay, it's over, I can't match this,'" she says.

It wasn't the risk that Egan envied; it was the experience. Around this time, in her mid-twenties, Egan discovered there was a way to finally get her treasured quarry: She could make it up. "In a way it was the perfect solution: I knew I could never satisfy my notion of experience otherwise."

Each one of Egan's books has taken her five or six years to write. She does it by hand, which might seem like an odd thing for a writer who is so interested in technology, but she doesn't know how to do it any other way. Also, each one of her books has been dramatically different. "In order to write I seem to have to start over from scratch," she says.

She's not far off. *The Invisible Circus* is a literary thriller in the mode of Robert Stone, who Egan says was a huge influence on her. *Look at Me*, her second novel, is a postmodern political novel about the way hard-line beliefs can warp into terrorism. *The Keep*, her third novel, a neo-gothic story in which all the things that typically happen to women in that genre—meltdowns, imprisonment—happen instead to a man.

In *A Visit from the Goon Squad*, Egan took this restlessness with form, not to mention the gender reversal of *The Keep*, and transposed it down to a structural level. Told in a series of stories, it's a book about people, set within the music industry, with time and mortality as its theme.

Egan began writing the book before she knew it was one book. "I just kept coming back to these characters," she says. With each story, she would leap forward or back in time, and the form changed: One story reads like detective fiction, another like romance. One of them is a series of PowerPoint slides. I ask if she was trying to conduct a postmodern clinic of narration and Egan replies, "I was just trying to keep myself entertained."

Even though one of the book's main characters is a man, and he rages against the dying of the light like a man, many of his worries—about his appearance, his weight, his whining about his likability—are all things normally ascribed to women. Egan expresses surprise when I point out this strong thread of thinking about women and power within her work. It was not something she set out to write about, even when she was deliberately trying, she says, to inject ideas into her fiction. "I feel that is more my project now than ever, even more than thinking about our image culture, per se, which is how I wound up writing about terrorism."

She's working on two books at the moment, one of which is a noir set within the Brooklyn Navy Yard, in which many of the characters, since it takes place during wartime, are women. I ask her if she likes making buried history visible, since periods of America's recent past appear in all her fiction, and she replies simply by saying, "Women are more easily forgotten."

"Black Box" is part of the other project she is working on. Egan is not exactly sure where it is going, in part because that section seems to have rewritten the rules of what can come after it. "I really felt that I reached some kind of outer edge of what I can make a story do." And so the woman who turned to writing to solve her hunger for experience has run into the limits of narrative. She won't be going back to travel anytime soon. "I've just finished three years of travel for *Goon Squad*," Egan says, "and it's nice to be in one place for a change."

January 2013

Acknowledgments

These pieces originally appeared, in slightly different form, in *The Age, The Australian, The Believer, The Dallas Morning News, The Denver Post, The Guardian, Hartford Courant, Herald Tribune, The Independent, The Jerusalem Post, Las Vegas Weekly, La Vanguardia, Metro Times, Milwaukee Journal Sentinel, Morgenbladet, Nerve.com, New City Chicago, Newsday, The New Zealand Herald, The Plain Dealer, Poets & Writers, La Reppublica, San Francisco Chronicle, Scotland on Sunday, The Seattle Times, South Florida Sun-Sentinel, The Star-Ledger, Star Tribune, St. Louis Post-Dispatch, St. Petersburg Times, The Sydney Morning Herald, The Times* (London), *Toronto Star, The Vancouver Sun,* and *Weekly Alibi,* and on Granta.com. I am grateful to the editors of these publications for giving me the chance to speak to so many extraordinary writers.

I would also like to thank Michael Heyward and Caro Cooper at Text, who saw that this was becoming a book long before it was one. Sean McDonald is as good an editor as he is a friend, and for both I am grateful. Thank you, too, to everyone at Farrar, Straus and Giroux for bringing me back into the fold after sixteen years away, and to Sophia Efthimiatou for saving me from myself. I am grateful for early reads from Ellah Allfrey, Ted Hodgkinson, and Yuka Igarashi. Sarah Burnes and Arabella Stein are friends with whom it is a pleasure to work. Their support for this book was beyond cheering. I would also like to thank, and apologize to, the woman who lived with these interviews as they were being written: often late at night, on planes, trains, and automobiles, over holidays, and even in the night-light-lit bathroom of a bed-and-breakfast. If there was any joy to giving up a deadline life, aside from, well, sleep, it has been sharing those newly free hours with you.